IN SEARCH OF THE LAST CONTINENT

AUSTRALIA AND EARLY ANTARCTIC EXPLORATION

IN SEARCH OF THE LAST CONTINENT

AUSTRALIA AND EARLY ANTARCTIC EXPLORATION

Andrew McConville

Australian Scholarly

For Dominique, and Mum and Dad, with love.

© Andrew McConville 2022

First published 2022 by
Australian Scholarly Publishing Ltd
7 Lt Lothian St Nth, North Melbourne, Vic 3051

Tel: +61 3 9329 6963 / enquiry@scholarly.info / www.scholarly.info

ISBN 978-1-922669-94-0

ALL RIGHTS RESERVED

Cover design: Lucia Sankovic
Cover image: Balleny Island, *Illustrated Australian News*, 1 April 1895

Contents

Introduction ***vii***

1. British and Russian circumnavigations **1**
2. Seals and discovery **10**
3. Enderby & Sons and the Third circumnavigation **21**
4. Three national expeditions **33**
5. Franklin, the Northwest Passage and the cooling of European interest in the icebound south **66**
6. HMS *Challenger*: An exploration beneath the waves **82**
7. Britain revisits the Arctic **86**
8. The Australian Antarctic Exploration Committee: The new champions of Antarctic exploration **91**
9. Northern whalemen and the London Agent General for Victoria **104**
10. Lords of the Imperial Treasury **111**
11. The Swedish Offer **119**
12. The NSW government subsidy **133**
13. Henrik Johan Bull and an accidental triumph **137**
14. Borchgrevink's ambition **158**
15. A minor journey **164**
16. The First Overwintering **166**
17. Henrik Johan Bull's later life **177**
18. Legacy of the voyage **185**

Afterword ***189***
Notes ***196***
Bibliography ***211***
Acknowledgements ***221***
Index ***222***

Introduction

The history of Antarctic exploration continues to fascinate. It has a purity that does not exist in the explorations elsewhere on the planet. In the Antarctic there were no indigenous peoples displaced or destroyed, no empires built, and few financial rewards.

Exploration was about the urge to conquer the unknown, imperial and national pride, scientific and geographical discovery, and sheer adventure.

Much of the focus on Antarctic exploration has been the heroic age of terrestrial discovery from 1901 to 1917. This was a period dominated by charismatic, driven men who raised their own expeditions, funded by societies, press barons and wealthy armchair adventurers. Government, too, became involved, occasionally with enthusiasm, more often with reluctance. Explorers usually returned to debts far more crushing than the icepack.

It is a period that has become a crowded field for publication. This book, though, is concerned with the era prior to terrestrial exploration, from James Cook's first circumnavigation (1772–75) and his shrewd assessment of the unseen continent he was circling, to the final years of the 19th Century with Carsten Egeberg Borchgrevink's ambitious and fractious first overwintering expedition.

Four of the great world powers, Russia, United States, France and England, all mounted significant national expeditions to the Antarctic in the first half of the 19th century.

From 1819–21 Faddei Bellingshausen[*] led a very successful Russian expedition, that again circumnavigated the continent without definitively sighting land.

In February 1819, a few months before Bellingshausen sailed, Englishman William Smith was blown off course on a voyage around Cape Horn for Valparaiso, Chile. Carried far south he discovered islands. Sharing a similar latitude to their northern namesake they became known as the South Shetlands. The shores of this remote island group were crowded with seals.

---

[*] Variable English spellings of forename – Thaddeus, Fabian, Faddei.

His discovery set off a brief and bloody frenzy amongst British and American sealers.

The unsuspecting seal population, serenely undisturbed by any previous human contact, were utterly decimated to the point of extinction in just a few years. As quickly as they arrived the sealing crews left, having so destroyed the seal populations that further voyages were uneconomic. Sporadically, further sealing expeditions set out for the sub-Antarctic Islands over the remainder of the century, but the boom had come and gone in a few years.

Between 1837 and 1843 expeditions from France under Dumont d'Urville, United States under Charles Wilkes, and England under James Ross, ventured south and made significant contributions to the knowledge of the continental nature of the Antarctic.

After the 1843 the great northern powers had lost interest in the icy and remote wastes of Antarctica and no significant national expeditions headed as far south as Bellingshausen, Dumont d'Urville, Wilkes, or Ross for the remainder of the century. Explorations to that point had confirmed Cook's initial view that the Antarctic was utterly remote, hostile, with no discernible strategic value, and with unlikely economic prospects. The commercial potential was limited to seals and that industry had been all but destroyed in a few years. For the rest of the century there was little enthusiasm for further exploration by the great powers, and only occasional interest from sealers.

Interest in exploration of the Antarctic was revived in the 1880s in Melbourne, Australia. One of the closest cities to the Ross Sea, Melbourne, had been transformed from a dusty collection of shacks next to the unprepossessing Yarra River in the late 1830s, to one of the richest and most ambitious cities in the world. The catalysts for this rapid development were massive gold rushes in the 1850s, coupled with the opening of large tracts of fertile grazing land, claimed with little regard to the indigenous population.

With geographical ambitions far beyond the mysterious vastness of the Australian continent, members of the Victorian (Melbourne) branches of the Royal Society and Royal Geographical Society formed an Antarctic Exploration Committee (AEC) in 1886 and made strenuous and determined attempts to mount an Antarctic expedition.

Mindful that a purely scientific expedition would be prohibitively expensive and hoping to court government investment by highlighting the potential of the untapped Antarctic whaling industry, the Committee proposed a joint commercial and scientific expedition. By the early 1890s, despite their best efforts, chances of funding became more remote as Melbourne's excessive boom gave way to an inevitable and savage economic decline.

At the same time as the AEC was energetically promoting the cause of Antarctic exploration, a Norwegian, Henrik Bull, sailed to Melbourne from Norway. In 1893, after failing to raise funds in Melbourne, he returned to Norway and was able to realise his dream of managing a whaling expedition to the Antarctic searching for the Right or black whales that James Clark Ross had reported as seeing in great numbers fifty years before.

The expedition was a commercial failure, Right whales were few and elusive in Antarctic waters, migrating populations having been devastated before they reached Antarctica and while Blue whales were plentiful, the technology and support was not available to catch and process these huge creatures.

The expedition, though, was important for several reasons. It was the first confirmed expedition to the Ross Sea since James Ross' final visit in 1842. The expedition made the first confirmed landing on the Antarctic mainland at Cape Adare and this created enormous interest. (While subsequent detailed interrogations of sealers logs have shown there were probably landings on the Antarctic peninsula as early as 1821, that information was only uncovered relatively recently and was unknown at the time of Bull's landing.)

The expedition also launched the Antarctic career of another ambitious Norwegian living in Australia, Carsten Egeberg Borchgrevink, who was able to use his experiences on Bull's expedition to raise funds and lead the first expedition to overwinter on the Antarctic continent.

This book assesses the early exploration of the Antarctic and pays special attention to the 1880s and 1890s and the activities of Melbourne's Antarctic Exploration Committee and Henrik Bull. Neither achieved their grand aims. They are not major names in Antarctic history, but both contributed in important ways to the subsequent exploration of the continent.

Chapter One

British and Russian circumnavigations

Gonneville land

In June 1503, Binot Paulmier de Gonneville sailed from the northern French port of Honfleur in command of the ship *Espoir*. Impressed by the wealth of the Portuguese spice trade he intended to sail to the East Indies seeking a share of the spice riches. Blown hopelessly off course by a ferocious Atlantic storm, a setback compounded by the death of his pilot Collin Vasseur, he stumbled upon what he claimed to be a great southern continent. He and his crew spent 6 months living with friendly indigenes.

When they set sail again in July 1504, Essomeric, one of the chieftain's sons, accompanied them. Needing supplies, and with a weakening and sickly crew, they made another landfall in October 1504. This time though the locals were decidedly unfriendly, killing several crew, purportedly for the dinner pot, and driving the *Espoir*'s company to sea again. Then, almost at the voyages end, in the English Channel, they were attacked by pirates. Several crew were killed, the ship was beached and all the records and cargo were lost. It is generally accepted that Gonneville's landfall was Brazil, although some have raised the possibility that the crew of *Espoir* may have been the first Europeans to make landfall in Australia.[1]

Gonneville's voyage, ending as it did with the loss of records and goods, was forgotten for a century and a half. Then Abbe Jean Paulmier, a French priest claiming to be a descendant of Essomeric, published a plea for a Christian mission to Gonneville's 'Terres Australes'.

The dream of this vast southern land, discovered by Gonneville and still awaiting the French flag, was awakened. It inspired a number of subsequent voyages and played its part in Cook's great Antarctic circumnavigation.

Bouvet's voyage

In 1664 Jean Baptiste Colbert, Louis XIV's finance minister, established the French Company of the East Indies. His King was the major shareholder. The fledgling company found itself in fierce competition with the powerful Dutch East Indies Company and struggled to return much profit. In 1719 it briefly became part of the Company of the Indies. The financial crash of 1720 saw it reconstituted as the French Company of the Indies, and with colonies of Mauritius (1721) and Malabar (1724) the company enjoyed several decades of success. An employee, Jean Baptiste Bouvet de Lozier, intrigued with the mysterious discoveries of Gonneville, proposed an expedition to find the fabled Gonneville Land. He argued persuasively for the commercial advantages of such a land with the possibility of vast untapped resources and a prime location to join the company's current colonies and assist in the exploitation of the riches of the southern hemisphere.

At that time, the Dutch East Indies Company was waning, but the rival British East Indies Company had twice the trade of the French. A fertile, resource rich, strategically located new colony might give them a decisive advantage over their rivals. The Company was convinced by Bouvet's arguments and in July 1738 the ships *Aigle* and *Marie* sailed from the Bay of Biscay port of Lorient under Bouvet's command. They approached 55° South and, at the very start of 1739, through the fog and sleet, sighted land. It being 1 January, Bouvet named the land he saw Cape Circumcision, for the feast day, believing it to be the distant edge of a great southern land. It was an icy and desolate place and there was no landing made. It was hardly the fertile and inviting lands Gonneville had described.

The Company didn't follow up Bouvet's discovery. He was appointed governor of Ile Bourbon (Reunion) and then Ile de France (Mauritius). He proved a sympathetic, humane and capable administrator. The Company's fortunes waned with the French defeat in the seven years' war with Britain. The war finally ended in 1763. In the years following the Company islands moved under government control. The Company's monopoly on Indian trade ended in 1769 and French commerce looked to the West rather than the East Indies. The Company limped on until its final demise with the French Revolution in 1789.

Bouvet returned to France later in 1763, he died in his 76th year in 1781, having, during his life, proved himself an admirable sailor, a kind and able administrator and a noble man.

His discovery didn't bring riches to the French Company of the Indies, but it did occupy the minds of many, including the British Admiralty, who saw the rediscovery of this northern edge of the great southern land as a key task for James Cook in his great Antarctic exploration of 1772–1775. For a time though the Cape proved as elusive as Gonneville Land itself. Cape Circumcision turned out not to be the tip of a great continent, but rather part of a small, forbidding and utterly remote island, named now, most appropriately, for the man who discovered it.

James Cook

In July 1772 one of history's great navigators, James Cook, set sail from Plymouth in command of the ships *Resolution* and *Adventure* (the latter captained by Tobias Furneaux). It was the second of Cook's three great voyages. The first, aboard *Endeavour*, took a group of scientists to Tahiti to observe the transit of Venus. Cook then sailed south-west and mapped New Zealand and then west again and charted the east coast of Australia. *Endeavour* suffered damage when negotiating the treacherous waters of the Great Barrier Reef. Cook beached his ship near modern day Cooktown in far north-east Australia for repairs. Despite this setback, to that point the voyage was an impeccable success, achieving the Admiralty's aims and maintaining good health amongst the crew. *Endeavour* harboured at Batavia to take on supplies. Batavia was an unhealthy place for Europeans and 30 of Cook's crew died of fever and dysentery.

Accompanying him on the *Endeavour* voyage was the gentleman botanist Joseph Banks. Banks was a personable and tough shipmate as well as a talented and adventurous scientist. His standing in society and flamboyant personality meant that once back in London he was the star of the voyage. The circumspect Yorkshireman seemed not to resent Bank's celebrity, and the Admiralty recognised the immense skill displayed by their captain. Cook was their choice to command a voyage into the high southern latitudes.

Banks, though, was central to the preparations for the second voyage. He anticipated a glorious triumph and intended to undertake the journey in some style. His staff grew to 17, including two French horn players, recruited to provide musical solace and inspiration to the labouring scientists. The vast entourage meant additional accommodation, but such wasn't available on *Resolution*. This presented no problem to Banks who set about organising the building of suitably generous additional quarters. The alterations, though no doubt comfortable, proved disastrous to the ship's handling. Amid fears of the ship capsizing before it cleared English waters *Resolution* was returned to her original state and Mr Banks withdrew to study plants in Iceland.

The Admiralty instructed Cook to 'proceed to the southward, and endeavour to fall in with Cape Circumcision',[2] to confirm whether it was part of a southern continent.

Beyond this Cook was to keep 'in as high a latitude as I could, and prosecuting my discoveries as near to the South Pole as possible'.[3]

His voyage has been written about extensively. It was an extraordinary feat of seamanship, in brutal unknown waters, under threat from icebergs, gales, fog and desperate cold. The ships left Plymouth Sound at 6 o'clock on 13 July 1772. They anchored in Table Bay at the end of October 1772. After three weeks at Cape Town, the ships headed south. By mid-December they were amongst icebergs and in the vicinity of the elusive Cape Circumcision. Despite careful, meticulous searching they didn't sight Bouvet's land. On 3 January 1773 Cook wrote:

> This longitude is nearly the same that is assigned to Cape Circumcision; and at the going down of the sun we were about ninety-five leagues to the south of the latitude it is said to lie in. At this time the weather was so clear that we might have seen land at fourteen or fifteen leagues distance. It is therefore very probable, that what Bouvet took for land, was nothing but mountains of ice, surrounded by loose or field ice. We ourselves were undoubtedly deceived by the ice hills, the day we first fell in with the field ice.[4]

Cook continued east, reaching latitude 61° 21', at this point 'surrounded on every side with huge pieces of ice equally dangerous as so many rocks'.[5]

Cook abandoned his aim of crossing the Antarctic Circle again and retreated north.

In February 1773, the two ships became separated. Cook's *Resolution* continued through the icy waters, then in March headed to a pre-arranged rendezvous at Queen Charlotte Sound at the top of New Zealand's South Island. The two ships met in Ship's Cove on 17 May.

During the southern winter they explored the South Pacific, Cook renewing old acquaintances among the people of Tahiti and visiting Tonga.

Again, the two ships became separated. This time *Adventure* was lagging well behind. With the summer fast approaching Cook had to head south again to complete his circumnavigation. He felt it unlikely that Captain Furneaux was near the rendezvous point, nevertheless, in one final search, he

> stood over for Cape Teerawhitte, and afterwards run along shore, from point to point, to Cape Palliser, firing guns every half hour; but all to no effect …
>
> Every one being unanimously of opinion that the *Adventure* could neither be stranded on the coast, nor be in any of the harbours thereof, I gave up looking for her, and all thoughts of seeing her any more during the voyage.[6]

On the 27 November 1773 they departed Cape Palliser and recommenced the circumnavigation.

Furneaux's ship finally made Ship's Cove on 30 November 1773, finding a message from Cook. Furneaux remained there several weeks preparing his ship. In mid-December a group of ten crew went ashore to forage for food. They were involved in a skirmish with local Maori and all ten were killed. Furneaux had no hope of a further rendezvous with Cook, and with the loss of ten men it was a melancholy crew that set the ship's course westward. They were running short of supplies and Furneaux decided to make for the Cape of Good Hope. They again searched for Bouvet Island without success. *Adventure* anchored in Table Bay on 19 March 1774 and arrived back in England on 14 July 1774.

Resolution, meanwhile, was in high southern latitudes. By 30 January 1774 they had reached 71° 10' South and lay only about 190 km from the West Antarctic coast (near what is now the Walgreen Coast of Marie Byrd Land).

This was as far south as the ice allowed. Cook, no doubt to the relief of his crew, headed north to Easter Island, Society Islands, Tonga, New Hebrides, New Caledonia and New Zealand. On 11 November 1774 Cook left New Zealand and headed for Cape Horn. On 29 December his ship passed the Cape and entered the South Atlantic.

He continued trying to sight the elusive Cape Circumcision, but after exhaustive searching concluded, on 21 February 1775, that having

… run down thirteen degrees of longitude, in the very latitude assigned for Bouvet's Land. I was therefore well assured that what he had seen could be nothing but an island of ice; for, if it had been land, it is hardly possible we could have missed it, though it were ever so small.[7]

In fact Cape Circumcision remained elusive. Bouvet's positioning had not been accurate, understandable given the conditions. Two Enderby Brothers vessels, *Swan* under James Lindsay and *Otter* under Thomas Hopper sighted land in the vicinity of Cape Circumcision on 6 October 1808. On 10 December 1825 it was 'discovered' again by another Enderby brothers' expedition with George Norris commanding *Sprightly* together with *Lively*. He named it Liverpool Island. The island's position was finally fixed accurately in 1898 by the German oceanographic expedition on *Valdivia*. Arriving on 25 November, they circumnavigated and charted the island. In December 1927 the Norwegian *Norvegia* expedition, promoted by Lars Christensen, stayed a month in the waters surrounding Bouvet Island. They landed, erected a depot house and raised the Norwegian flag. They visited again in December 1928 and in October and November 1929. On 23 January 1928 it was annexed to Norway by Royal Proclamation, and on 19 November Britain renounced all claim to the island.

This remote and forbidding island has no permanent residents, however Norway has maintained a presence and scientific staff spend time there. In 2006 the station built to house scientific staff disappeared, probably blown into the sea after a nearby earthquake may have compromised the building's foundations. It was uninhabited at the time. In February 2012 the highest point of the island was summited for the first time.

Towards the end of February *Resolution* crossed their outward route of December 1772, thus completing the first circumnavigation of the Antarctic. *Resolution* anchored in Table Bay, Cape Town on 21 March 1775.

From his observations on the voyage Cook concluded that it was probable 'there was a land of considerable extent' around the South Pole.

However, it was likely a land of 'inexpressibly horrid aspect … a country doomed by Nature never once to feel the warmth of the sun's rays, but to lie buried in everlasting snow and ice.'[8] On 30 July 1775 he anchored at Spithead, completing this great voyage. He proudly noted: 'Having been absent from England three years and eighteen days, in which time, and under all changes of climate, I lost but four men, and only one of them by sickness.'⁹

It truly was a remarkable achievement by one of history's great navigators.

Faddei Bellingshausen and the Russian Antarctic and Arctic expeditions

Russian Faddei Bellingshausen,[10] born shortly before the death of Cook on his third voyage, commanded the second circumnavigation of the Antarctic. The ships *Vostok*, under Bellingshausen with Ivan Zavodovski second in command and *Mirnyi*, captained by Mikhail Lazaref, left the port of Kronstadt in mid-July 1819.[11] Bellingshausen's instructions from the Ministry of the Navy were broadly to explore in as high a latitude as possible, seeking any land and to get as near as possible to the South Pole. The expedition was only to turn back if they met 'insurmountable obstacles'.[12]

Bellingshausen was well qualified for such a daunting task. From an aristocratic family he became a naval cadet at age ten. At 25 he served as fifth lieutenant on the first Russian circumnavigation of the world under the command of Admiral Adam Johann von Krusenstern. The voyage set sail in 1803 and rounded the world by way of the Cape Horn, the Marquesas, Kamchatka and Japan and then home via the Cape of Good Hope. Remarkably there were no casualties either to illness or accident and all returned safely to Mother Russia in 1806.

Bellingshausen's voyage was one of two despatched by Emperor Alexander 1 in 1819 in an ambitious attempt to solve some of the mysteries of both poles. Two ships *Otkryitie* and *Blagonamyerenni*, under Captain Lieutenant-Commander Vasilev and Lieutenant Gleb Shishmarev, were sent north to the Arctic.[13] Their task was to explore the waters of the Siberian and Alaskan Arctic, especially to find a passage between the Atlantic and Pacific oceans returning in 1822. These dual voyages represented a great national undertaking, mirroring Cook's 2nd and 3rd voyages from half a century earlier.

In late January 1820 Bellingshausen crossed the Antarctic Circle. There has been forensic investigations by historians and geographers trying to establish who was the first to sight the Antarctic continent. Bellingshausen certainly sighted plenty of ice. His ships did approach the Princess Martha Coast. If not for the poor weather, they may have affected the first landing.

In mid-February he noted substantial 'stationary' icebergs with ice stretching beyond sight.[14]

This was likely land, though he was a cautious man and didn't claim a definitive sighting. That was the closest they got to the continent that year. They crossed north of latitude 60° by mid-March, Bellingshausen advising Lazarev (captain of *Mirnyi*) that the two ships should separate where Captain Cook broke off his course. He advised Lazarev the reason for leaving the high latitudes were the increasingly difficult conditions – ferocious weather, ice and the encroaching darkness.

On 11 April 1820 (G) *Vostok* arrived at Port Jackson. *Mirnyi* arrived a few days later. They narrowly missed an encounter with the ships of the northern expedition *Otkryitie* and *Blagonamyerenny*, who, on the long voyage to approach the Arctic from the Bering Straits, had been at Port Jackson several weeks earlier.

On 19 May (G) the ships sailed from Port Jackson and spent much of the southern winter exploring New Zealand, Tahiti and Polynesia. Bellingshausen discovered several islands giving a touch of Russia to the South Pacific. Some of his names haven't survived but it is cheering to see, on modern maps, Vostok Island, lying north of Tahiti.

Vostok returned to Port Jackson on 21 September 1820, and *Mirnyi* the following day. Bellingshausen's account includes his outline of the fledgling colony of New South Wales. On the 12 November 1820 both ships sailed southward again to complete their great undertaking[15]. On the 21 January 1821 (G), having reached latitude 69° 53'S they discovered land, an island they named in honour of Peter the Great.

Peter 1 Oy remains barely accessible and it is utterly hostile. After Bellingshausen, the island was not encountered again until Jean Charcot's 2nd French South Polar Expedition (1908–1910) aboard *Pourquoi Pas?* sighted the island on 14 January 1910. 'In the fog which melts away two or three miles from us there appears suddenly an enormous black mass enveloped in clouds.'[16] It was not until the Lars Christensen sponsored expedition of *Norvegia* in 1928–1929 that anyone set foot on Peter 1 Oy. On 1 February 1929, *Norvegia* lay off the island and they managed a landing. A small depot house was erected, and the Norwegian flag was raised at Framnes Head. This remote, bleak and forbidding island was annexed by Norwegian Royal Proclamation on 1 May 1931.

At the end of January 1821, Bellingshausen discovered another island (abutting the Antarctic Peninsula). He named it for Tsar Alexander 1. In early February they sighted the South Shetland Islands and by mid-February they completed their circumnavigation. In early April they reached Rio de Janeiro and by early August they passed through the Baltic Sea and made port at their departure point of Kronstadt, having travelled over 57,000 miles in a voyage of just over two years. During the voyage Bellingshausen had lost only two men from *Vostok*, both on the Pacific cruise in the southern winter of 1820. Blacksmith Gubin died in May from injuries received in a fall from a mast at Port Jackson. He had spent time in hospital in Sydney but despite Bellingshausen's misgivings the Staff Surgeon declared him fit, only for him to succumb several weeks later as the ships explored the Pacific. Phillip Bykov was lost overboard in September. A crewman from *Mirnyi* Fedor Istomin has been identified as having died of typhoid in February 1820.

Thus ended one of history's great voyages of exploration and discovery. These concurrent Russian polar expeditions, seeking as they did to explore both frozen ends of the earth, were amongst the greatest of the 19th century's maritime endeavours.

Despite surveying great areas of the northern coast of the Americas and Asia, and recording ethnographic data from these first encounters with the Inuit tribes, the northern explorations of Vasilev and Shishmarev were considered a failure by the Russians at the time as severe ice conditions thwarted any attempt to find a passage to the Atlantic. Both expeditions remained little known in the West. The first English translation of Bellingshausen's journals didn't appear until 1945 and very little has been published about the Northern expedition (either in Russian at the time or subsequently).

Chapter Two

Seals and discovery

The whaling and sealing industries during the 18th and 19th centuries were voracious, lucrative and competitive. Companies funded adventurous fleets that slaughtered seals and whales from the Arctic to the South Seas as they progressively hunted out populations. These rough, tough sealers were involved in a boom-and-bust industry that seems rather distasteful these days. There was no thought of sustainable harvests. There were no enforceable regulations. Hunts were conducted at the remotest, unknown corners of the earth, well out of sight of the prosperous classes who required the products of the bloody industry. There was no need to understand the process of obtaining whale bones when a lady purchased a corset, or the manner of producing oil to light booming cities and grease the machines of the industrial revolution, or the story behind a fine seal fur coat – little different to 21st century fashions made in sweatshops and bought unquestioningly in the West.

These bold and brutal hunters set upon the sub-Antarctic islands in a frenzy of clubbing, lancing, skinning, flensing and boiling until, in the space of a few years, the seals were all but destroyed. Around the Antarctic continent the whales fared better until the 20th century. The whales able to be harvested with early 19th century technology were Right whales, in scarce supply in Antarctic waters. The giant blue whales, requiring greater technology to kill and then to process, were safe in the deep south until factory ships and shore processing settlements enabled their plunder in the Antarctic in the early 20th century. However this industrialisation of Antarctic whaling was a century away when sealing ships made their way south.

Sealing was rudimentary, requiring the stomach and stamina for killing unsuspecting creatures dozing on the wildest and most inhospitable shores. There was nothing scientific about it. As King Island sealer John Boultbee observed: 'Then begins the slaughter, the men hitting right & left as fast as they can with their clubs, until there is not a seal left'[1]

The first in the field made a very bloody fortune and subsequent vessels were less and less successful until the seal population was so close to extinction as to make further hunting in that location unprofitable. Thence the ships sailed on to more remote locations visiting the same slaughter before moving ever further southward.

The fur seal had the misfortune to possess a very valuable pelt. Populations were exterminated with remarkable ferocity, almost in a season. The only thing that saved them was that they were very quickly reduced to uneconomic numbers.

The docile creatures, awkward and trusting on land and with no experience of land predators, lay quietly as sealing crews approached. The male would roar to protect his harem and was often left to last so his harem didn't disperse. The fur seals were then skinned, the skins were salted and their bloody carcasses left for the birds. The enormous numbers of seal skins obtained on the virgin shores of the South Shetlands brought great profits for a few years.

Also in demand were elephant seals. These giants were valued for their oil. They were despatched and lumps of blubber rendered down to liquid in big pots, then stored in barrels. They were killed often with a lance and the blubber from the animal cut into chunks. These were then boiled down on shore or towed back to ships where the boiling was done. Francois Peron, a member of Baudin's expedition 1800–04, witnessed the elephant seal industry on King Island (Bass Strait) in 1802.

> Withdrawn on to wild and lonely islands, these great seals could without enemies, without fear, multiply and increase there as they wished … Everything has changed for them now … they will not escape the mercantile avidity that seems to have sworn the complete destruction of their race.[2]

He noted that 'some blows and sometimes one blow only, of a stick applied heavily on the end of the snout of these amphibians, is enough to kill them instantly'.[3]

He was rather disgusted by the industry:

> Seeing a cruel sailor, armed with a heavy stick, run sometimes for fun through the midst of these marine herds, killing as many seals as he hits, and soon surrounding himself with their corpses, one cannot help bemoaning

the kind of lack of foresight or the cruelty of nature which seems only to have created such a strong, gentle and unfortunate beings in order to deliver them to all the blows of their enemies.[4]

He noted, though, that the normal method of killing the elephant seals was with the use of 3 metre lances with very sharp blades, thrust under the left flipper and piercing the heart. This had the advantage of releasing 'torrents of blood'.[5] This bleeding was felt to improve the quality of the oil, and Peron was impressed with the oil. It was clear and odourless and 'it lasts longer than the other products of the same nature: for a sixth of a pint is enough to keep an ordinary wick alight for twelve hours'.[6]

Bloody, destructive and ruthless as this industry was, the fearlessness of the wandering crews was impressive. In battered ships, amongst wild and uncharted oceans, these men were making new discoveries often with little regard, as they single-mindedly pursued their prey to the very end of the world. Jeremiah Reynolds, providing background information to the Committee on Naval Affairs, House of Representatives, United States, in 1828 wrote of them:

> These long and difficult voyages give a hardihood and enterprise to American seamen which will continue as long as we are engaged in this trade. The length of the voyage, the difficulty of the navigation, the large size of the vessels, the science and care necessary for sailing them in safety, and the vicissitudes of the voyage, make the youngest on board a navigator, a seaman, a pilot, a gunner.[7]

By the late 18th century, the seal colonies of the Falklands were being decimated by United States and British crews. Following James Cook's account of fur seals on South Georgia, the voracious industry moved there. Other islands, like Amsterdam and St Paul, and later Kerguelen and the Prince Edward Group, were also plundered.

In February 1819, merchant captain William Smith, was transporting goods between Buenos Aires, and Valparaiso on his ship *Williams*.

> Fancying that the passage round Cape Horn might be weathered better by preserving a more than usual southerly course, being on the 19 February 1819 in Lat 62°W South, and Long 60°W, imagined he saw land at the distance of two leagues.[8]

He hauled off northward for safety overnight and then confirmed his discovery the next morning. On his return voyage from Valparaiso in May, he sailed to 62° 12' South, but difficult winter ice conditions forced him northward without sighting land. Initially his claims were ridiculed 'all endeavouring to persuade him that what he had seen was no more than ice-islands'.[9]

In late September 1819 he returned again from Montevideo to Valparaiso. Again he went well south as he rounded the Cape. On 15 October he found land again. He sent a boat ashore to claim the islands for the crown and spent several more days surveying his discovery. The islands were christened the South Shetlands after their northern namesake.

On his arrival at Valparaiso in November Smith confirmed his discovery to the British naval commander, Captain Shirreff. This time there was excitement amongst the English community.

> Everyone became struck with the advantages a British settlement would offer, not only our whale fisheries, but to our commercial interests in this part of the globe.[10]

Shirreff chartered Smith and his ship and had Edward Bransfield RN, accompanied by three midshipmen from his ship *Andromache*, join the ship to survey the new discoveries. They sailed on 19 December 1819 and reached the islands on 16 January 1820, exploring amongst them until 21 March. They most probably sighted the top of the Antarctic Peninsula which they named Trinity Land.

An account published in the *Literary Gazette and Journal of Belles Lettres* over three issues (3, 10, 24 November 1821) described the sighting:

> They now, in consequence of the weather, steered southward, and seemed to be running from the land; but at three o'clock in the afternoon, after having their attention attracted by three immense icebergs, the haze clearing they very unexpectedly saw land to the S.W.; and at four o'clock were encompassed by islands, spreading from N.E. to E. The whole of these formed a prospect so gloomy that can be imagined, and the only cheer the sight afforded was in the idea that this might be the long-sought Southern Continent, as land was undoubtedly seen in latitude 64°, and trending to the eastward. In this bay or gulph there was a multitude of whales, and a quantity of sea-weed, apparently fresh from rocks. A round island was

called Tower Island, latitude 63° 29', longitude 60° 34', and the land Trinity Land, in compliment to the Trinity Board.[11]

They reached Valparaiso on 15 April 1820.

News seeped out. References to the discovery were made in United States as early as April and in England in May. By August the discoveries were being excitedly reported by the press, expecting 'incalculable advantages to our trade in the South Seas'.[12] Smith's islands were being described as the coast of a continent and seen to have great political advantages in the international climate of the time.

> Our South Sea Traders, who, during hostilities between this country and Spain, have been subjected to the greatest difficulties and privations, will now be independent of Spain or any other power possessing South America.[13]

These islands, at the edge of the Antarctic Peninsula, didn't prove to be the place for a vast new British Colony. However, they quickly attracted British and American sealing ships intent on a fast commercial bonanza. Two ships from Buenos Aires, *Espirito Santo* and *San Juan Nepomuceno* plundered seals at the time Bransfield was surveying the islands for the British Crown. The first United States vessel to arrive was *Hersilia* captained by James Sheffield. The second mate was Nathaniel Palmer who was to become a notable contributor to early Antarctic exploration. The owner, Edmund Fanning, had his son William Fanning accompany the ship. The ten-month voyage began in July 1819, returning to Stonnington, Connecticut in May 1820 with a haul of 9,000 seal skins. This heralded the commencement of the frenetic, lucrative, voracious and brief plunder of the fur seal population of the South Shetlands.

Frederick and *Free Gift* sailed from Stonnington in the same month as *Hersilia* returned. In August 1820 Sheffield sailed south again in *Hersilia*, accompanied by *Express* captained by Ephraim Williams and *Hero* captained by newly promoted Nathaniel Palmer. United States sealers also left New York and Nantucket. Among the Nantucket sealers was *Huntress* under Christopher Burdick, while from New Haven sailed *Huron*, together with the tender *Cecilia*, under John Davis. Various British sealers also sailed to the South Shetlands in 1820, among them Andrew McFarlane aboard *Dragon*.

These early visitors to the South Shetlands were ever searching for a beach free of rivals and teeming with seals. In such close proximity to the Antarctic Peninsula, it is little wonder that there are various accounts and references that suggest possible landings in this vicinity.

The first sightings of the Antarctic continent

The sealers were secretive, and little interested in geographical firsts. These were incidental to the relentless search for new sealing sites. Few ship logs have survived, many writings are vague, and new discoveries have come to light only relatively recently. In the late 1930s vigorous debate raged for several years about the moot point of who was first to sight continental Antarctica. There were two major contenders initially. Bellingshausen, who wasn't sure himself if he had sighted land, though he almost certainly sighted continental ice, and Smith and Bransfield's survey voyage, which is generally considered to have sighted the Trinity Peninsula, at the northern extremity of the Antarctic Peninsula. Based on quite vague writings of Nathaniel Palmer, several American academics, particularly William Hobbs and Lawrence Martin, opened a robust and antagonistic debate for their man's claim. Patriots on both sides argued about dates, latitudes, longitudes and obscure observations in old logbooks. William Hobbs 1939 paper was described by ex RN Lt Cdr R.T. Gould as a 'most regrettable commentary, acridly bitter in tone, painfully wrong in its facts, and scurrilous in language'.[14] Gould declared the 'high mountains covered with snow' charted by Bransfield south-westward of 'Hope Island', are 'obviously Mount Bransfield and Mount Jacquinot' at the north-east extremity of Trinity Peninsula. He triumphantly declared: 'In other words, *Bransfield was the first man to discover and chart a portion of the Antarctic Continent*' (his italics).[15]

The Hobbs article particularly, throwing around accusations of hoax maps, false accounts, conspiratorial suppression of facts by the Admiralty, and generally finding the British to be an untrustworthy and underhand lot, deliberately altering records to deny the honourable Yankee sealers of their rightful discoveries, seems designed to be deliberately provocative. By overlaying the veneer of nationalistic barracking to the discussion, Hobbs has in fact undermined the achievements of the notable mariners involved in the area in the 1820s. The debate became more about Hobbs and his approach. Perhaps that suited him better.

On balance it seems the pro Bransfield/Smith supporters may be correct, although it was many years after these disputed observations that the peninsula was actually proved conclusively to be that and not a series of islands. The debate was probably best summed up by Hunter Christie:

> It is a pity that two men (Bransfield and Palmer), both of whom did excellent work in their own ways, should have become involved long after their deaths in such fruitless controversy.[16]

The first landing

Rather more interesting than this dispute was the discovery in 1952 of the log of Captain John Davis accounting the voyage of the United States sealer *Huron* to the South Shetlands in the 1820–21 season. The logs of *Huntress* and *Hero* also survive. The three logs were used by maritime historian Edouard Stackpole to outline the probable first landing on the Antarctic Continent.

The competition for seal pelts between British and 'Yankee' sealers was fierce, and as the rich seal rookeries were plundered on Livingston Island, tempers frayed. Several American sealers reported threats, harassment, and robbery by the English. Nine sealing captains met on *Huron* to plan their response. They gathered a formidable party and sailed to meet the British at Shirreff's Cape. They rendezvoused at Blythe's Bay. One of their number Captain Bruno, joined them with news that quickly defused the situation. He had checked the beaches around Shirreff's Cape and found them so bereft of seals that there appeared no spoils worth fighting over. These were practical men and the risks involved in pitched battle, with scant reward on offer for the victor, convinced them to withdraw and spend their energies in searching for as yet unfound and unexploited seal rookeries.

In fact such disputes weren't defined by national rivalries. The crew of British sealer *Hetty*, in late 1820, had been driven away from Blythe's Bay by countrymen from other ships. There were also stories of crews taking to each other with sealing clubs, perhaps delivering some justice on behalf of the slaughtered seals. It is likely Captain Davis would have been particularly annoyed at the antagonism of the British having himself rescued a castaway crew (probably from *Lady Troubridge* that foundered on 20 December

1820) and delivered them to British sealers at Rugged Island just prior to the new year.

At the end of January 1821, Captain Davis took his shallop *Cecilia* and sailed south. At the southerly Smith Island the crew of *Lynx*, out of Sydney, were busy skinning seals. Davis continued east to Low Island where his crew took almost 1,000 sealskins. Davis continued below the Shetlands, into the unknown, in search of any land that may have untouched seal rookeries. They sailed into what is now known as Hughes Bay. There, on 7 February 1821 he observed 'land high and covered intirely (sic) with snow … I think this Southern Land to be a Continent.'[17] The shallop's boat was launched to search the beach for seals. It is most likely that this was, at the extremity of the Antarctic Peninsula, outside the Antarctic Circle, the first landing on the continent. This achievement was not particularly noteworthy for Captain Davis, more importantly he notes that there were no signs of seals. Davis and his crew sailed the little shallop out of the bay and north. Three days later they had reached the safety of Yankee Harbour and *Huron*.

Captain Fildes, whose own ship *Cora* had been wrecked at the South Shetlands, wrote about another possible landing by Andrew McFarlane in his ship *Dragon*. He noted that in good weather land was visible to the south of Deception Island. Captain McFarlane confided that he had landed there but disappointingly no seals were found. According to Fildes, Captain Usher, skipper of *Caraquet* (also *Caraquette*) investigated the same land but again found empty beaches.[18]

While these are sketchy evidences, there is little reason to think that these and possibly other intrepid sealing men, on a clear day being able to see the Antarctic Peninsula from Deception Island, would not have ventured to those shores to search for the ever diminishing fur seal. They had little reason to exaggerate their claims, most of which went unread and unknown. Geographical firsts were not their business, seals were, and they went wherever they thought more seals could be found. The South Shetlands were soon abandoned and the areas the sealers hunted and voyaged were barely sighted again until near the new century.

While Davis had been venturing south in *Cecilia* Captain Burdick of *Huntress* had encountered William Smith, the discoverer of the South Shetlands, who had returned with two ships and 60 men and had collected

45,000 skins.[19] (The number of skins may have been exaggerated and is likely to have been 30,000 – still substantial and valued at £7,500).[20] His arrival back in England, though, heralded financial ruin. His partners were in financial trouble. He was bankrupted, and faded into obscurity, writing letters to the Admiralty requesting some financial recognition for the discovery of the South Shetlands. His requests weren't acted upon. He died in 1847.

Towards the end of February 1821, as the weather became worse, many of the sealers headed north. Captain Davis remained until the end of March finally sailing for the Falkland Islands in company with other American ships *Charity*, *Aurora* and *Henry*. He wasn't the last to leave though. A sealing crew from the British ship *Lord Melville*, were stranded on King George Island, when their ship couldn't return to pick them up. The men survived a grim winter and were collected the following season.

After wintering at the Falklands, Captain Davis took *Huntress* and *Cecilia* again to the South Shetlands. The obliteration of the fur seals was so complete that they had to satisfy themselves mainly with Elephant seal blubber to be rendered to oil.

Substantial numbers of British and American ships came to the South Shetlands for the 1821–22 season but the returns were vastly diminished. Sealers in lesser numbers came for subsequent seasons. In a few years the 'gold rush' had ended. There were virtually no seals left to hunt. Those sparse survivors were left to try and re-establish their population.

Nathaniel Palmer sailed back to the South Shetlands for his third straight season. He fell in with British captain George Powell and his ship *Dove*. Jointly they discovered and charted the South Orkneys, sighting land on 6 December 1821. The islands proved disappointingly free of fur seals.

Another regular visitor over several seasons was English sealer James Weddell. His greatest voyage was the penetration of the Weddell Sea to 74° 15'S. Many subsequent voyages found the Weddell Sea unnavigable due to extreme ice conditions. Weddell's voyage has drawn the wrath of the redoubtable Professor Hobbs who dismissed his 'alleged' voyage as 'fictitious', a claim again vigorously contested by British geographers and historians at the time.[21] Weddell's voyage did meet with some scepticism by those who came immediately after him, especially Dumont d'Urville who encountered impenetrable ice in 1838. Weddell's account of his voyage, though, is now generally considered reliable. In answer to the Hobbs article Professor Rudmose Brown concluded 'Weddell was lucky, and luck is a great factor in navigating polar seas. There is not a vestige of justification for doubting his word.'[22] Various geographers and historians have also pointed to the fickle ice conditions that may differ markedly in particular seasons. Since 1973 satellites with passive microwave sensors have enabled scientists to gain a clearer picture of variable ice conditions. Seemingly frozen seas have been found to have vast ice-free regions (polynyas) within them. A winter polynya, 350 km by 1,000 km, was observed via satellite in 1974 and 1975 off Coats Land in the Weddell Sea.[23] Weddell's stated positions on the voyage were on water. Sometimes mariners who exaggerated their positions (such as Benjamin Morrell) were later found to be sailing on land!

The voyages of sealers were often little known. Their aim was strictly commercial and geographical firsts were incidental (the Enderby approach being a notable exception). Many logs and diaries have been lost or destroyed and some remain undiscovered. As surviving logs are studied, they have progressively revealed the extent and achievement of these pioneering Antarctic voyagers. Their influence on subsequent Antarctic exploration was limited though as most were secretive about where they had been and disinterested in geographic goals.

Further notable voyages around this time were firstly that in 1831 of *Venus* skippered by Samuel Harvey. Harvey wrote a letter to the Captain Kelly, Harbourmaster at Hobart. The letter casually mentions that Harvey's ship penetrated to 72º south before being thwarted by 'fogs and thick weather'.[24] While no other source can confirm his latitude, it is likely he was in the vicinity of the Ross Sea a decade before its discoverer James Ross.

In July 1833, *Magnet*, under the command of Peter Kemp, sailed from Britain. They sailed to the Kerguelen Islands. At the end of November 1833, they headed further south. At the end of December they were about 60 kilometres off the Antarctic continent, at about 58ºE, in the area now named for Kemp. They sailed back to the Kerguelens to hunt seal. In late March 1834 they set sail for South Africa. On 21 April 1834, Kemp was lost overboard.

Levant under Mercator Cooper's command sailed deep south looking for whales and seals. A landing was made on sea ice in the vicinity of Cape Adare on 27 January 1853. Whether the men set foot on land or the adjacent ice shelf is unclear.

As more logs from sealing voyages are found and studied it would be unsurprising if further possible landfalls are uncovered. In terms of influencing subsequent explorations, such landings were of no consequence for they remained unknown until well into the 20th Century (or later).

Chapter Three

Enderby & Sons and the Third circumnavigation

In amongst the sealers untamed slaughter there were some great geographical advances. Several of these advances were not incidental. The greatest promoters of exploration among the commercial vessels were the Enderby family company. For three generations they hunted whales and seals, but also sought to expand the map of the world.

The balance between exploration and commerce shifted more towards the former under the stewardship of Samuel's grandson Charles. His quixotic ambitions led to great geographical advances by ships with empty holds. This eventually led his company into bankruptcy. But there was a grandeur to his eventual failure.

The firm was founded by Samuel (1717–97) and was initially involved in the Arctic whaling trade. His ships also carried whale oil and wax from New England, returning to America with other goods.

The revolutionary war curtailed his American trade so he sent his fleet south to new and lucrative whaling grounds. This voracious industry constantly needed to expand its area as whale and seal populations were decimated. In 1787–1788 the Enderby ship *Emelia* became the first British whaler to round Cape Horn. She reached 59°S and returned with a profitable cargo of oil.

Enderby ships helped transport convicts to Sydney as part of the third fleet. This gave them an outward cargo. Once they had disembarked the convicts, enterprising captains could then seek out the Pacific whaling grounds.

In 1792 Enderby despatched former RN ship *Rattler* to explore potential whaling grounds in the southern Atlantic and east Pacific. Such intrepid exploratory voyages became an integral part of the Enderby's operations. Samuel Enderby died in 1797 and the business passed to his sons with Samuel (junior) the principal.

In 1806 the Enderby ship *Ocean*, captained by Abraham Bristow, discovered the Auckland Islands, south of New Zealand. This was the first major land discovery for the firm, and one that would eventually lead to their downfall. In 1807 Bristow returned to the islands. This time he landed and planted the Union Jack, adding to his Majesty's overseas possessions. In 1808 it was Enderby ships (*Swan* under James Lindsay and *Otter* under Thomas Hopper) that finally rediscovered the elusive Bouvet Island, such a cause of much fruitless searching by Cook and others. In fact another Enderby vessel, *Sprightly*, under George Norris, accompanied by the intrepid cutter *Lively*, rediscovered Bouvet Island again in 1825. Norris also noted the nearby volcanic island he named Thompson. Joseph Fuller, captaining *Francis Allyn*, made brief reference to sighting both Bouvet Island and Thompson Island during his 1893–1895 voyage. Thompson Island has not been sighted since, and it has been theorised that it may have disappeared due to a volcanic eruption.[1]

Charles Enderby's explorations

In 1829 the junior Samuel Enderby died and his son Charles took over the company. Charles was a founding fellow of the Royal Geographical Society and a fellow of both the Royal Society and the Linnean Society. He actively promoted geographical exploration in concert with more commercial goals. His ambitions were ultimately thwarted partly because of a number of geographically notable, but commercially disastrous voyages. Finally, an ill-judged attempt to establish a colony on the remote and inhospitable Auckland Islands put the family firm into bankruptcy.

John Biscoe

Soon after his father's death Charles despatched Enderby captain John Biscoe on a whaling, sealing and exploratory voyage to the Antarctic (1830–33). On 14 July 1830 two Enderby brothers' ships, the 150-ton *Tula*, accompanied by the 50-ton cutter *Lively*, set sail from the Port of London. Charles Enderby delivered to John Biscoe his final instructions. These included not just commercial outcomes, but also 'to endeavour to make discoveries in a high southern latitude'.[2]

The two vessels cleared the Channel on 30 July. Their first Port was Boa Vista, Cape Verde. The ships lost touch as they headed south. They rendezvoused at Port Louis, Berkeley Sound, Falkland Islands on 10 November 1830. At the end of November, the ships set sail again towards the Antarctic. *Lively* had a new captain – Mr Avery. Captain Smith had left the expedition in the Falklands after being scolded by Biscoe for losing touch on the voyage from Cape Verde.

Initially the ships set out in search of Aurora Islands, thought to lie between the Falklands and South Georgia. These mythical islands, now thought to be the bleak Shag Rocks, were originally 'discovered' by Joseph de la Llana, master of the Spanish ship *Aurora*. In 1790, another Spanish ship *Principessa*, reported sighting the islands. In 1794 the Spanish expedition aboard *Descubierta* and *Atrevida* seeking to ascertain the exact position of the islands, located three rocks at 53°48'W.

Unsurprisingly Biscoe didn't locate the Aurora Islands. He sailed on. On 20 December he sighted one of the South Sandwich group.

> Its appearance being very discouraging ... being nothing more than a complete rock, covered with ice, snow, and heavy clouds, so that it was difficult to distinguish one from the other.[3]
>
> They continued southeast. By 7 January 1831 they were closely skirting the field ice the whole way, and examining every inlet, in hopes of finding a passage to the southward ... In this, however, they were constantly disappointed.[4]

On January 28 they reached their farthest south at 69°.[5] They continued east. By late February they had managed to manoeuvre close enough to sight land. 'At length, on the 27th, in Lat 65°57'S, Long 47°20'E, land was distinctly seen, of considerable extent, but closely bound with field ice.'[6] They named it Enderby Land.

It was a century before Enderby Land was again sighted. *Norvegia* under Riiser-Larsen and Douglas Mawson's BANZARE expedition both confirmed the details of Biscoe's sighting.[7] The two expeditions in fact met near Cape Ann on 14 January 1930.

Biscoe's sighting was attended by an appearance by Aurora Australis, spectacular enough to take their attention from the precarious position of the ship.

> At times rolling as it were, over our heads in the form of beautiful columns, then as suddenly changing like the fringe of a curtain, and again shooting

across the hemisphere like a serpent; frequently appearing not many yards above our heads, and decidedly within our atmosphere. It was by much the most magnificent phenomenon of the kind that I ever witnessed; and although the vessel was in considerable danger, running with a smart breeze and much beset, the people could scarcely be kept from looking at the heavens instead of attending to the course

The ships were now hit by ferocious weather. A heavy gale on 5 March, continued

> increasing to a perfect hurricane, till the 7th. In the course of it, the two vessels again separated, the Tula was much injured, several of her men were severely hurt, and their health seriously affected by exposure to the cold.[8]

Still, though, Biscoe doggedly pursued land. He sighted and named Cape Ann. The choice of name has long been considered obscure, but the best guess appears to be that he named it for his mother.[9] On board *Tula*, the situation had become dire. They had not seen *Lively* since 6 March, and there were great fears for the little cutter's safety. Their own vessel was

> now a complete Mass of Ice, only 3 of the crew who can stand & likewise being well convinced that any Land to the Southward of that lat'd [61°S] would be inaccessible I find myself from these most imperious circumstances obliged although very reluctantly to give up any further pursuit this season …[10]

It was a grim voyage to Van Diemen's Land (Tasmania). Two crew had already died and the others being so reduced that the ship was entirely navigated by the three officers, one man and a boy.

> The nights, during most of the period, were so dark, except when occasionally illumined by the aurora, that in the helpless state of the crew, and their utter inability to meet any sudden exigency, it was deemed expedient to lie to every evening till the following morning.[11]

Tula reached Hobart on 10 May 1831.[12] Biscoe remained there for 5 months. His battered ship was refitted and his ailing crew recuperated. There was no sign of *Lively*. As time passed hopes faded.

Lively, though, had survived. The little vessel finally struggled up the Derwent in September 1831 with a great tale to tell.[13]

Most of the crew died, and Captain Avery was left with only a man and a boy to sail the ship. The boy's hand had been shattered in an accident and the three were too debilitated to remove the last two dead crewmen whose bodies remained below. Eventually the captain was able to rig a rope and tackle to hoist the bodies on deck before 'launching them into the deep'.[14] He managed to manoeuvre the ship through the treacherous entry to Port Phillip Bay. This large bay is the location of the city of Melbourne, but in 1831 there was no European settlement.

They were able to get to shore to forage for food, but as if they hadn't faced enough adversity, *Lively* drifted away. They walked nearly 40 miles, finally locating the grounded cutter. They were able to refloat her and make their way to Hobart.

Reunited the two ships set forth again on 8 October 1831. They spent some time in the waters around New Zealand and the Chatham Islands in the hope of catching some seals 'with very indifferent success'.[15] They headed south again and made further discoveries in the area of the Antarctic Peninsula including some islands, later named for Biscoe, and an island he named Adelaide, for the Queen. This great voyage of discovery did also have a commercial motive, and his crew attempted some sealing at Smith Island, in the South Shetland group, but with little success.

The expedition arrived at the Falkland Islands towards the end of April 1832, thereby completing this third Antarctic circumnavigation. Ill fortune stalked them. *Lively*, having battled so much danger and adversity to complete the circumnavigation, was wrecked at Mackay's Island (Falklands). The crew, though, were saved. Biscoe's voyage finally ended at East Country Dock on 8 February 1833. It was a great geographical and nautical success, but rather less so commercially, delivering a paltry cargo of 30 seal skins. Charles Enderby seemed unperturbed by the financial loss. He was already planning to send Biscoe off again on a further exploratory voyage in July.

> The probability seems thus to be revived of the existence of a great Southern Land, yet to be brought upon our charts ... so strongly, indeed, are Messrs Enderby impressed with this probability, that, undeterred by the heavy loss which they have incurred by the late voyage, they propose again sending out Captain Biscoe this season, on the same research ... And the Lords Commissioners of the Admiralty have resolved to send an officer of the Royal Navy, Mr Rea, as passenger in his ship, to assist him in those scientific

observations which, whatever may be the fate of the commercial speculation confided to him, will probably make his next voyage still more valuable than that just concluded.[16]

Alas, for reasons unclear, Biscoe didn't, finally, take charge of that voyage. At all events it proved unsuccessful. William Lysle captained *Hopefull* (with RN officer Rea onboard), while John Tobias Mallows captained *Rose*.

Rose was crushed in the ice pack at 60°S, 53°W. The crew were saved but the expedition was discontinued. Another bold, but very costly endeavour by the Enderbys.

John Biscoe married in 1836 and sailed to Sydney, later moving his expanding family to Hobart. His epic circumnavigation had taken a toll on his health. In 1842 he was forced to retire from the sea. A public subscription funded his return to England aboard *Janet Izat*, embarking on 15 February 1843. Biscoe, though, didn't live to see England again, expiring during the long voyage.

John Balleny

Undaunted by such considerations as profit, Charles Enderby organised another expedition, that again proved rather greater in geographical than commercial returns.

Charles Enderby proudly acknowledged this to the Royal Geographical Society:

> Nothing discouraged by this failure, [referring to *Hopefull* and *Rose* expedition.] and the heavy loss already incurred, Messrs. Enderby, in conjunction with some other merchants, determined on another South Sea sealing voyage, giving special instructions to the commander of the expedition that he was to lose no opportunity of pushing as far as he could south, in the hopes of discovering land in a high southern latitude.[17]

In June 1838 the Enderby's purchased *Sabrina*, a Cowes cutter of 47 tons. In July there followed the purchase of the 134-ton schooner *Eliza Scott*. In recognition of the companies deteriorating finances 53 of 64 shares in each vessel was on sold to other London merchants. At the outset of the voyage there was some uncertainty about the captaincy of the two ships. John Balleny appears to have been a very late appointment as captain of *Eliza Scott* as was Thomas Freeman of *Sabrina*. The ships left London on 14 July 1838.

By early December the ships had reached New Zealand. They headed south in early January and anchored for several days in Perseverance Harbour, Campbell Islands. There was another ship there at the time, *Emma* [sometimes referred to as *Lady Emma*], coincidentally captained by John Biscoe on an expedition from Sydney. Biscoe's epic circumnavigation had been ruinous to his health, and he had spent his time in Australia mainly in the coastal trade. Here though he was setting forth on a sealing trip far to the south. He had sailed on 7 December 1838 and didn't return to Sydney until 13 May 1839. Balleny, in his log, wrote 'I find Capt Biscoe is in search of land as well as ourselves'.[18]

Where Biscoe went and what he discovered remain unclear. On his return to Sydney, the *Gazette* made reference to this mysterious 'voyage of discovery', suggesting Biscoe has sailed

> ... as a far south as 75°. Owing to the secrecy of the trip we are unable to give our readers any information. During her voyage she started her upper works and was obliged to put into the Orkneys to have them fresh treenailed, which occasioned a detention of one month.[19]

Apart from Balleny's remarking on their encounter at the Campbell Islands, this appears to be the only significant reference to the voyage. There appears to be no log in existence. The claim of 75°, if true, would have reflected a truly sensational voyage, surpassing Weddell's furthest south. A.G.E. Jones speculates that he may have made this high latitude in the south Pacific or the Weddell Sea.[20] But, as remarkable as such an achievement would be, it is more likely the product of a journalist's illegible notes or faulty hearing. The voyage remains a tantalising mystery. Perhaps more reliable light is shed on it by Dumont d'Urville who met Biscoe in Hobart on 26 December 1839. He wrote that Biscoe 'told me that he had lately tried to get further south along the meridian of New Zealand; but that ice had stopped him at 63° South'.[21]

Balleny continued south. On 1 February 1839, they achieved their highest latitude at 69°S. On 9 February they sighted land.

> At 11A.M. Noticed a darkish appearance to the S.W. ... At noon the sun shone brightly: saw the appearance of land to the S.W. Extending from west to about south – ran for it: at 4h. Made it out distinctly to be land. At 8h P.M. (having run S.W. 22m) got within 5 miles of it, when we saw another piece of land of great height, bearing W. by S. At sunset we distinctly made

them out to be three separate islands of good size, but the western one the longest. Lay-to all night off the middle island.[22]

On 12 February they attempted a shore landing on Young Island. There was no suitable landing spot, but Captain Freeman jumped from the boat 'got a few stones but was up to the middle in water'.[23] They continued westward.

On 2 March, at 8p.m., Balleny recorded distant land near the area now named Sabrina Coast. At noon that day he recorded his position as 64°58'S, 121°08'E. At that point while the coast of the continent was due south of his ship, it was many miles distant.

On 21 March 1839, 'the autumnal equinox of these latitudes was rendered brilliant by a magnificent display of Aurora Australis'.[24] Alas its brilliance may have been a portent of approaching doom. In the afternoon of 24 March, a gale sprung up. Balleny last saw the cutter *Sabrina* burning a blue distress light at midnight, but the ferocity of the storm didn't allow him to get any closer. His own vessel was 'labouring and pitching violently'.

At 9 a.m. the next morning

> a heavy sea broke on board the schooner, staving both boats, and sweeping everything from the decks, and laying the vessel on her beam ends: for ten minutes she appeared to be settling in the water, but she gradually righted ...[25]

There was no further sign of *Sabrina*. Despite Balleny's hope that she may have escaped and found her way to safety independently, as *Lively* had on Biscoe's voyage, she was never seen again, lost with all hands. Captain Freeman's soggy landing at Young Island a lonely epitaph for he and his anonymous crew.

Balleny sailed north. At the end of April *Eliza Scott* reached Madagascar and remained there for a month as his crew recovered from the gruelling voyage. They sailed again in early June, arriving back in England on 18 September 1839. James Clark Ross was in port preparing his ships *Terror* and *Erebus* for a voyage south in search of the magnetic pole. Balleny was able to pass on a copy of his chart and notes from his log.

Balleny's voyage did excite interest from other notable men. Charles Darwin was particularly interested in a report that a rock had been observed in an iceberg. He interviewed *Eliza Scott*'s second mate John McNab, having previously questioned John Biscoe about his observations in the Antarctic.

Darwin felt that

> every fact in the transportation of fragments of rock by ice is of importance, as throwing light on the problem of 'erratic boulders', which has so long perplexed geologists.[26]

In *The Voyage of the Beagle* Darwin again refers to the 'gigantic boulder embedded in an iceberg in the Antarctic Ocean, almost certainly 100 miles distant from any land, and perhaps much more distant'.[27]

Mawson's expeditions of 1911–14 and 1929–31 explored the area where Balleny had reported 'Sabrina Land' and found it to be non-existent. The land directly south though, Mawson sighted and appropriately named for the lost cutter *Sabrina*.

> We were then in the vicinity of Balleny's supposed landfall recorded in the year 1839. We proved quite conclusively that land does not exist in that neighbourhood.

Mawson then went up in the plane and observed in the SSW

> what appears to be ice-covered low land. Should the latter prove to be the case on further investigation, we propose that the term Sabrina Land be applied to it to commemorate Balleny's effort.[28]

Charles Enderby's summation of the voyage was that

> the results of this voyage must tend to keep alive the supposition of the existence of either a great southern land or a vast mass of islands, whose northern limits would seem to range between the 67th and 69th parallels, a part of which we trust, ere long, to see laid down in our charts, and not improbably rendered subservient to the interests of science, if not to the prosperity of our fisheries.[29]

In the space of a decade Charles Enderby had sent out, under Biscoe, under Lysle, and under Balleny, expeditions with bold geographic intent, (and success in Biscoe and Balleny's case), but had lost a ship on each expedition and each were significant commercial failures. At the time of Balleny's voyage the Enderby's financial situation was such that they had sold 80% of the shares in their vessels to other London merchants. The geographic achievements of the voyages didn't include discovery of significant exploitable new whaling and sealing grounds.

Antarctic historian Hugh Robert Mill wrote:

> There is, perhaps, no other instance of a private mercantile firm undertaking so extensive a series of voyages of discovery without much encouragement in the way of pecuniary returns.[30]

In the 1840s the days of the vast Enderby shipping fleets sailing the southern oceans were past. They had become merchants in Australian wool, and rope manufacturers in Greenwich. In 1845 disaster struck the brothers business when their factory and storehouses were destroyed by fire. The main factory 'a noble looking building overlooking the Thames' collapsed. The building contained recently installed and extensive machinery. Various other buildings in the factory complex were severely damaged and the newspapers estimated damage in excess of £40,000, only £6,000 was covered by insurance.[31]

By 1849 the situation of the family company was dire. In October 1849 the *The Times* of London reported that the 'Messrs Charles, Henry and George Enderby … have announced themselves unable to meet their engagements'. Their rope works had been disposed of and 'it is feared that various members of the family will in the aggregate suffer severely'.[32] But by the time of the report Charles Enderby was already at sea, enacting plans to restore the family's fortunes with a new company, the Southern Whale Fishery.

He looked to the bleak and remote sub-Antarctic Auckland Islands, 465 kilometres south of New Zealand's South Island. Discovered by an Enderby captain Abraham Bristow and claimed by him for the crown in 1807, the islands had been left alone, disturbed only by sealing crews and the occasional shipwreck. The seal populations were quickly reduced almost to extinction, but Charles Enderby saw potential. He planned a settlement that could farm livestock and grow vegetables. He envisaged a fleet that could hunt coastal and ocean whale populations. A dockyard could provide commercial facilities for refitting passing ships.

In 1849 a paper titled *Revival of the Southern Whale Fishery – The Auckland Islands*, and liberally quoting Charles Enderby, painted a very positive picture. The islands were

> covered with wood and have a very rich virgin soil, capable of feeding on one acre of land as many sheep as can be fed on six acres in Australia; the land is equally suitable for feeding cattle, horses,&c; it is also capable of

growing all such products as are usually grown in England.[33]

Enderby negotiated a 30-year lease with the British Crown and the Queen appointed him Lieutenant Governor on 16 June 1849 of this new British colony. In November and December 1849 three shiploads of settlers arrived at the Auckland Islands.

The settlement was a failure. It was difficult to grow anything in the bleak climate and poor soils. There were few passing ships to make use of the dock facilities, and whales were scarce. Fergus McLaren summed up the failure succinctly:

> Possessing a vile climate, land unsuitable for cultivation, and no natural resources, a less suitable situation for the new colony could hardly have been chosen.[34]

Settlers began abandoning the colony. The London directors of the Southern Whale Fishery Company became increasingly perturbed at the vast imbalance between expenditure and income. Finally, late in 1851, they sent two special commissioners to the Aucklands. The two commissioners, George Dundas and Thomas Preston, considered the situation dire and in direct defiance of Charles Enderby's determined optimism were adamant that there was no future for the colony. It came to an acrimonious end and was officially closed on 5 August 1852.

There was one more foray to the high southern latitudes by an Enderby ship when *Brisk*, under Captain Thomas Tapsell, sailed from the Auckland Islands on a Southern Whale Fishery expedition. He sighted the Balleny Islands in February 1850 and then westwards to longitude 143° in a reportedly higher latitude than Charles Wilkes without sighting land.

After three generations the Enderby family company was bankrupted. They had, though, made an enduring contribution to Antarctic discovery. Many Antarctic names recognise Enderby captains, ships, and the family. Herman Melville, in *Moby Dick* writes:

> Ere the English ship fades from sight, be it set down here, that she hailed from London, and was named after the late Samuel Enderby, merchant of that city, the original of the famous house of Enderby & Sons; a house in my poor whaleman's opinion, comes not far behind the united royal houses of the Tudors and Bourbons, in point of real historical interest.[35]

Charles Enderby was embittered by this final failure and engaged in furious correspondence with the company directors regarding the behaviour of Preston and Dundas.

On 22 February 1858, he presented the logs of John Biscoe and John Balleny to the Royal Geographical Society of London. He died in London, intestate, at age 78 on 31 August 1876. In his last years he had been living at his sister's house.

Chapter Four

Three national expeditions

After the predations of the sealers had decimated any accessible seal populations to the edge of the Antarctic Circle, discovery of the continent moved back to the hands of large, government sponsored, naval expeditions.

In April 1828, the RN sloop *Chanticleer* sailed from Spithead on a voyage south under Henry Foster. It was a scientific expedition with aims to 'determine the specific ellipticity of the earth, ascertain the chronometric difference of meridians of the principal stations of the Atlantic; and make observations in magnetism, meteorology'.[1]

The voyage ranged across the Atlantic and spent some time in the South Shetlands at Deception Island. Vague references were made to a landing 'on the most southern tract of land on the globe'.[2] Unfortunately Foster was drowned while canoeing the Chagres River in Central America. The expedition returned under the command of Lt Horatio Austin, later a commander of one of the Royal Navy expeditions searching the Arctic for the lost Franklin ships.

In the late 1830s French, United States, and British expeditions sailed south, primarily in the service of science. At the time they set sail there had already been much activity at the South Shetlands and the vicinity of the Antarctic Peninsula. James Weddell had recorded a voyage beyond 74°S in the sea bearing his name. Balleny had found islands within the Antarctic Circle south of Macquarie Island and reported sighting land further west (Sabrina Coast). Biscoe had discovered Enderby Land and had sighted and named Graham Land (one of several sightings of parts of the Antarctic Peninsula up to that time). There was a strong belief in the existence of a southern continent. The three national expeditions were able to give greater shape to the continent. Ross penetrated the sea and reached the great ice barrier, both now named for him, setting a new furthest south of 78° 10'. Wilkes sailed westward along the edge of the continent from just beyond the Balleny islands for 2,700 kilometres. At times he sighted land, and continental ice, at times he made educated guesses. He returned from the polar regions sure that he had been at the edge of a vast continent. Dumont d'Urville was in the same area as Wilkes. Dumont d'Urville too sighted land, his men also made a landing on a tiny islet just off the coast of what is now known as Adelie Land.

Dumont d'Urville and the French Expedition 1837–40

Jules Sébastian César Dumont d'Urville, possessing a name as elaborately impressive as his predecessors de Gonneville and Bouvet, was born in 1790 at a time of great revolutionary tumult in France. A voracious reader and serious student, he joined the French Navy in 1807. Not one for social frivolities, 'aloof, brusque ... and without social graces'[3] he was not always popular with his naval contemporaries. But he was ambitious, single-minded, intelligent and inquiring.

From the late 18th century into the first part of the 19th century La Pérouse, d'Entrecasteaux, Baudin, Fréycinet and others led scientific, geographic and potentially colonial expeditions from France to explore the Pacific and beyond.

In 1785 La Pérouse set sail on an ambitious voyage that was planned to explore both hemispheres. After encountering Arthur Phillip's convict flotilla in Botany Bay the French expedition disappeared into thin air.

Bruni d'Entrecasteaux, who, in 1791, was sent to locate any trace of La Pérouse, explored the Australian and New Guinea coastline finding no sign of the lost expedition. D'Entrrecasteaux died during the voyage, in 1793. In 1794 his successor as commander, Jean-Louis d'Hesmity d'Auribeau, handed the expedition ships to Dutch authorities at Surabaya (East Java) rather than return them to the control of the new republican government in France.

On 19 October 1800 ships *Géographe* and the *Naturaliste*, under the command of Nicolas Baudin sailed from Le Havre, France. Illness and death cut a swathe through the large contingent of expedition scientists, artists and gardeners with only a handful completing the voyage.

The two ships sailed into Port Jackson and spent time at Sydney Town in late 1802. *Naturaliste* then sailed for France while *Géographe* continued to investigate the Australian coast.

The expedition completed detailed geographic and scientific studies of Australia and gathered significant collections of flora and fauna. On the return voyages of *Naturaliste* and *Géographe* the ships must have resembled Noah's Ark with a collection of the strangest animals, and the ships decks covered in plants. Keeping this extensive collection of flora and fauna alive, crossing the vastness of several oceans, through wild seas and doldrums, fierce heat and storms, was a near impossible challenge. Aboard *Naturaliste* the attrition rate of both plants and animals was very high. Nicolas Baudin, on *Géographe*, demanded much greater care. Unfortunately, Baudin, like many of the captured animals, failed to complete the return journey, dying in Mauritius in 1803. Despite the losses on the long journey home, the natural history collections that arrived in the two ships were extraordinary.

Amongst the menagerie that arrived safely in France were two distinct dwarf emu sub-species that had lived in splendid isolation on King Island and Kangaroo Island for thousands of years. Several emus from both islands were collected by Baudin's scientists just as the arrival on the two islands of European sealers and farmers were pushing this sub-species to rapid extinction.

The plants and the surviving animals were destined for the gardens of Malmaison, the magnificent estate of Josephine, wife of the soon to be crowned emperor Napoleon Bonaparte. For the rest of her life Josephine developed a magnificent garden including many plants from Baudin's expedition. Roaming the gardens were various exotic creatures.

The final surviving King and Kangaroo Island emus lived out their lives as the last of their kind in the lonely splendour of imperial France, firstly at Malmaison and then at the equally grand Jardin des Plantes. They outlived their benefactor Empress Josephine (*d.*1814), and their collector Nicolas Baudin.

Louis de Fréycinet had been the surveyor on the Baudin expedition and then led his own expedition to the South Seas in 1817, despite the loss of one of the expedition ships in the Falklands (*L'Uranie*), he was finally able to return to France with a further exceptional collection of natural history and scientific observances.

Dumont d'Urville's career started more modestly, but as it happened, fortuitously for the collection at the Louvre. In 1819 he joined the ship *Chevrette* for a surveying voyage in the Mediterranean. *Chevrette* arrived at the

Greek island of Melos shortly after a local farmer had uncovered an ancient sculpture. It was the Venus de Milo and Dumont d'Urville was integral in France acquiring it.

In 1822 he commenced the first of three substantial voyages to the southern seas, as second in command on *Coquille* under Louis Isadore Duperrey.

Duperrey had been Fréycinet's second in command. The expedition extended from 1822 to 1825 and explored potential sites for a French colony around the Australian coast. In part Duperrey's instructions were to investigate the South-West of the continent, particularly the area of the Swan River and King George Sound, with a view to establishing a French colony. Despite Duperrey's instructions (and much to Dumont d'Urville's frustration), little time was spent investigating potential colonial sites on the Australian south-west coast. The expedition did though make a significant contribution to the science of magnetism and natural history.

The year following his return, Dumont d'Urville was given command of his own expedition, again looking to further French interests in Oceania. *Coquille* was renamed *Astrolabe* in honour of one of the lost ships on the La Pérouse expedition. Dumont d'Urville set sail from Toulon on 25 April 1826, with a crew of 79 men. His instructions set out an itinerary that commenced with a voyage to Port Jackson (Sydney) where the crew could recover from the long voyage and address any issues with the ships. From there he was to proceed to investigate the north of New Zealand and then sail to Tonga, Fiji, New Caledonia, New Guinea, Ambon Island (Indonesia), and then Palau returning via Mauritius. As with other early 19th century French expeditions part of Dumont d'Urville's task was to follow up any leads to the mysteries around the disappearance of La Pérouse.

La Pérouse commanded an expedition that left France on 1 August 1785 with two ships *La Boussole* and *Astrolabe*. It was an ambitious voyage investigating the South Pacific, then sailing north to Alaska for one of many investigations of a possible Northwest Passage to the Atlantic. La Pérouse then sailed south and east to the coast of China, then the Philippines, and Japan, further north to Siberia where he despatched journals and maps overland to France. They sailed south to Samoa, where the crew of *Astrolabe* were involved in a skirmish with the locals, losing 11 men including that ship's captain Paul Antoine Fleuriot de Langle.

La Pérouse sailed into Botany Bay just a few days after Arthur Phillip and his 11 shiploads of convicts, soldiers and crew had arrived to establish a British penal colony. The two parties exchanged cordial greetings. The French expedition left Botany Bay on 10 March 1788 and vanished.

In October 1826 Dumont d'Urville's expedition reached the west coast of Australia. He was determined to explore King George Sound in a manner that his superior Duperrey had failed to do on the *Coquille* expedition. After nearly three weeks his conclusion was that 'it would be difficult to come upon a more favourable place to found a colony'.[4] Dumont d'Urville relentlessly pursued the planned itinerary with, in his own words, 'stubborn determination, some will say blind recklessness'.[5]

The expedition spent the last half of December 1827 in Hobart and here Dumont d'Urville heard stories of a possible discovery of La Pérouse's fate. Peter Dillon, an Irish trader in the Pacific, had come upon artefacts and stories that the La Pérouse ships had been wrecked at Vanikoro in the Solomon Islands. On 5 January 1828, Dumont d'Urville left Hobart to investigate. Finally he was able to confirm the fate of the La Pérouse expedition. The ships had been wrecked on reefs. Men were able to get to shore and while their fate is unclear, no survivors were found 40 years later by Dumont d'Urville. He was able to recover many relics of the expedition and build a monument to the lost crews.

On 25 February 1829 the expedition docked in Marseille, just two months short of 3 years after departure. Dumont d'Urville had completed virtually everything in his original instructions and had solved the mystery of La Pérouse.

Despite his achievements it was not until 1837 that he commanded another expedition. He spent a number of years preparing reports of his *Astrolabe* expedition for publication, and his fractious personality may have irritated his superiors. However on 7 September 1837 the ships *Astrolabe* and *Zélée* sailed from Toulon. His instructions again had the expedition exploring widely across the Pacific including advice to 'direct your route towards the 23rd parallel of latitude, coasting the whole string of islands, Ducie Pitcairn, Gambier Rapa, Rourontac, Mangia, Raratonga'. However his first challenge was to explore 'towards the Pole as far as the polar ice will permit'.[6]

His first foray into the ice was frustratingly unsuccessful. Hoping to emulate James Weddell he set course for the Weddell Sea. The first sight of ice was awe inspiring.

> Austere and grandiose beyond words, while stirring the imagination, it filled us with an involuntary feeling of dread, nowhere else can man feel so strongly the sense of his own impotence ... It is a new world unfolding before our eyes, but a world that is inert, mournful and silent, where everything threatens man with annihilation.[7]

With his ships caught precariously in the ice having made very little distance and contemplating death on icefloes if the ships were crushed, Dumont d'Urville found himself sceptical of Weddell's furthest south.

> Either Weddell struck an exceptionally favourable season, or he played on the credulity of his readers ... I still had great trouble believing that such solid and extensive ice as we had just encountered could ever yield passage to ships.

Dumont d'Urville wrote these comments after he returned and was aware of James Ross furthest south on the other side of the continent and so stopped short of completely discarding Weddell's claims, allowing that if any ship advanced six degrees beyond his position he would accept Weddell's claims.[8]

They escaped the ice but the crew of his companion ship *Zélée* were savaged by scurvy. The ships struggled into Talcahuano Bay, Concepción, Chile, where they remained for nearly 7 weeks. They then sailed across the Pacific, north of New Guinea, stopping at Guam as he had ten years previously, and visiting several islands in the Moluccas. The ships ventured into the Torres Strait from the west, stopping for several days at Port Essington, a British military outpost on Australia's north coast. They returned to the Moluccas, then Singapore, Borneo, and the Philippines before sailing south to Hobart in preparation for another voyage to the Antarctic. Their time in the tropics left them with a dysentery epidemic with crew on both ships confined to their bunks and several sailors dying. The two ships gratefully reached Hobart on 12 December 1839, having lost 16 men to illness. Several more died in Hobart.

Dumont d'Urville's original instructions had only specified one foray into the Antarctic, their unsuccessful time at the edge of the Weddell Sea. The commander was frustrated and disappointed with that attempt. He had met with polar veteran John Biscoe in Hobart. Biscoe related having spoken with Charles Wilkes regarding the Antarctic ambitions of his United States Exploring Expedition. British Arctic veteran James Ross, commanding *Terror* and *Erebus*, had embarked from England several months earlier, also determined to unravel the mysteries of the Antarctic. No doubt Gallic pride was pricked by the glories these expeditions were likely to garner. At that point Dumont d'Urville had barely penetrated the ice and had sailed over much the same area of the Pacific as his previous expedition a decade earlier.

The ships and the crew had been at sea for two arduous years. There had been deaths, illness, deprivation but d'Urville resolved that before setting a course for New Zealand as per his instructions, he would make another voyage south. The decision is perhaps best summed up by his secretary, César Desgraz who noted that with Ross and Wilkes in the field it would be 'embarrassing' and 'painful' for their expedition to remain 'aloof from this noble struggle'.[9]

And so, on 2 January 1840, their two ships sailed south from Hobart. Much like Wilkes, Dumont d'Urville's enduring fame was primarily for an Antarctic voyage which encompassed only a short part of his entire expedition, in this case one month of a voyage of over 3 years.

On 16 January 1840, they sighted ice and on 19 January they sighted land, named by Dumont d'Urville for his wife Adélie. Two days later several crew set foot on one of the small islands, just offshore. Their voyage south, to that point, had been quite smooth, on 24 January though, they encountered a fierce Antarctic gale that almost sunk *Astrolabe*.

To add to their worries, the compasses were rendered next to useless by their proximity to the South Magnetic Pole. After a desperate 22 hours, the gale abated, with both ships having survived, to continue their exploration of the Adélie Land coastline. On the 29th quite remarkably they encountered one of the ships from Wilkes US Exploring Expedition.

The US ship *Porpoise* had lost contact with the other ships of the US expedition when they sighted two vessels. In the vastness of the Antarctic they had come upon the French expedition. The ships passed without exchanging compliments or information, both claiming surprise at the others ignorance of protocol. Wilkes described the French action as a 'cold repulse'.[10] Dumont d'Urville, though, expected the American ship to exchange greetings. As

Porpoise was travelling quickly Dumont d'Urville ordered the mainsails be reset to keep abreast of the visitor, but *Porpoise* continued without acknowledging the French ship.

Given Wilkes tendency to be secretive and sinuously ambiguous, and given Dumont d'Urville's austere, prickly but honourable character, and great sea borne experience, it is unlikely the Frenchman would have avoided the encounter or misrepresented the circumstances. Dumont d'Urville graciously suggested that it might well have just been a misunderstanding of each ship's intentions.

No doubt much to the relief of his exhausted crew, on 1 February 1840, d'Urville set a course northward. They reached Hobart on 17 February 1840, a brief sojourn after the dangers and deprivations of the ice. A week later they set sail again for New Zealand, investigating the sub–Antarctic Auckland Islands and then sailing north along the east coast of the South and North islands. The voyage continued to the Torres Strait, where disaster struck when, on 1 June 1840, both ships were caught on reefs. Dumont d'Urville was assailed with fears that having 'emerged victorious from their battles in the ice to perish miserably on some nameless reef'.[11] After a tense four days, when at times it seemed the fate of La Pérouse may also be theirs, the tide and the winds conspired to free both ships. It was the final serious drama of an epic voyage, the last of the great French scientific expeditions by sail. On 7 November 1840 they reached Toulon, 38 months after they had set out. Less than two years later, on 8 May 1842 Dumont d'Urville took his family on an outing to Versailles. On the short return journey to Paris their train derailed. Dumont d'Urville, his wife and son were amongst the many who died in the disaster.

Symmes Theory, Charles Wilkes and the United States Exploring Expedition

A year after Dumont d'Urville's expedition commenced the ambitious United States Exploring Expedition set sail.

The Ex-Ex had a long gestation. In fact it could be claimed that the long road to the expedition started with a fantastical theory that might have come straight from the pages of Jules Verne. In April 1818 a sincere and serious former soldier, John Cleves Symmes, a resident of St Louis, published and distributed his theory proposing that the earth was hollow and beyond the ice at the extremities of the globe were warm climates and entrances to the earth's core.

> I declare the earth is hollow, habitable within; containing a number of solid concentrick spheres; one within the other, and that it is open at the pole twelve or sixteen degrees. I pledge my life in support of this truth, and am ready to explore the hollow if the world will support and aid me in the undertaking.

The Arctic was the place to prove his theory.

> I ask one hundred brave companions, well equipped to start from Siberia, in the fall season, with reindeer and sledges, on the ice of the frozen sea; I engage we find a warm and rich land, stocked with thrifty vegetables and animals, if not men, on reaching one degree northward of latitude 82; we will return the succeeding spring.[12]

His theories were generally ridiculed, but he was not swayed from them and lectured widely gaining some acolytes. One was prominent Ohio businessman James McBride who helped promote Symmes theory all the way to Congress where various petitions were submitted on Symmes behalf. Symmes himself boldly petitioned the Senate via Mr Johnson of Kentucky stating his belief of the existence of an inhabited concave to this globe; his desire to embark on a voyage of discovery to one or other of the polar regions; his belief in the value and honour to his country of the discoveries he would make; that his pecuniary means are inadequate to the purpose without public aid; and suggesting to Congress the equipment of two vessels, each of 250 or 300 tons, for the expedition; and the granting such other aid as government may deem requisite to promote the object.

Congress ultimately declined his offer but he continued proselytising. His theory resonated with the young and dynamic editor of the *Wilmington Spectator*, Jeremiah Reynolds. Reynolds was so taken with Symmes ideas that in October 1825 he joined him lecturing to a sceptical public at halls in small towns and large, including major centres such as New York, Philadelphia and Boston. The ambitious Reynolds, an engaging speaker, assumed a more central role and the two men parted ways within 6 months. Symmes continued the grind of lecturing with little reward and much ridicule and disinterest. Discouraged and ill Symmes withdrew back to Cincinnati and then to the family home in Hamilton, Ohio. He died 29 May 1829.

His theory has been revisited several times. In 1873 a lecture he had given at Union College during the winter of 1826–27 was recounted from memory by a former student who had attended. The writer was still a believer and recalled confirmation in William Edward Parry's observations of twilight:

> Captain Parry and others speak of the brilliant twilight of the North, as being sufficient to enable them to read ordinary print distinctly. This curious fact is wholly inexplicable upon Newtonian theory, but is easy of explanation upon this. This twilight coming from the north may be caused by the sun's rays thrown into the interior through the southern opening, which by two refractions, one at each opening, and two or three reflections from the inner concave surface, would pass out at the north over the verge, and produce there this strong twilight.[13]

Symmes, though, received the most enthusiastic and enduring support from his son Americus. Half a century after his father's death Americus was still championing his cause. In the 1885 publication *The Symmes Theory of Concentric Spheres*, he remarkably claimed some support for his father's ideas in the travels of Adolf Nordenskiöld and Adolphus Greely. Greely's expedition was one of 14 from 12 nations sent to undertake co-operative scientific programs in both the Arctic and Antarctic as part of the first International Polar Year of 1882–83. Greely and his men established a station far north at Lady Franklin Bay on Ellesmere Island. They were stranded when in successive summers relieving ships couldn't get through the ice. Americus Symmes opined that Greely's party of 25 were in the 'fertile land of Symzonia where there is more game than can be found anywhere else in creation'.[14] In fact Greely, following pre-arranged protocols, left the station and led his men south in the hope of rendezvousing with a relief ship. They didn't find Symmes' predicted abundant game. In hellish conditions the men slowly starved. One was executed for stealing food, another drowned. When relief belatedly arrived only Greely and 6 companions remained alive. One died on the sombre return home while those remaining survivors, on their return, faced dark speculations of cannibalism. They had certainly not discovered the benign land of Symzonia.

Americus Symmes received some coverage in the *New York Times*, under the title 'Arctic theory gone mad'. The article suggested that 'there is no question now that Mr Symmes is insane on the subject of his father's theory'.[15] His beliefs unshaken he had a monument erected over his father's grave with a hollow globe atop. His was a long and increasingly lonely vigil.

Back in 1826 Jeremiah Reynolds had begun to question some aspects of the theory. After his break with Symmes, he moved away from strict orthodoxy with the hollow earth theories. He began to enthusiastically promote the idea of an American Antarctic expedition and encouraged any interested parties to lobby Congress. Many memorials were forwarded urging exploration of the South Seas. Reynolds provided detail of the advantages of an expedition to the House committee on Naval Affairs. He reminded Congress of the benefits in national prestige, scientific discovery and potential commerce:

> And what place is left for us to explore, but this southern polar region? This has never been thoroughly done by any nation. It is almost an unknown region yet, and opens a wide field for enterprise for us, at a most moderate expense. There are more than a million and a half of square miles entirely unknown.[16]

In 1828 a Bill was introduced 'To provide for an exploring expedition to the Pacific Ocean and South Seas'. It asked for an appropriation of $50,000. In 1829 Andrew Jackson became president at the expense of John Quincy Adams. At that time the new administration was not supportive of such far flung expeditions and the voyage did not go ahead. Undeterred Jeremiah Reynolds joined a privately funded sealing voyage organised by veteran sealing captain and shipowner Edmund Fanning.

The expedition received government sanction but no public money. It was notable in that it included several scientific observers, including Reynolds, John Watson and James Eights. The marriage of commerce and science was attempted several times towards the end of the century with mixed success. Two ships were despatched, one *Annawan*, under the command of pioneer of the South Shetlands, Nathaniel Palmer. The other, *Seraph*, captained by Benjamin Pendleton. A third ship, the sealer *Penguin*, kept company with *Annawan* in deep southern latitudes. She was captained by Alexander Palmer, Nathaniel's brother.

The expedition met with little success. Various elusive landfalls proved non-existent, or at least unfound. The ice conditions were very difficult, and the sealing was disappointing. The fractious crew, disinterested in exploration for its own sake and fearing a poor financial return for their labours, forced the captains to abandon further exploration in favour of sealing around the coast of Chile. Jeremiah Reynolds, along with John Watson, explored Chile on land while the ships sought seals. The most notable outcome of the voyage was the work of James Eights who published a range of pioneering scientific papers from his observations on the voyage. He was later appointed to the scientific staff on Wilkes expedition but lost his position when the staff was cut as expedition funds diminished with the long delays.

Reynolds remained in Chile. He wrote disappointingly little about the expedition, although he did pen a tale he heard in Chile regarding '*Mocha Dick or the White Whale of the Pacific*',[17] thought to be a source for Melville's great whaling tale. In Chile he joined the US frigate *Potomac*, as secretary to the commodore.

When finally he returned to the United States, Reynolds buoyantly pursued the notion of a grand national expedition, and though the wheels of government turned slowly, they were turning back in his favour. In April 1836 he addressed Congress. An appropriation of $150,000 was approved by both Houses. Reynolds enthusiasm though was matched by bureaucratic inertia. This was particularly the case with the Secretary of the Navy Mahlon Dickerson. Initially placed in charge of the scientific staff, Reynolds became increasingly frustrated at the delays in preparations and increasingly infuriated by what he saw as Dickerson's obstructionism. In an ill-considered move he initiated a tetchy exchange of letters with Dickerson in the daily newspapers. These were attributed to 'Citizen' (Reynolds) and 'Friend to the Navy' (Dickerson). The first letter by Reynolds in mid-1837 gets straight to the point:

> In the freedom of my soul, I must say I have long doubted your capacity for the high office you [Dickerson] hold; and I have often wondered you did not gratify the whole community by retiring from duties you must find so difficult to perform ... I never heard a sentence from your lips, or read a paragraph from your pen, that gave me the impression that the compass of your mind, on public measures, was not better adapted to raze or to cut down than to build up and adorn![18]

Clearly these two men couldn't continue working together. After being the key champion of the expedition, Reynolds was removed from its staff.

Dickerson himself resigned from his position in 1838, his unenthusiastic and negative approach having thwarted quick progress.

Preparations ground on. Several experienced commanders resigned, overwhelmed by the turgid wheels of an unsympathetic bureaucracy, and frustrated by a lack of will from the government's representatives. Others, fearful of the project's stagnation, refused the offer of command. Finally, leadership fell to the inexperienced, but exceptionally ambitious, Lt Charles Wilkes. He was a talented hydrographer but had limited experience at sea. He proved single minded and determined in achieving the expedition's aims, but was also a poor leader of men. Vain, imperious, highly strung, over the long voyage he managed to alienate most of his fellow officers and, through his undignified scrabble for recognition, glory and acclaim, to undermine the considerable achievements of the expedition.

The expedition slowly took shape. Despite the delays the ambition of the expedition was vast, and a fitting reflection of a vibrantly developing world power. It was to involve six ships and would spend four years exploring the world's oceans, returning with a huge quantity of scientific data. The ships though were poorly prepared, especially for the rigours of the deep southern latitudes. The flagship of the expedition fleet was *Vincennes*, accompanied by *Porpoise*, *Peacock*, *Relief*, a lumbering stores ship, and two New York pilot boats, the schooners *Flying Fish* and *Sea Gull*. These were small, fast vessels, likely to be well suited to exploring the coastline of Pacific Islands, but vulnerable to the mountainous seas and harsh conditions south of Cape Horn.

The expedition sailed from Chesapeake Bay on 18 August 1838. Their time in the Antarctic represented only a minor period of the journey. It was, though, the source of much controversy. On 25 February 1839 while *Relief* and *Vincennes* stayed to explore the coastline at the base of South America, the other four vessels left Tierra del Fuego, and, despite the lateness of the season, sailed south.

Porpoise, with Wilkes on board, and *Sea Gull* sailed directly south, like Dumont d'Urville a few years earlier, they hoped to find the conditions Weddell had experienced in 1823 when he set a 'furthest south' of 74° 15'. Wilkes was to be disappointed. The conditions were ghastly and by 5 March he decided *Porpoise* and *Sea Gull* should sail north. *Peacock* and especially its' small companion *Flying Fish*, achieved much more. Their aim was to exceed Cook's furthest south of 71° 10'. They didn't get underway until a day after the other two ships, and then the following day they were separated in a fierce gale. The little schooner *Flying Fish* got as far as 70° South. *Peacock* hadn't penetrated the ice quite as far and the crew were greatly concerned, fearing *Flying Fish* had been lost. On 25 March, the ships sighted each other and gratefully they headed north. *Peacock* sailed directly to Valparaiso, Chile, while *Flying* Fish rendezvoused with *Sea Gull* and *Porpoise*, and *Vincennes* at Orange Bay, Tierra del Fuego. On 17 April *Porpoise* and *Vincennes* set sail for Valparaiso. *Sea Gull* and *Flying Fish* were to remain for ten more days for any sign of the store ship *Relief*. As it happened *Relief* arrived in Valparaiso in mid-April. *Flying Fish* and *Sea Gull* set sail from Tierra del Fuego towards the end of April.

Sea Gull didn't arrive in Valparaiso, lost with all hands somewhere off the South American coast. It was an unhappy end to the expedition's first experience of the Antarctic, and a portent of the entirely unhappy future the expedition had under a leader lacking the authority of rank and experience. Wilkes had already developed a poisonous relationship with many of his officers, and ordered *Relief* to return to the United States, together with various officers he wished to be rid of.

The remaining four ships sailed across the Pacific, exploring the Polynesian islands and arriving in Sydney at the end of November 1839.

On 26 December 1839 the expedition sailed from Sydney to explore the high latitudes directly south. Initially sailing together the ships soon lost contact with *Vincennes* and *Porpoise* leaving the other two behind. They encountered their first iceberg on 10 January 1840 at 61°S. *Peacock* was sighted on 16 January. After that date there has arisen some confusion about what they did or didn't see and where and when. Certainly, they sailed west along the coast for considerable distance, but whether all the claimed sightings of land were actual sightings, or educated guesses has been a matter of some controversy.

Porpoise lost contact with the other ships when at the end of January Dumont d'Urville's two French vessels were sighted. As detailed above, either misinterpreting the French intentions, or deliberately avoiding them, *Porpoise* sailed on without exchanging a greeting, or any information.

D'Urville records the date as 29 January while Wilkes account records the date as 30 January.

Dumont d'Urville recorded having sighted land on 19 January and landed on a rocky island just offshore on 21 January. This landing, unknown to Wilkes until he returned to Sydney, would lead to suspicions about some of Wilke's subsequent claims. Discrepancy in dates added to the subsequent confusion. Some 70 years later Dumont d'Urville's dates were disputed by US Rear Admiral John Pillsbury. He made a close study of the ship's positions, particularly when the *Porpoise* sighted the two French ships and proposed that Dumont d'Urville hadn't accounted for crossing the 180th meridian and his calendar was therefore a day behind.[19] Most histories continue to date Dumont d'Urville's sighting of land as 19 January rather than 20 January.

Wilkes continued sailing amongst icebergs through treacherous gale swept waters, with a crew in deteriorating health, until finally heading north on 21 February 1840. He had completed one of the great Antarctic voyages and discovered convincing further evidence of the continental nature of the Antarctic. Apart from the eastern fringes of their journey, this area would not be visited again until the next century. However, as with many actions throughout the voyage, these courageous and single-minded achievements would be overshadowed by Wilkes temperamental need to ensure the greatest glory fell to himself.

On 21 February 1840, the *Hobart Town Courier* reported the exciting news that Commodore Dumont d'Urville's expedition had discovered land in the Antarctic.

> On the evening of the 19th of January, in latitude 66°S and about 130° east longitude, land was descried; and on the 21st the two corvettes approached to within five or six miles, and two boats crews put off to collect specimens of rock from a point which was clear of ice.[20]

Peacock, much disabled from encounters with the ice, struggled back to Sydney arriving on 22 February. *Vincennes* reached Sydney on 11 March, and Wilkes received the unwelcome news of Dumont d'Urville's sighting of the area he named Adelie Land (for his wife), in exactly the same area as Wilkes had sighted land, and just days before him. Wilkes, though, suddenly decided his crew had also actually sighted land on that same day (19 January), even though it wasn't entered into the ship's log. This claim formed one of the charges of his subsequent court martial trial, (though it was deemed an unproved charge).

On 13 March 1840 the *Sydney Herald* carried a story under the headline '*Discovery of the Antarctic Continent*'. The article carried Wilke's claim to have sighted land on 19 January also, though further north and east of Dumont d'Urville's sighting. (The newspaper quoted the position as 64° 20' South and 154° 18' East. Wilkes quotes 66° 20'S, 154° 18'E.)[21] This would place Wilkes at a substantial distance from the nearest land. Ironically the *Herald* reprinted the *Courier* report of Dumont d'Urville's discovery directly below the Wilkes article. To further complicate matters there were suggestions that two officers on *Peacock* sighted land on 16 January at 65°S, 160°E. Their captain, William Hudson, was dismissive and didn't see fit to record this 'sighting' in the ship's log.

In his narrative, published 9 years later, Wilkes claims land was sighted from *Peacock*, *Porpoise* and *Vincennes* on 16 January. His claims are presented in quite equivocal language though:

> On this day (16th January) appearances believed at the time to be land were visible from all three vessels, and the comparison of the three vessels, and the comparison of the three observations, when taken in connexion (sic) with the more positive proofs of its existence afterwards obtained, has left no doubt that the appearance was not deceptive. From this day, therefore, we date the discovery which is claimed for the squadron.[22]

In a lengthy, stern and anonymous review of Wilkes voluminous narrative from 1845 the author notes that

> we learn from the 'Narrative' as well as from other equally authentic sources, that the discovery of land is not recorded in the log-books of the vessels and journals of the officers until about the 28th of January, though it is dated, upon other authority, on the 16th of that month. Captain Wilkes accounts for this unusual omission of the most important fact of the cruise in every record of its incidents by saying, that the discovery was not anticipated ...[23]

The reviewer finds this very suspect reasoning. He adds:

> We leave here the subject of the land for the present, merely adding an expression of our regret, that the inconsistencies of Captain Wilkes should have promoted and justified, both at home and abroad, such discussions

and doubts respecting the date and extent of this discovery, as involve, though we trust they will not in the end impair, the national honour.[24]

The British expedition under James Clark Ross was soon to arrive in Hobart. Prior to departing Sydney, Wilkes decided to write to Ross with information about his discoveries – a generous act but given Wilkes rather ungenerous nature it is hard to put it down to magnanimity. It is likely Wilkes wanted to emphasise his achievements to one of the most notable polar commanders, and to ensure there was no confusion as to priority for discoveries when Ross returned. Whatever the motivation, it added another layer of controversy and argument to an already complex situation. Ross sailed over some of the 'land' marked on the Wilkes map and made some ungenerous and imperious observations about this rival expedition.

In his narrative Wilkes wrote:

> How far Captain Ross was guided in his search by our previous discoveries, will best appear by reference to the chart, with a full account of the proceedings of the squadron, which I sent to him ... Although I have never received any acknowledgement of their receipt from him personally, yet I have heard of their having reached his hands a few months prior to his Antarctic cruise. Of this, however, I do not complain, and feel justifiable desire to maintain the truth in relation to a claim that is indisputable.[25]

Ross was already annoyed that both the French and American expeditions were exploring in the vicinity of the South Magnetic pole, an area he rather presumptuously regarded as his own bailiwick. Given that Wilkes had sailed from the United States at the same time as the British Association for the Advancement of Science was meeting to discuss the need for an expedition, and well before any British expedition had been organised or a commander appointed, Ross's haughty resentment seems completely unjustified. As it happened the presence of Wilkes and Dumont d'Urville had a favourable outcome as the course Ross chose enabled him to reach a new furthest south.

Ross sailed over land indicated at the edge of Wilkes map, in the vicinity of the Balleny Islands. Inevitably a dispute erupted with Wilkes subsequently claiming that these areas were not actually from his own observations but from Balleny's. Ross was unimpressed and devoted several pages of the account of his own voyage to contesting Wilke's version.

His account starts with the ominous title '*Search for supposed land*'.

> As we advanced on our course in eager expectation of 'making the land', our surprise and disappointment may be imagined when no indications of it were to be seen at sunset, although we were not more than 12 or 13 miles from its eastern extreme, as laid down on Lieutenant Wilkes chart; and we began to suspect that from having had but little experience of the delusive appearances in these icy regions, he had mistaken for land some of the dense well-defined clouds which so continually hang over extensive packs of ice.[26]

With visibility of '60 to 70 miles'[27] no land was sighted. The next day they found themselves sailing 'very nearly in the centre of the mountainous patch of land laid down in Lieutenant Wilke's chart as forming a part of the Antarctic continent'.[28] Ross includes a quite lengthy argument regarding Wilkes claims, and concludes with the rather pointed statement:

> I cannot refrain from observing that the practice of 'laying down land, not only where we had actually determined it to exist, but in those places also in which every appearance denoted its existence' is not only entirely new amongst navigators, but seems to me likely to occasion much confusion, and even to raise doubts in many minds whether the existence of some portions of land that undoubtedly were seen might not also be of an equally questionable character with those laid down from appearances only ...[29]

When Robert Scott left the Ross Sea on his return from his first expedition in 1904, he travelled along the edge of the ice in the vicinity of the Balleny Islands and at the eastern extent of Wilkes voyage. Unable to sight land he concluded, rather ungenerously, 'once and for all we have definitely disposed of Wilkes Land'. Given the extent of Wilkes landfall claims this overstatement by Scott is perhaps more indicative of the lingering British scepticism since Wilkes' spat with Ross. Scott went on to claim 'there is no case for any land eastward of Adelie Land'. Given the limited extent of Scott's investigations, this is a bold and ill-considered statement, and one that proved incorrect.[30]

Unsurprisingly American historian Edwin Balch was incensed.

> There was land twenty degrees longitude distant from Captain Scott, which he was so anxious to expurgate from the map – undoubtedly because it was an American discovery – that he sails nineteen degrees of longitude towards it. The day before reaching it he pretends to have qualms of conscience about his coal – a handy excuse for stopping- and just before reaching the spot

where the land is charted, he stops, alters his course, and steams away. He neither sails over the spot nor alongside; he simply runs away. Nevertheless, he is so determined that this land shall not exist he says squarely, 'thus once and for all we have definitely disposed of Wilkes Land'.[31]

Wilkes Land was not revisited until Mawson's Australasian Antarctic Expedition of 1911–14 and his British, Australian and New Zealand Antarctic Research Expedition of 1929–31. Part of the point of the second expedition was to establish Australia's primacy in the areas he had explored in 1911. While these areas were in the vicinity of Wilkes Land the threat to Australian claims was not from the United States, who had shown little interest in the Antarctic since Wilkes had sailed away in February 1840, but rather the Norwegian whalers, who under Lars Christensen, were exploring the same area, and were looking to advance their already thriving Antarctic whaling industry, and to avoid any royalties charged by rival national claimants to sectors of the Antarctic.

After his expedition Mawson presented a paper to the Royal Geographical Society of Australasia (SA Branch) that gave his assessment of Wilkes Land sightings. He carefully analysed Wilkes claims from his own experience of two expeditions from sea and on land and using aircraft and concluded with a list of land definitely sighted; may have been sighted; unlikely; and cannot have been sighted. At that time he placed the sightings of 16 January 1840 and 19 January 1840 in the 'cannot have been sighted' category.

In an address to the Australian and New Zealand Association for the Advancement of Science in August 1932 Mawson felt 'Wilkes had come in for an undue amount of censure', and while it has subsequently appeared that Wilkes and his officers may have mistaken icebergs and low cloud for land:

> … he certainly located, elsewhere, considerable stretches of true coastline. The result has been that even some of his correctly diagnosed land discoveries have been discounted.[32]

This is exactly the problem Wilkes created for himself. Greedy for glory and unwilling to share it with anyone, either his own crew or other expeditions, he opened himself up to suspicion that tainted his substantial achievements. His pursuit of personal glory has rendered his successes to be viewed as inglorious, his desire to be feted has overwhelmed all the things he could rightly be feted for. Mawson notes that all those who, at sea in more modern vessels, have weathered out an Adelie Land hurricane will be ready to assist in securing for Wilkes in his Antarctic achievement, the fullest possible credit ...[33]

But few who encountered Wilkes were moved to assign him credit.

William Hobbs, fresh from the antagonistic battles around who first sighted the Antarctic, mounted a strident defence of every Wilkes sighting, even asserting that Mawson's judgements confirmed all the sightings. Hobb's initial response in 1932 was reasoned. In 1940 his increasing shrillness obscured the depth of his assessments of Wilkes sightings. He made very sound observations regarding a consistent tendency amongst many explorers (including Mawson) to misjudge distance due the extraordinary clarity of the Antarctic air.

Mawson felt that Hobbs was 'characteristically ingenious' in his support of some of Wilkes claims and that his arguments were 'beyond all reasonable expectation and deduction'. With a sense of exasperation Mawson concluded that

> evidently Hobbs cannot agree that Wilkes was human and subject to the same misinterpretation of cloud and ice formations as other mortals.[34]

Finally in 1959, Wilkes claims received greater vindication when Phillip Law (Director Antarctic Division of the Australian Dept of External Affairs) and B.P. Lambert (Director of Division of National Mapping, Australian Dept of National Development) delivered a paper at an Antarctic Symposium held in Buenos Aires in November 1959. Law and Lambert developed a new map using surveys of the US Operation Highjump (that took aerial photographs of the coast eastward of Cape Freshfield) and the Australian National Antarctic Research Expedition of 1958–59 under Phillip Law, that also used aerial photography between Horn Bluff and Cape Freshfield (1958) and reconnaissance of Oates Land from the sea and the air (1959). They found that 'the whole question of the reliability of Wilke's observations along this sector might well be reviewed'. They confirmed most of the Wilkes expedition's equivocal landfalls (the exception being features Ringgold reported on 16 January 1840 from *Porpoise*) and found that the shortcomings of Wilkes' maps were understandable and variations in latitude and distances were not unusual given the challenges of sometimes 'abnormal atmospheric refraction' in the Antarctic.[35]

Subsequent historians and geographers have not been quite so generous as Lambert and Law and raised continuing doubts about a number of the landfalls.[36] But after a century of controversies Law and Lambert had provided a vindication Wilkes would have yearned for during his lifetime. There was never any doubt about his skill as a hydrographer but Wilkes had substantially contributed to the controversies that surrounded his Antarctic discoveries. The failure to log sightings, the charges against him by his own officers, his own expressed view that land was marked where it was found and where it was suspected, his evasiveness, and the fact that he was an unsympathetic character all meant that where there was doubt it would rarely be accompanied by benefit.

Regardless of the sightings and dates, the Wilkes expedition's great successes in these deep southern latitudes was to sail over 2,400 kilometres in the vicinity of the Antarctic Coast and provide a more certain identification of it as a continent from the observations of their cruise.

Wilkes perceptively described his discovery thus:

> From our discoveries of the land through 40° of longitude, and the observations made during this interesting cruise, with the similarity of formation and position of the ice during our close examination of it, I consider that there can scarcely be a doubt of the existence of the Antarctic continent extending the whole distance of 70° from east to west.[37]

He has been proved correct and certainly the Ex-Ex provided substantial further evidence of the continental nature of the Antarctic. It is a stretch to credit him with the discovery of the continent though, as some are wont to do. Early maps had theorised of a Great Southern Land. Bouvet thought he had reached the tip of the great southern continent when he sighted the point he named Cape Circumcision. Cook had ruminated on the likelihood of a continent as he circumnavigated without sighting land, William Smith's discovery of the Shetlands was hailed as the discovery of a continent, and John Davis in his landing at Hughes Bay thought he was on a continent. The land sightings of Biscoe, Balleny and Kemp added to the growing belief of a substantial body of land. Dumont d'Urville's nearly concurrent sighting and then Ross's subsequent explorations continued the development of understanding of the geography of the Antarctic. It wasn't until the 20th century that the outline of the continent was given substantial shape. Wilkes had completed one of the really significant Antarctic voyages, and this was just one part of a vast scientific and geographic exploration.

The unhappy expedition continued on. *Vincennes* left Sydney on 19 March and rendezvoused with *Porpoise* and *Flying Fish* at the Bay of Islands, New Zealand, at the end of March. Newly repaired *Peacock* met them in Tonga in May 1840. The ships sailed on to Fiji, where two men were killed on Malolo Island after a disagreement with the locals. Wilkes disproportionate response was to kill 80 natives (perhaps more) and to burn their village.

In his narrative he blithely outlines his orders: 'Move upon Sualib, destroying all plantations they should meet along the way, sparing none except women and children'.[38] The village of Arro was destroyed.

This was a shocking act of mass murder but in his narrative Wilkes offered no equivocation:

> The punishment inflicted on the natives was no doubt severe; but I cannot view it as unmerited, and the extent to which it was carried out was neither dictated by cruelty nor revenge.[39]

His actions on Malolo formed one of the charges in the fractious court martial proceedings that were conducted on the expedition's return. William Stanton notes that crewman Bob Johnson admitted at the court-martial that the attack was revenge, not self-defence.[40]

The expedition next visited the Hawaiian Islands, and then to the West Coast of North America, charting Puget Sound and investigating the Columbia River, where *Peacock* ran aground on a sand bar and was wrecked. Wilkes purchased a replacement ship, *Oregon*, and sailed to San Francisco Bay. The ships sailed west to the Philippines and then on to Singapore, where the schooner *Flying Fish* was sold. She had done splendid service on the arduous journey, but the thought of her joining *Sea Gull* at the bottom of the sea in the storms off South Africa when so close to home precipitated the decision. The remainder of the fleet continued their desultory journey. Wilkes ordered *Oregon* and *Porpoise* to return via Rio de Janeiro to complete some minor observations. It was most likely an arrangement that suited Wilkes vanity, allowing his ship to arrive first and alone. In June 1842 *Vincennes* reached New York. The other two ships straggled in several weeks later. The expedition, after almost four years of voyaging, was over. They had completed a vast scientific program and made significant discoveries. This should have been a triumphant homecoming, instead the substance of their achievements was overwhelmed by a welter of recriminations.

This culminated in a series of court martial actions immediately on their return. Various charges were brought against Wilkes, and he, in turn, brought a number of charges against several crew. After four years governmental interests and priorities had moved on, and the bitter personal feuds played out in public undermined sympathy and appreciation of what was, on so many levels, a grand adventure.

Wilkes was vain, temperamental and peremptory. He managed to alienate almost everyone on the expedition. Of the six ships that set out, the lumbering stores ship *Relief* was sent back, with a complement of officers and crew that were on Wilkes ever growing list of men he felt were troublemakers. *Peacock* was wrecked, and the small schooner *Sea Gull*, vulnerable to the whims of the ferocious seas of the Southern Ocean, was lost with all hands. The other schooner *Flying Fish* achieved the expedition's furthest south and her survival for the journey, especially in the treacherous conditions around the Antarctic, were a testament to the ship and the skills and toughness of the captain and crew. The expedition had set out with 83 officers and 342 enlisted men. Aside from the loss of *Sea Gull* the death rate was very small, considering the length and difficulty of the voyage, however the expedition lost many to desertion.

There were several major problems that undermined the expedition. The delays in preparation lost them several commanders and the energetic and articulate Jeremiah Reynolds. Whether Reynolds would have been an effective leader of the scientists is uncertain, (in fact some of the scientists were adamant he wouldn't)[41], and whether he would have had any chance of working amicably with Wilkes is most doubtful, but his literary skills would have shown the expedition in a far better light than Wilkes turgid and occasionally vitriolic account. One reviewer opined drily that the 'radical faults of his [Wilkes] mind impart themselves to his style, and his book seems in reading even longer than it is'.[42] – (It ran to 5 very long volumes).

If the Secretary of the Navy, during the preparations, had been a dynamic champion of the expedition, instead of the obstructive and disinterested Mahlon Dickerson, the voyage may have got underway quicker, better prepared and with a more experienced leader. Wilkes insecurity, pettiness, vanity and need for personal recognition, despite his great hydrographic skills and single-minded determination, undermined the legacy of the voyage.

The contemporary reviewer of his narrative in the *North American Review* has some interesting insights into Wilkes personality. The article has been attributed to Charles H. Davis, a naval officer who achieved the rank of Rear Admiral.[43] At the time of the Wilkes expedition he served on the *Independent*. Wilkes sought volunteers from that ship when in Brazil, but rejected Davis, then a lieutenant with a scientific bent. Wilkes also alienated *Independent*'s commander, his superior in rank, John Nicholson, with his peremptory demands. The author was clearly not sympathetic to Wilkes, but the article makes many perceptive observations. Perhaps echoing Ezekiel 25:15 he finds Wilkes too often influenced by 'the evil spirit of a revengeful heart'.

> One defect of Captain Wilkes's character as a commander appears to have been a want of true dignity, a puerile irritability of temper ... an ignorance of the spirit of the profession.

The reviewer goes on to condemn his appointment:

> It is due, however, to the navy to say, that the selection of Captain Wilkes for this most responsible and distinguished post was not directed by any peculiar fitness he was supposed to possess as a naval commander, but, as we understand it, by his skill as a hydrographer and his proficiency in the manipulation of magnetic and astronomical instruments, qualifications very respectable and useful, but not those the country will look to when it shall need the services of its naval captains.[44]

The reviewer claims that in February 1843 38 lieutenants on the naval list had seen more service than Wilkes. 'Knowing this, it is less a matter of surprise, that he has shown himself so ignorant of the genius of the naval service, and so incompetent to administer its discipline.'[45] As a naval man, particularly one who has had first-hand experience of the wrong side of Wilkes personality, the author has an axe to grind. But his is an interesting and articulate view. The publication in a respected and widely circulated journal of such a scathing personal assessment of a serving naval officer, particularly one who has just commanded such a monumental expedition, is certainly unusual and indicates the breadth of antipathy towards Wilkes.

Wilkes, in his report to the Secretary of the Navy, despatched from Sydney after his return from the Antarctic, (and published later in newspapers) lauds his crew:

> I cannot close this report without bringing to your notice the high estimation in which I hold the conduct of the officers, seamen and marines, during the Antarctic cruise, the manner and spirit, together with the coolness and alacrity, with which they have met the dangers and performed their duties. I trust that they will receive from the government some notice of it. All I can say in their favour would fall far short of what they deserve.[46]

This seems far removed from his behaviour towards the crew over the voyage. If he had been able to conduct himself with this level of sincerity and respect in his personal dealings with the men, his standing after the cruise and his ongoing reputation may have even surpassed the level that he considered he deserved.

The court martial of Wilkes only sustained the charge of excessive punishment for which he was reprimanded. But the public airing of the other charges, including that of falsely claiming a sighting of land in the Antarctic on 19 January 1840, with conflicting evidence presented by naval officers, often boasting greater sea experience than Wilkes, could only have damaged his reputation and the reputation of the expedition. Midshipman William May, the subject of a petty court martial charge brought by Wilkes, reputedly remarked: 'He who would survey the world must first sound the depths & shallows of his own character'.[47]

Most recent assessments of Wilkes suggest that he was a poor leader of men but had great talents as a hydrographer and was able, against massive obstacles, to achieve the very ambitious aims of the expedition. Some historians are more sympathetic. Kenneth Bertrand describes him as 'an able, forceful, and resolute man'. Bertrand felt that 'malcontents' amongst the crew 'found encouragement in Washington, where Wilkes, the "stormy petrel" of the Navy, had enemies as well as friends among his brother officers'.[48]

Certainly, the qualities Bertrand identifies are those one would expect of any successful commander of such an arduous expedition. Few comparable commanders, though, presided over such a disputatious and disharmonious voyage. Historian William Stanton poses the question. 'What indeed is one to make of this man who commanded an expedition of six ships and hundreds of men yet was neither seaman nor leader?' He recalls the expedition geologist,

James Dana's view:

'Wilkes was conceited and overbearing, stingy with praise, ready to blame, and often unjustified' but doubted 'we would have fared better, or lived together more harmoniously' under another commander.

Stanton adds: 'Without Wilkes incredible energy and byzantine mind the Expedition's achievements might have been no more lasting than the wake of its ships upon the waves of the world.'[49]

Wilkes was a man whose personal achievements were genuinely great, but whose personal traits appeared often to be ignoble. He spent much of the next 20 years in Washington, overseeing the publication of the expedition results to a mainly disinterested public. He returned to the sea during the Civil War when he attained the rank of acting Rear Admiral in September 1862, commanding the West India Squadron. Operating in the Caribbean his lack of respect for the politics of neutrality led to several incidents that embarrassed the Union and threatened to drag Britain into the conflict. The Navy Secretary Gideon Welles had had enough. Wilkes was relieved of his command. When he furiously and publicly contested the decision in a letter to the *New York Times*,[50] Welles instigated court martial proceedings against him. This time Wilkes was found guilty of five charges of disobedience, disrespect and insubordination and was suspended from duty for three years. This sentence was reduced to a single year, but it marked the end of his active duty. He died on 8 February 1877. His expedition had provided the strongest evidence to that time of the continental nature of Antarctica. The fractious commander is commemorated in the area known as Wilkes Land.

James Clark Ross

In the August 1838 meeting of the British Association for the Advancement of Science a number of resolutions were passed regarding the need for observations of terrestrial magnetism at various points of the earth. Resolution 4 led directly to the embarkation of the Royal Navy expedition to the Antarctic under James Clark Ross.

It reads:

That the Association considers it highly important that the deficiency, yet existing in our knowledge of terrestrial magnetism in the southern hemisphere, should be supplied by observations of magnetic direction and intensity, especially in the high southern latitudes between the meridians of New Holland [Australia] and Cape Horn; and they desire strongly to recommend to Her Majesty's government the appointment of a naval expedition expressly directed to that object.[51]

From this resolution, things moved remarkably quickly. The Admiralty were listening and acted:

> the science of magnetism may be essentially improved by an extensive series of observations made in high southern latitudes, and by comparison of such observations made at certain fixed stations, and whereas practical navigation must eventually derive important benefit from every improvement in that science; we have, in consideration of these objects, caused Her Majesty's ships Erebus and Terror to be in all respects prepared for a voyage for carrying into complete execution the purposes above mentioned.[52]

French and American expeditions had already been despatched to the Antarctic. This may have influenced the sharp movement of the bureaucracy in approving and embarking the expedition.

James Clark Ross was commissioned to command, aboard *Erebus*, on 8 April 1839. His friend Francis Crozier, a comrade from several Arctic expeditions, was appointed his deputy and placed in charge of the second ship, *Terror*.

James Clark Ross had exceptional experience for the task. He hadn't sailed beyond the Antarctic Circle, few had, but he had distinguished himself in extensive travels in the Arctic. In 1818 he sailed on an expedition to Lancaster Sound under his uncle John Ross. He then accompanied William Edward Parry (John Ross' deputy in 1818) on three separate expeditions into the Arctic, searching for a Northwest Passage across the top of the Canadian Arctic, and a fourth expedition attempting the North Pole. In May 1829 he joined his uncle on another Arctic expedition that spent four years stranded in the ice before returning home in October 1833. Over a period of 15 years James Clark Ross had spent almost a decade deep in the Arctic.

For this expedition his instructions from the Admiralty required him to establish magnetic observatories at St Helena, Cape of Good Hope, Hobart, and Sydney, and complete magnetic observations at other points of their journey. He was also instructed to proceed south and attempt to locate the magnetic South Pole. The second summer season Ross was to continue his Antarctic explorations and confirm Biscoe's land sightings (Enderby and Graham Land) if possible. This was a very focussed scientific expedition.

The ships set sail on 5 October 1839. The first rendezvous was the island of Madeira. On 31 January 1840 the ships made St Helena. A location was chosen for the establishment of the magnetic observatory, but it was soon noted that any results would be disappointing due to influence of the magnetic rocks of the island. On 6 April they sailed again, this time for the sub–Antarctic Crozet Islands. There they encountered a seal gang who had been working there for several years.

> Mr Hickley, their leader, came on board, and he, as well as his boat's crew, looked more like Esquimaux than civilized beings, but filthier far in their dress and persons than any I had ever before seen. Their clothes were literally soaked in oil and smelt most offensively.[53]

On 13 May *Terror*, which had become separated, was able to safely enter the harbour at the Kerguelen Islands where *Erebus* was anchored. The party completed a range of magnetic observations in the bleakness of this sub–Antarctic Island group, finally leaving on 20 July 1840.

Terror made Hobart on 15 August, *Erebus* arrived the following day. After the wild isolation of the sub-Antarctic, the rough and ready settlement of Hobart must have been welcome. Ross went ashore to Government House to meet the governor, Arctic explorer John Franklin.

With the enthusiastic support of Franklin, no doubt glad to have the company of a man with a similar background and experiences to himself amongst the rough and combative folk of a remote convict colony, Ross, aided by a large party of convict labourers, set about establishing his observatories.

On arrival in Hobart, Ross learned more about the movements of the French and United States expeditions. He was rather unreasonably angry that they had been investigating the exact area where he intended trying to locate the South Magnetic Pole. Ross was correct in suggesting the Antarctic presented a rather large field for exploration which afforded vast areas for three expeditions to operate without running into each other or covering the same areas, but merely by announcing an expedition didn't give Ross priority over the areas directly south of Australia.

As it happened these expeditions, influencing his decision to sail further east, enabled his discovery and exploration of the relatively ice-free sea named after him, and to set a new farthest south beyond 78°. It may be that he had already thought of sailing further east before he heard of the discoveries of his two rival explorers. As discussed above, Wilkes sent him a map of his claimed landfalls which would initiate a lingering controversy and cross Atlantic arguments that lasted for a century beyond the two protagonists' engagements.

Historian of early Antarctic voyages A.G.E. Jones has proposed a tentative theory that the ship *Venus* on a whaling expedition out of Sydney under Captain Samuel Harvey may have penetrated the Ross Sea to 72° in 1831. This claim is based on a letter written by Harvey to Hobart harbour master James Kelly. The ship's log was destroyed seven years after being handed to the Customs in London. A.G.E. Jones further speculated that Ross may have heard of Harvey's voyage.[54] That was just speculation, though. It appears likely that Ross made his decision based on having been so recently forestalled further west by Wilkes and Dumont d'Urville, and their confirmation, (together with Balleny's report of Sabrina Land), that there was no way further south in the areas they had explored. Balleny had also observed open sea at 69° South.

The ships sailed for the Antarctic on 12 November 1840. On 20 November they anchored at Auckland Islands where they conducted another series of observations. They remained for a month and sailed due south on 17 December. Icebergs were sighted on 27 December. They reached the pack on New Year's Day, and with their strengthened ships were in a mood to try and barge their way into the ice. By 8 January 1841 they found themselves in open sea beyond the pack. They explored this wonderland in an almost leisurely manner sailing right to the Great Ice Barrier (later named for Ross). On 12 January a difficult and hasty landing was made on one of two small icebound islands they named ' Possession'.

On 2 February they reached their furthest south at 78° 4'S, 4° further south than Weddell's voyage on the other side of the continent. They sailed eastward, exploring the great ice barrier, then turned north and pushed their way through the gathering ice to the open sea north of the pack. This was a remarkable voyage, pioneering the route that Amundsen, Scott and Shackleton used to approach the Pole. The only disappointment for Ross was his inability to be able to sail to the South magnetic pole (it was located on land at the time). His explorations continued, confirming Balleny's Islands and sailing over some of the 'land' marked on Wilkes's map.

The ships made a triumphant return to Hobart, docking on 7 April 1841. The observatory had operated in his absence under Lieutenant Kay. Portable observatories were set up and the ships refitted.

Second voyage

After a spectacular bon voyage ball in their honour, the expedition left Hobart on 7 July 1841 and reached Sydney on 14 July where they again were able to enjoy colonial hospitality in the form of another ball and dinner. On 5 August they set sailed for New Zealand where they anchored in the Bay of Islands. More magnetic observations were taken over the next 3 months. The ships sailed again on 23 November 1841, bound for the Antarctic. By mid-December they sighted icebergs. They worked their way through thickening ice but it was a much more difficult task than the previous year.

On 19 January 1842 they encountered a storm. Chunks of floating ice were hurled against both ships, causing damage to *Erebus* and smashing *Terror*'s rudder. Finally on 2 February, after seven weeks of weary and tense manoeuvring at the mercy of the whims of the wind and the ice, they cleared the pack and sailed into Ross's open sea. They recorded a latitude of 78° 9' 30"S on 23 February, exceeding their previous year's furthest south. They retreated north, finally escaping the pack on 1 March.

Just after midnight in the early hours of 13 March, in strong wind, the two ships, severely threatened by icebergs, came the closest to disaster for the entire voyage. Unable to avoid each other in their desperation to skirt away from the icebergs, the ships collided. The crews were prepared for the worst, but providentially, the ships managed to extricate themselves from each other and avoid being dashed to pieces by the icebergs. Repairs were conducted and the ships continued east. On 4 April, rounding Cape Horn, Ross launched five bottles of different weights in the hope of testing currents and winds. The lightest washed ashore at Cape Liptrap (near the most southerly point of the Australian mainland) to be found by a beachcomber in September 1845.[55] On 6 April 1842 the ships and their grateful crews anchored at Port Louis in the Falkland Islands.

Third Voyage

They were to remain in the grim settlement for the winter of 1842, Ross being fearful of desertions at a more hospitable port. The only break was a visit to the utterly remote Hermite Island, at the foot of Tierra del Fuego, to make more observations. They left the Falklands on 8 September and returned on 12 November.

A third Antarctic voyage was an unwelcome prospect for most of the crew, but Port Louis was not popular so most were happy to at least be quitting there, even if they would have preferred sailing north rather than south. They set out on 17 December 1842. This third Antarctic voyage tried to follow Weddell into the depths of the sea named for his voyage beyond 74°S. It was to prove a dispiritingly impossible task. Like Dumont d'Urville and Charles Wilkes before him and many mariners since, Ross found the ice conditions impenetrable. The ships entered the ice on 12 January 1843, in sight of their newly named and claimed Cockburn Island, hoping for a similarly easy passage as they had the first year into the Ross Sea. After 13 days the ice was carrying them northwards and they could still see Cockburn Island. The furthest they reached was 71° 30'S, 14° 51'W, on 5 March 1843.

Their last task was to try and locate Bouvet Island. The island had eluded James Cook's methodical searching and Ross also failed to locate it. He was at one stage within 30 kilometres and with favourable conditions would have undoubtedly sighted the island. It was such a dot in the vastness of the ocean that it is more remarkable that Bouvet happened upon it in the first place. When Ross returned to England Charles Enderby told him that several of his ships had located the island at some distance from Bouvet's recorded location.

On 4 April 1843 the expedition reached Simon's Bay, South Africa, and finally sighted England on 2 September 1843, the voyage completed after four years. Unlike his rival Wilkes, Ross returned to a knighthood and acclaim.

The expedition had been able to break through the pack ice into an open sea and travel beyond 78°S and had opened the way for the initial explorations of the continent in the next century. They were the first to view the Great Ice Barrier, one the world's most remarkable geographical sights.

The expedition had conducted a thorough scientific program carefully observing terrestrial magnetism and recording the weather and studying the oceans. A two-volume account was published on the zoology of Antarctica as observed on the voyage.

Accompanying the expedition had been William Hooker. Just 22 when he set sail on *Erebus* as assistant surgeon and botanist, he published in six volumes a detailed account of his botanical observations from the voyage. He went on to a distinguished career succeeding his father as director of Kew Gardens and was a close friend and supporter of Charles Darwin. As the only survivor of the grand period of British Polar exploration before Franklin he became an eminence grise of Clements Markham's determined and often dispiriting attempts to raise interest in further British exploration of Antarctica in the second half of the 19th century. Hooker lived long enough to observe the explorations of the new century. He died aged 94 in 1911.

James Clark Ross took one more journey into the high icy latitudes when in 1848, he led the first expedition sailing in search of his old friend John Franklin and the two ships that had served him so well in the Antarctic. His was the first of many relief expeditions that returned without finding a trace of Franklin and his men, and their ill-fated attempt to finally forge a Northwest Passage through the Arctic Ocean above Canada. It marked Ross' seventh and last voyage to the Arctic.

Ross died on 3 April 1862, a few weeks short of his 62nd birthday.

Following the return of Ross's Antarctic expedition, Colonel Sabine pushed for another expedition to complete the terrestrial magnetism observations in that portion of the Antarctic that had not been traversed by Ross, between the Greenwich meridian and longitude 120°E, beyond latitude 60°S (the very southern portions of the Indian Ocean).

Edward Sabine was an army officer, physicist and veteran of several Arctic expeditions. He was astronomer in John Ross' 1818 expedition and accompanied Parry on his 1819–20 expedition.

He spearheaded the 'magnetic crusade', drawing together the British Association for the Advancement of Science and, the Royal Society, Admiralty and Army Ordnance to launch an extensive and co-ordinated program to try and unlock the secrets of the earth's magnetism.

He was an influential figure and another expedition was organised. Lt. Thomas Moore was appointed in command. He had previously sailed with *Terror* on the Ross expedition. The ship *Pagoda* had been hired and sailed

False Bay, near Cape Town, on 9 January 1845, returning to Simon's Bay, Cape Town, on 20 June 1845.

The assistant surgeon Walter Dickson noted:

> Though no brilliant discovery was made, nor many striking incidents encountered, yet a perilous navigation was successfully achieved, good service was rendered to science, and the chief end of the expedition was accomplished.[56]

Moore went on to command HMS *Plover* patrolling the Bering Straits in support of the search for Franklin. Later he was a governor of the Falkland Islands.

Chapter Five

Franklin, the Northwest Passage and the cooling of European interest in the icebound south

After the triumph of James Clark Ross amongst the icebergs and peril of the South, and the continuing British progress to unravel the mysteries of the Arctic, the time was ripe for the British to finally solve the centuries old obsession with a commercial route north of Canada, between the Atlantic and Pacific Oceans. Each exploration seemed to bring the dream of a navigable Northwest Passage closer to reality. John Barrow, the second secretary of the Admiralty, had set Britain's sights firmly on the North. Overland and sea expeditions had greatly increased the knowledge of the coastline and islands at the top of the world but the prize of the Northwest Passage had not been won. Barrow determined to send the biggest, best equipped, most modern expedition, to finally solve the puzzle.

John Barrow was a talented and capable man of humble origins, who rose to his position of great influence through intelligence, diligence, appropriate deference and administrative skill. At the Admiralty he championed Arctic exploration, and particularly the dream of the Northwest Passage. In 1818 two expeditions were launched. David Buchan on board *Dorothea* together with his second in command John Franklin on *Trent* were to attempt to attain the North Pole. Despite determined efforts to break through the ice, unsurprisingly they didn't get beyond 80°N.

John Ross led an Admiralty expedition with two ships, *Isabella* and *Alexander*. Following William Baffin's voyage of two centuries before and reaffirming the existence of the vast body of water that bears Baffin's name, the ships entered Lancaster Sound. John Ross was confronted by a distant mountain range. He named the range for the first secretary of the Admiralty

John Wilson Croker. Despite his officers doubting that what they were viewing in the distance was in fact a mountain range, Ross ordered a retreat. This mountain barrier proved to be illusory. The naming of such a non-existent range for Croker no doubt amused his political enemies, but Ross was never again entrusted by the Admiralty with such a major expedition. John Barrow was withering in his assessment of Ross' explanation for his retreat.

> This can only be looked upon as a pitiable excuse for running away home, and is a most clumsy perversion of his instructions, the obvious meaning of which he has not only misconceived, but misquoted.[1]

Ross's second in command on that voyage, William Edward Parry, proved a bold and adventurous explorer spending a good part of the next decade in the Arctic. He made three attempts to find the Northwest Passage – 1819–20 in the ships *Hecla* and *Griper*; 1821–23 in *Hecla* and *Fury*; and using the same ships again in 1823–25. On the third expedition he had to abandon one of his ships, *Fury*, and a large cache of stores, in Prince Regent Inlet. This later proved fortuitous for his former commander John Ross. Parry attempted the North Pole in 1827, reaching 82°45' North. His deputy was James Clark Ross who had been on his uncle John's 1818 voyage and Parry's three previous expeditions.

The attempt on the pole set a furthest north record that lasted for decades. In 1875 the Admiralty Arctic Committee were still proudly recalling that journey:

> ... it is remarkable that our own Parry, in his boat and sledge journey, made in 1827 from the northern part of Spitzbergen, attained the highest latitude yet reached, and that the credit due to the geographical achievement of the position nearest the North Pole still remains with England.[2]

John Ross, spurned by the Admiralty for his seemingly timid capitulation to an imaginary mountain barrier in Lancaster Sound, showed great resilience and commanded several private expeditions. In 1829, sponsored by gin baron, Felix Booth, Ross set out aboard *Victory* in what became one of those great unlikely adventure stories typical of polar exploration. This was a different type of expedition, with a crew of only 23. In Prince Regent Inlet Ross was able to supplement his supplies from stores Parry had left when his ship *Fury* was abandoned. Ross sailed south into a gulf named for his sponsor. In October his ship was iced in. They were unable to escape the next summer or the one following. The crew, understandably, became more fractious, but the commander's nephew, James, spent the time fruitfully. He explored and mapped the coastline by sledge and small boat and discovered the north magnetic pole.

Victory remained hopelessly trapped and was finally abandoned in May 1832. The desperate crew struggled on foot towards Fury Beach, and the remaining abandoned stores. Stalked by the spectre of starvation, they reached the beach and the stores in June. Constructing a hut they faced another bleak Arctic winter. Finally in August 1833 they were able to launch three of *Fury*'s whale boats that had been abandoned by Parry. The food situation was parlous. Their only hope was to be sighted by a ship in this remote desolate part of the earth. At the end of August they were rescued by *Isabella*, a ship that by coincidence had previously been captained by Ross. It was a miraculous escape after four years in the Arctic, and remarkably only three sailors died. Perhaps a lesson in the advantages of small-scale expeditions.

John Barrow at the Admiralty was not only interested in seaborne exploration, he also sent out several land expeditions. In 1819, John Franklin set off into the wilderness of north Canada. Franklin was a navy man with a good record, but no experience of the overland conditions he would have to endure. He had joined the Royal Navy at 14. He served at Trafalgar in 1805 and the battle of New Orleans in 1814. As noted above he had Arctic experience captaining *Trent* in Britain's first attempt on the North Pole.

From York Factory on Hudson Bay Franklin trekked west to the Great Slave Lake and then north to the Coppermine River and the Arctic Coast. Together with his British party he recruited indigenous guides and hunters, and French-Canadian voyageurs as porters. The journey was a nightmare. Unprepared for the harshness of the climate and the terrain, the party was reduced to eating the leather of their shoes. 11 men died. One of the voyageurs was suspected of murder and cannibalism and was shot by Dr Richardson.

Despite the troubles of the first expedition Franklin had managed to fight his way to the Arctic coast and to survive, and he was chosen to lead a second journey to the same area. The expedition set out in 1825 and returned in 1827. It was much more successful and he was knighted in 1829.

In 1836 he received the thankless appointment of Lieutenant-Governor of the rough and ready convict colony of Van Diemen's Land (Tasmania). He was a good man, used to the structure and discipline of the Royal Navy, but inexperienced in the politics and power struggles of this rugged and remote British outpost. After a difficult and demanding time dealing with the intrigues and conflicting factional interests, he was recalled to Britain in 1843.

Meanwhile John Barrow was still vigorously prosecuting the case for the discovery of the Northwest Passage and was planning the Admiralty's grandest assault. *Terror* and *Erebus*, so successful under sail in James Clark Ross's epic Antarctic exploration, were to be completely refitted. They would have the additional power of locomotive engines and the 'comfort' of steam heating. The expedition would be lavishly provisioned. Included would be the newly invented sealed canned food.

Barrow's first choice for command of this mighty endeavour was William Edward Parry. Parry, though, declined, as did James Clark Ross. Surprisingly the command fell to John Franklin. Despite a solid career, his only seaborne Arctic experience was on *Trent* 27 years before, and most notably, he would be 59 years old when the expedition commenced. Nevertheless, nothing could shake the confidence of the Admiralty in this best prepared, provisioned and crewed Arctic expedition.

On 19 May 1845 the expedition set sail accompanied by the confident assumption of a successful voyage. Fittingly it would be a British expedition that would, after centuries, sail the Northwest Passage.

In late July, in Baffin Bay, sailing towards Lancaster Sound, *Terror* and *Erebus* were sighted by two whalers, *Prince of Wales* and *Enterprise*. Franklin and his officers accepted an invitation to board *Prince of Wales*. This convivial visit was the last reported sighting of the two ships. The expedition had vast provisions and the ships were considered the most able vessels to resist the pressures of the ice. No-one expected them to be back anytime soon. However, after two years had elapsed a sense of foreboding superseded the initial confidence. Franklin's wife Jane's began lobbying for a rescue attempt.

In 1848 John Richardson, an old colleague of Franklin's from his two Canadian journeys, led an overland expedition. He was joined by John Rae, an Orkney islander, who studied medicine in Edinburgh. Rae had signed on as a ship's surgeon in 1833 with the Hudson Bay Company vessel *Prince of*

Wales (later sold and the last ship to encounter the Franklin expedition as above) and then was appointed surgeon at the company's Moose Factory, St James Bay, a position he held for a decade. In 1844 he led an expedition to survey the northern coast of North America. This completed the work done earlier by Franklin, James Ross and other explorers.

In 1848 Richardson and Rae conducted an efficient and effective search but they didn't find any sign of Franklin.

At the same time James Clark Ross commanded a seaborne search aboard *Enterprise* accompanied by *Investigator*. Meanwhile *Plover* was despatched to the Bering Strait to be joined by *Herald*, redirected from survey work off California. Several years passed. Each of these expeditions returned without discovering any sign of Franklin or his ships. *Plover* remained patrolling the Bering Strait region until 1854 in the vain hope they could provide assistance if Franklin emerged from the Northwest Passage.

In 1850 the Admiralty sent out four ships, supported by 4 towing vessels and a supply vessel. (These five accompanying vessels didn't venture into the Arctic beyond Disko Island, Greenland). The expedition was under the overall command of Horatio Austin. One of these ships, *Assistance*, was captained by Erasmus Ommanney. Also aboard was a young midshipman, Clements Markham. These two would later champion attempts to raise interest in a British assault of the South Pole. Another notable figure in the promotion of British polar ambitions, Sherard Osborn, commanded *Pioneer*.

A party from Ommanney's ship discovered the first sign of the Franklin expedition, with remains of an encampment on Beechey Island.

Searching in the same area were two further vessels under whaling Captain William Penny. At Beechey Island one of his crew discovered three graves with inscribed headboards recording the deaths of three men from the expedition in early 1846. In response to Lady Franklin's pleas several American ships had also joined the search in this area.

The redoubtable John Ross, at age 73, captained a further search ship, *Felix*, privately funded by Lady Franklin.

The Times reported that

> ... Lady Franklin, with all the fervour of a devoted wife, is at present engaged in a pious pilgrimage to the ports whence the whale ships are likely to proceed to Davis's Strait, with a view to plead her anxieties and

distresses, and to animate the daring and generous commanders of these ships in her cause ... the appearance of Lady Franklin, and the mention of her most touching case, cannot fail to excite the same generous ardour, and we may confidently anticipate such practical results as, under Providence may tend to dispel the dark cloud that has already nearly weighed her down, and which presses heavily on the mind of every thinking individual in the kingdom.[3]

Two further Royal Navy vessels under overall command of Richard Collinson (*Enterprise*) with second in command Robert McClure (*Investigator*) also sailed in 1850, approaching from the west through the Bering Strait. McClure became separated from Collinson and missed a rendezvous in Honolulu. To catch up he took the dangerous route through, rather than around, the Aleutian Islands, beating his commander to the Arctic. Not for him to await at the northern rendezvous point. He saw an opportunity to grab the prize of the Passage for himself, and almost succeeded. Caught in impenetrable ice in Prince of Wales Strait, the ship finally reached shelter of sorts to the northeast of Banks Island. His ship was never released, so while he proved there was a sea route around the top of Canada, he fell just short of completing it by ship. His crew were faced with several brutal winters before being rescued.

In 1853 the Admiralty launched a five-ship expedition under Edward Belcher. Four ships were beset by ice. Fortuitously, a sledging party from one of the ships, *Resolute*, came upon McClure's trapped *Investigator*, and her crew of starving men. Their adventure was not over though. Belcher's expedition remained ice bound. In mid-1853 *Phoenix*, under the command of Edward Inglefield (who in 1852 had captained Lady Franklin's *Isabel* searching along Smith Sound) and accompanied by *Breadalbane* and *Diligence*, sailed north to restock the supply ship *North Star*.

Anchoring in Disko Bay on 8 July 1853, they observed the wrecked whaler *Rose*, and encountered her desolate crew. Inglefield decided to send *Diligence* back to England, crewed by the stranded whalers, while *Phoenix* and *Breadalbane* continued on. They were able to rendezvous with *North Star* and transfer stores, but on 21 August, off Beechey Island, the starboard bow of *Breadalbane* was stoved in by ice. The ship sank in 15 minutes. Inglefield was able to rescue the crew. They sailed from Beechey Island on 24 August. The wreck of *Breadalbane* was discovered in August 1980 and is now the site of tourist cruises.

The loss of *Breadalbane*, unavoidable as it was, was but a prelude to what would be a disastrous and humiliating period in the Arctic for the Royal Navy. Four of Belcher's ships were stuck fast in the ice. The captains of the respective ships didn't see the situation as dire. Their ships were sound and well provisioned, and they expected to be released by the ice. Their commander Belcher, though, was not of a mind to remain for a further winter. Despite the pleas of his ship's captains, he took the unprecedented action of ordering the abandonment of four of the ships, *Assistance*, *Pioneer*, *Resolute* and *Intrepid*.

Belcher's original confidential letter to his captains, according to Sherard Osborn, captain of *Pioneer*, contained 'a long string of erroneous predictions and verbose ambiguities'.[4] Belcher would brook no arguments and had Sherard Osborn, captain of *Pioneer*, relieved of command and confined to his cabin for questioning his judgement. With McClure's *Investigator* abandoned too, it meant five additional crews were precariously housed in the one remaining ship, *North Star*. Fortunately, just as they set off for home they were met by *Phoenix*, returning again under Edward Inglefield, accompanied by *Talbot* (under Captain Jenkins). The crews were redistributed amongst the three ships and the desultory group sailed for home in August 1854.

Belcher had, perhaps, taken too literally some points in the Admiralty Sailing Orders. In part they stated:

> We have equal confidence in the care to be exercised by you for those employed under your orders; but there is one object which in the exercise of that care will naturally engage your constant attention, and that is, the safe return of your party to this country.[5]

Presumably they hoped 'safe return' would be aboard the ships they sent out.

Further the Admiralty surmised:

> We are sensible, however, that not withstanding a wish to keep this part of your duty prominently in mind, yet, that an ardent desire to accomplish the object of your mission, added to a generous sympathy for your missing countrymen, may prevail in some degree to carry you beyond the limits of a cautious prudence.[6]

While several of his captains were keen to go beyond the 'limits of a cautious prudence', Belcher was having none of it.

On his return Belcher faced court martial, and while he managed to avoid censure, he was discredited and never held such an important post again. Undaunted he published his account of the expedition with the grandiose title *The last of the Arctic voyages*. As pompous as the title sounds, it was prophetic. The disaster of Belcher's command, after the tragedy of the loss of Franklin and his men and ships, and the expense of so many fruitless searches, left the Admiralty and the government with no appetite for further polar adventures. An American reviewer found Belcher's book to have 'a magnificence of aspect, in singular contrast with the paucity of the results which his expedition accomplished'. The reviewer's view of Belcher is damning. 'He had able subordinates, as his narrative amply shows, but it as amply shows that he was an inefficient, querulous, and feeble chief.' The reviewer goes further, 'his incompetency to lead such an expedition under such perilous circumstances manifests itself through almost the entire voyage'.[7]

To emphasise the folly of his decision of the 'needless abandonment of four fine ships',[8] in September 1855 one of the deserted ships emerged from the ice. *Resolute*, unmanned and empty, broke free of the ice and managed to sail, without sailors or commanders, to Davis Strait, just north of the Arctic Circle. She had been abandoned at 74°41'N, 101°22'W, and drifted to 67°N. There she was spotted and claimed by James Buddington, the skipper a US whaler *George Henry*. The captain sailed his prize back to New London, Connecticut. The salvaged ship was purchased from Buddington by the US government, refitted and sailed back to England where she was presented as a gift to Queen Victoria. When the ship was finally broken up, her timbers were used to make a writing desk, presented as a gift to the US president in 1880.

In a much later footnote to the expedition the well-preserved wreck of HMS *Investigator*, that had so nearly completed the Northwest Passage from west to east, was discovered in late July 2010.

Richard Collinson and his ship *Enterprise*, left behind by his ambitious subordinate Robert McClure aboard *Investigator*, completed a remarkable journey of his own. He negotiated the narrow, treacherous channels between continental Canada and Victoria Island and wintered in the ice of Cambridge Bay. The ship arrived back in England in May 1855 after a cruise of 3 ½ years.

Collinson lost few crew and didn't expose them to anything of the reckless danger and deprivation of McClure. It was his misfortune to have been unwittingly forestalled by John Rae (see below) and McClure, and to have not uncovered any new information on Franklin. His voyage was underestimated and uncelebrated, while McClure, having failed to rendezvous with Collinson, then setting out by himself, losing his ship, and almost his entire crew, was feted as the first man to achieve the Northwest Passage (albeit partly on foot).

Views of Collinson's leadership are varied. He had a fractious and at times poisonous relationship with many of his officers and only deft work by the Admiralty managed to calm court martial demands by both sides. Collinson has been accused of excessive caution, particularly in his decision to spend the first winter in Hong Kong rather than choosing a rather more northerly position. His prudence, though, allowed him to return with his ship and crew and without assistance. McClure's boldness almost led to the loss of his entire crew, and if sledging teams from *Resolute* had not happened on his ship, the Admiralty would have had another Franklin like disaster to deal with. Meanwhile, at the same time, Belcher was abandoning four sound ships to the ice.

With an ounce of luck, Collinson's expedition could have been the one that finally found a written record of Franklin, and remains of his crew. The Inuit interpreter Miertsching was intended to accompany *Enterprise* but had been temporarily accommodated with McClure on *Investigator*. This arrangement became permanent as the two ships failed to rendezvous at Honolulu, or at Cape Lisburne (at the northern end of the Bering Strait). Without an interpreter Collinson and his crew were unable to understand the Inuit's descriptions of ships abandoned at King William Island.

No less an authority than Roald Amundsen, in his account of his first successful traverse of the Northwest Passage by sea, describes Collinson as

> one of the most capable and enterprising sailors the world has ever produced. He guided his great, heavy vessel into waters that hardly afforded sufficient room for the tiny Gjoa. But, better still, he brought her safely home His recompense for the heroism shown was, however, but scant.

Regarding the Northwest Passage, Amundsen's view was that

> McClure found a Northwest Passage that was not navigable; Collinson found one which was practicable, although not suitable for ordinary navigation.[9]

At the same time Belcher's ships were static in the ice and McClure was pressing for the Northwest Passage, and while Collinson was embarking on his careful voyage along the northern Canadian coast, the enterprising John Rae was conducting a much different search across the wilds of northern Canada.

Living off the land, Rae's small expedition included William Ouligback, an Inuit interpreter, who spoke 'English fluently; and, perhaps, more correctly than one half of the lower classes in England or Scotland.'[10]

Rae and Ouligback were told that

> in the spring four winters past (spring 1850) a party of white men, amounting to about 40 were seen travelling southward over the ice and dragging a boat with them ... by signs the natives were made to understand that their ship, or ships, had been crushed by ice and, that they were now going to where they expected to find deer to shoot ... At a later date the same season, but previous to the breaking up of the ice, the bodies of some 30 persons were discovered on the continent, and five on an island near it, about a long days journey to the N.W. of a large stream, which can be no other than Back's Great Fish River.[11]

This story was told by Inuit who had heard about, but not witnessed, the events. Rae purchased some items from the Franklin expedition. When he returned to England with his story it created a sensation, and not just because it was the first substantial evidence of the fate of Franklin and his men.

His report was delivered to the Admiralty and then published in the *The Times*. Few people in Britain held out genuine hope of the expedition's survival but one paragraph of Rae's report was met with outrage.

> From the mutilated state of many of the corpses and the contents of the kettles, it is evident that our wretched countrymen had been delivered to the last resource – cannibalism – as a means of prolonging existence.[12]

Lady Franklin rallied her forces to refute the claim. Leading the charge was Charles Dickens. Rae was not a man to court sensational publicity or to take much notice of the newspapers. He was comfortable in the extremes of Northern Canada and found little need to get entangled in the controversy.

Dickens politely took him to task:

> ... There is no reason whatever to believe, that any of its members prolonged their existence by the dreadful expedient of eating the bodies of their dead

companions. ... Quite apart from the very loose and unreliable nature of the Esquimaux representations ... we believe we shall show, that close analogy and the mass of experience are decidedly against the reception of any such statement, and that it is in the highest degree improbable that such men as the officers and crews of the two ships would, or could, in any extremity of hunger, alleviate the pains of starvation by this horrible means.[13]

Dickens expresses the innate view that the Inuit were unreliable, and that Englishmen would never resort to cannibalism to ward off starvation. Letter writer 'E.J.H' wrote: 'Where Esquimaux can live – where Dr Rae's party could find abundant means – what should have prevented Sir John Franklin and his party subsisting too?'[14] Another correspondent suggested that the men had been murdered by the Inuit.[15]

John Rae had lived for 20 years in the far north, had learned the Inuit skills which enabled him to be such a capable explorer, had absolute faith and trust in his interpreter and knew the desperate extremity of the conditions. He addressed the arguments of Charles Dickens and various correspondents in a letter to *The Times* (31 October 1854, p. 8) and in *Household words* (23 December 1854). Dickens added a rather patronising addendum to Rae's article, quoting an episode from Franklin's second expedition to the northern reaches of Canada when his party were involved in a skirmish with the Inuit. It is generally (but not universally) accepted that Franklin's last surviving men may have attempted to survive by eating the flesh of dead companions. Rae was merely honestly recounting what he had heard, however he surely would have realised the controversy that his casual inclusion of the suggestion of cannibalism would have caused. Perhaps, for the sake especially of the bereaved families of the lost men, this need not have been published. It dominated the public reaction to his report and overshadowed the substance – the likelihood of the remnants of the expedition perishing in the vicinity of Great Fish River (Back River).

However the Admiralty and the British government, especially after Belcher arrived back without his ships, were no doubt relieved to finally have the inevitable confirmation of the demise of all Franklin's men. They need not send out any more expensive and fruitless search parties.

The search for Franklin continued through private funding and public appeal. The Admiralty, having spent vast amounts on many searches and having lost a number of ships, felt enough had been done. Rae's report seemed to confirm what they had feared for some time. The party had all perished.

In February 1857 Charles Woods, 1st Lord of the Admiralty, was reported as stating 'Her Majesty's Government will not give any encouragement to the proposal to send out another Arctic Expedition'.[16]

The Times editorialised in support:

> We rejoiced in the recent determination of the Admiralty not to throw away good lives after bad, and to refuse absolutely the countenance of the Government to any further explorations in the Polar Seas with the hope of recovering that which had long since perished.[17]

The formidable Lady Franklin continued to press, but in the wake of the Admiralty's firm decision to cease the search, she was forced to again raise funds for a private expedition. This time it was under the command of experienced Royal Navy man Leopold McClintock. He had distinguished himself in previous searches, particularly with his sledging skills. This time he commanded *Fox* which set sail on 2 July 1857 with a crew of 24, including Allen Young who donated funds for the expedition and took up the position of sailing master and supplemented by two Greenland Inuit. *The Times* deemed the expedition 'quixotic'. Opining that 'We can form no favourable expectations as to the results which may be looked for from this last Arctic Expedition'.[18] The newspaper, though, was wrong.

Inuit told McLintock stories about two ships abandoned years before. They sold him artefacts from the Franklin expedition. They directed him to King William Island. One of his crew, Lt Hobson, found a cairn. Within was a sealed tin containing the only written record of the voyage ever discovered. A message from 28 May 1847 reported all well, but a second message in the margins, added on 25 April 1848, told a different story. It reported the deaths of 24 men, including John Franklin, the abandonment of the ships and an attempt to walk to Great Fish River at the top of Canada. In the vicinity of the cairn, Hobson found discarded equipment, lifeboats, and skeletons. These discoveries were as close as anyone would get to solving the mystery of the lost Franklin expedition, and the note indicating the survivors were attempting to reach Great Fish River confirmed the Inuit stories that John Rae had brought back. The expedition docked at Portsmouth on 21 September 1859, having lost three men to illness and injury. McLintock hastened to London and reported the success of the expedition to the Admiralty. On 23 September his findings were published in *The Times*.

Adventurers continued the search, found more equipment, and bones, and heard more Inuit stories, but the search was over as far as the Admiralty and government was concerned. They were left to ponder the cost of Franklin's expedition, in the lives of the men of the two ships, the prestige of the Royal Navy, with its best equipped attempt on the Northwest Passage ending in tragic failure, the many rescue expeditions over a decade, costing vast amounts to fit out, not to mention the loss of a number of ships and the embarrassment of the abandoned *Resolute* finding her own way out of the ice.

There were great geographical benefits from so many ships traversing the Arctic. Huge areas were discovered and mapped. But on balance, the Admiralty and the British Government had had enough of polar adventures. In the period between 1847 and 1859 many expeditions, both government and private, had joined the Franklin search. Some estimates place the number higher than 70. A more accurate estimation from W.G. Ross is 7 overland and 32 maritime expeditions, involving 47 ships, over that 13-year period.[19]

In the midst of the Franklin search, Great Britain, after four decades, found herself once more engaged in a European war in the Crimea. The formerly underemployed Royal Navy did not have spare time for geographical expeditions of uncertain value and high risk. The great champion of naval exploration, John Barrow, had died in 1848.

The Franklin expedition is one of the enduring mysteries of the ocean and attempts to solve the mystery have never really ceased. The wrecks of *Breadlbane* (August 1980) and then *Investigator* (July 2010) have been discovered. Finally, nearly 170 years after Franklin's expedition disappeared, in September 2014, Parks Canada discovered the well-preserved wreck of *Erebus*. Two years later, in September 2016 the well-preserved wreck of *Terror* was discovered by the private Arctic Research Foundation, in the aptly named Terror Bay, on the southwestern side of King William Island. So finally we are close to the final chapter of one of maritime explorations greatest puzzles.

It was 1875 before the British government considered serious funding of further Arctic exploration and they saw even less value in further exploration in the frozen south. The other great national contributors to Antarctic exploration to that point had their own reasons for abandoning further voyages.

Russia was as far from the Antarctic as a country could be and Bellingshausen's great expedition was exceptional. There were few other 19th century examples of such adventurous and far-reaching explorations by the Russians, and with the vast and barely known icy wastes of the Arctic at their doorstep they had little incentive for travelling to the other end of the world for polar adventures.

France had been pioneers in the region too, with Bouvet and Kerguelen's 18th century discoveries and Dumont d'Urville's later sighting of the continent. Dumont d'Urville's tragic death cost the country a revered Antarctic veteran and the colonial powers had, by mid-19th century, carved the Pacific territories into colonial outposts. France's turbulent history overwhelmed whatever desires there may have been of further adventures in the southern ice.

The Americans, through their sealing fleets, had been very active in the 1820s and sealers continued to visit the Antarctic fringes, albeit in fewer numbers, optimistically chasing after the greatly diminished seal population. The fraught and bitter aftermath to the US Ex-Ex obscured the great achievements of the voyage. There was, though, a champion of further Antarctic exploration – the highly respected pioneering oceanographer Matthew Fontaine Maury. In May 1860 he wrote to the President of the British Association, Lord Wrottesley, to enlist support in an international effort in the Antarctic. Maury hoped that

> the time is not too far distant when circumstances will be more auspicious than at present they seem; for, as soon as there appears the least chance of success, I shall urge the sending from this country an exploring expedition to the eight millions of unknown square miles about the South Pole.

His letter was an effort to 'enlist your influence with Her Majesty's Government and the English people in the cause of Antarctic exploration'. He ended his appeal 'trusting and hoping that you will join with me in the cry, 'ho for the South Pole'.[20] A year later, in April 1861, undaunted by the lack of any official progress towards the south, he wrote to the grandly titled Envoy Extraordinary and Minister Plenipotentiary of Great Britain, Washington, Lord Lyons. The letter was again a plea for Antarctic exploration.

> If, in pleading the cause of Antarctic exploration, I be required to answer first the question of cui bono? Which is so apt to be put, I reply, it is enough for

me, when contemplating the vast extent of that unknown region, to know that it is a part of the surface of our planet, and to remember that the earth was made for man; that all knowledge is profitable; that no discoveries have conferred more honour and glory upon the age in which they were made, or have been more beneficial to the world, than geographical discoveries; and that never were nations so well prepared to undertake Antarctic explorations as are those that I now solicit.[21]

These sentiments would find support amongst the British Association but would meet a stonier reception among the hard heads of Treasury, or the Admiralty, still counting the vast cost of the Franklin episode.

Soon the American states were plunged into a bloody and debilitating Civil War. Maury had to set aside any dreams of geographical discoveries in the Antarctic. A southerner, he served the Confederacy. Following the Confederacy's defeat in the war he chose exile in both Mexico and then England, returning to the United States in 1868. He died in 1873, his hopes for further Antarctic exploration unfulfilled.

England, the 19th century's superpower, with the world's greatest navy, appeared the most likely to be able to launch explorations as the century progressed. However, apart, from the ambitious oceanographic expedition of HMS *Challenger* which roamed the seas for nearly four years, including a brief sojourn in the high southern latitudes, no official British expeditions ventured across the Antarctic Circle until the end of the century.

The truth was, that though the Antarctic was greatly unknown, what little that was known suggested there would be no economic or strategic benefits, and considerable danger to crews, ships and the public purse, in further exploration of such an inhospitable, impenetrable and remote area of the world. James Cook's initial view seemed utterly accurate.

The thoughts of the British Royal Societies were in the far north rather than the far south. The driving force behind Britain's next polar expedition was Sherard Osborn, a Royal Navy veteran of the Franklin search. He had been part of Austin's fleet and commanded one of the ships abandoned by Belcher (HMS *Pioneer*).

On return from the Arctic he commanded ships in the Crimean War and the 2nd Opium War. On 23 January 1865 he presented a paper to the Royal Geographical Society advocating further British exploration in the Arctic.

He condemned the 'rest and thankful men' who might use of the loss of Franklin's expedition as an excuse to not continue exploration in the region. He felt there was no more reason to turn away from 'Arctic Regions because Franklin died off King William's Land, than you would wish them to do so to an enemy's fleet, because Nelson fell at Trafalgar'.

He pointed to the achievements of previous expeditions and suggested critics should confront

> our knowledge of 1864 with that of 1800 upon natural history, meteorology, climate, and winds of the Arctic Regions. They must remember that it was there we obtained the clue, still unravelled, of the laws of those mysterious currents which flow through the wastes of the ocean like two mighty rivers – the Gulf Stream, and the Ice Stream.

He was dismissive of any citing of danger as a drawback. 'I will not dwell upon the personal hardships or risks incurred – they can be easily discounted at any Insurance Company in the City of London.'

He reasonably pointed out that

> more sailors have been thrown to the sharks from the diseases incident to service in China and the coast of Africa, within the last four years, than ever fell in thirty years of Arctic service.[22]

His robust arguments were embraced by the RGS and supported strongly by another champion of polar exploration, Clements Markham. However, it was another decade before the expedition sailed, sadly just 3 weeks after Osborn's premature death. In the meantime, another expedition had been organised and despatched. This was the vastly ambitious and successful HMS *Challenger* study of the oceans.

Chapter Six

HMS *Challenger*:
An exploration beneath the waves

The Challenger Expedition, one of pure scientific research, had a much quicker gestation period than Osborn and Markham's protracted efforts to mount an Arctic expedition. Edward Forbes, a Scottish naturalist, had for many years been studying and theorising on the distribution of marine species. In 1841 he accompanied a Royal Navy expedition to the Eastern Mediterranean which he felt helped confirm his theory that there were eight progressively deeper zones of marine animal life. Further to this he posited his azoic theory that no life existed in the deep sea (beyond 300 fathoms). Forbes died young, just seven months after he was appointed to the Regius Chair of Natural History at Edinburgh University in 1854.

While there was initial acceptance of the 'azoic theory', as the fledgling study of the depths of the ocean developed, Forbes theory came under increasing scrutiny. In 1866 another Scottish naturalist, Charles Wyville Thomson, visited Norway where Professor Michael Sars showed him life forms retrieved the previous year by his son Georg (who also became a pioneering marine biologist), dredging in the vicinity of the Lofoten Islands to depths up to 450 fathoms.

The Sars, father and son, were investigating reasons for variability in the Norwegian Fish catch. Previously Peter Christen Asbjørnsen, (now better known as a collector of Norwegian folklores, but also a notable pioneer of marine biology), had dredged in Norway's extensive Hardandgerfjord to 200 fathoms, bringing up starfish.

These examples confirmed Thomson's developing doubts at Forbes' theory, indicating as they did that animal life is abundant in the ocean at depths varying from 200 to 300 fathoms, and beyond.

Thomson was determined to conduct his own investigations and prevailed upon his friend, Dr William Carpenter, at the time a vice president of the Royal Society, to lobby the Admiralty for use of a Royal Navy ship to conduct dredging. The influence of the Council of the Royal Society had the desired effect, and the gunboat *Lightning* was made available. Thomson and Carpenter (and his son Phillip) made a short exploration of the ocean between the Shetland and Faeroe Islands in the northern summer of 1868.

The following year they were given the use of HMS *Porcupine* for May to September and were able to conduct three separate cruises. Other duties prevented Thomson and Carpenter accompanying each voyage. The first, under scientific direction of Gwyn Jeffreys, with assistance from another of Carpenter's sons, William Lant, explored the area west of Ireland and Scotland between 18 May and 13 July. The second cruise, under Thomson and commencing 17 July, investigated west of Ushant Island (Brittany) and around the edge of the Bay of Biscay. The third cruise, under Carpenter and again with his son Phillip, and with Thomson along as 'supernumerary', investigated the same area north of Scotland as the expedition aboard *Lightning* of the previous year.

The investigations were continued in 1870, again in HMS *Porcupine*. The first voyage was directed by Gwyn Jeffreys accompanied by Swede Joshua Lindahl and William Lant Carpenter. They sailed from Falmouth to Gibralter where Dr Carpenter took over for the second voyage. In August 1871 George Nares commanded *Shearwater* in a further voyage investigating the currents in the Straits of Gibraltar with Dr Carpenter.

Clearly the Admiralty were in a mood to support the scientific investigations of Carpenter and Thomson, providing, in several successive years, the use of Royal Navy ships with indulgent commanders and acquiescent crews. In a time of peace, it was a reasonable use of the Admiralty's ships, exposed to few of the dangers or potential disaster of attempts on the North Pole or the Northwest Passage, or the icy regions of the Southern Ocean.

Thomson and Carpenter were ready for a far more adventurous and ambitious use of the Royal Navy's resources. With again the backing of the Royal Society, Thomson and his allies were able to convince the Admiralty and the government to support, provide a ship, commander and crew, and funds for a purely scientific exploration of the world's oceans. It was a smooth and quick process compared with Markham and Osborn's longstanding efforts to mount an Arctic expedition.

The Times, referring to the voyages of *Porcupine* and *Lightning* viewed

> the great scientific and practical importance of the facts revealed by these short and imperfect inquiries was such as to render their continuance a matter of national concern ... [Mr Lowe (Treasury)] fully recognizes that matters which it is fitting for the country to undertake should be carried through with every advantage that money can secure ... [and Mr Goschen (Admiralty)] lent himself heartily to the scheme.[1]

The ship was HMS *Challenger*, powered by both steam and sail, and captained by experienced Royal Navy man George Nares, who had been captain of *Shearwater* during the dredging in 1871 (and who was a veteran of the Franklin searches). *Challenger*, a ship built for battle, was adjusted for her new peaceful purpose. Many of her guns were removed to make space for scientists and their laboratories and equipment.

The expedition sailed from Portsmouth on 21 December 1872 with a small scientific team supported by over 200 officers and crew. They traversed the oceans, methodically and laboriously dredging to uncover the mysteries of the great depths.

It wasn't an Antarctic expedition, but they spent time at Heard Island and the Kerguelen Group and ventured across the Antarctic Circle on 16 February 1874, the first steam powered ship to do so, (although their time in the Antarctic was mainly under sail to preserve coal). Rocks released by icebergs were dredged up providing more confirmation of the continental nature of the Antarctic.

The final result of the Challenger expedition, after three and a half years voyaging, were 50 volumes of reports, the last publication arriving 19 years after the completion of the voyage. It was a scientific watershed, establishing firmly the sciences of oceanography and marine biology and greatly increasing the world's knowledge of the sea. The scientists with the expedition were led by Thomson. Young German zoologist Rudolf von Willemoes-Suhm died during the voyage. The other scientists went on to distinguished careers.

John Murray, the dominant personality of the scientific staff, became the most well-known and lent his considerable influence to British attempts to mount an Antarctic expedition. In a satisfying piece of symmetry, in 1910 he travelled with young Norwegian marine biologist, Johan Hjort, in a dredging voyage from May to August aboard a vessel called *Michael Sars*. Murray had provided finance for the expedition from profits derived from exploiting phosphate deposits on Christmas Island. The voyage investigated some of the areas visited by the pioneering voyages of Carpenter and Thomson 40 years before. Fittingly the final voyage was from Glasgow to Bergen, investigating the depths between the north of Scotland and the Faeroe Islands, just as Carpenter and Thomson had in *Lightning* in 1868, the first of the series of voyages that led to the *Challenger* voyage.

Another on the *Challenger* expedition was John James Wild, who travelled as Thomson's secretary and as the official artist. He later found his way to Australia and was involved in attempts in Melbourne to mount an Antarctic expedition.

On 24 May 1876 *Challenger* arrived at Spithead, the voyage was completed. It was an outstanding success, in contrast to the judgement of Nares Arctic voyage that arrived in England 6 months later.

Chapter Seven

Britain revisits the Arctic

While *Challenger* cruised the oceans with her crew of scientists dredging up creatures never seen before and gathering data for the extensive scientific reports, Clements Markham and Sherard Osborn, with the backing of the RGS, continued to champion a recommencement of British exploration in the Arctic.

Following Osborn's 1865 paper to the RGS, Markham wrote several articles promoting the cause. Osborn read another paper at the RGS in April 1872, and a further paper at the August meeting of the British Association in the same year. Markham, appointed as editor of the *Geographical Magazine* in July 1872, was able to include articles pushing the benefits of Arctic exploration. In 1873 he published in instalments *Threshold of the Unknown Region* which was then published as a monograph, running to 4 editions by December 1875.

Finally, public and government interest was being aroused. To allay fears of the dangers of ice navigation, Osborn despatched Markham's cousin Albert, an experienced navy man, on a journey with an Arctic whaler from May to August 1873. His narrative of the voyage was published in 1874. In the introduction Sherard Osborn took another opportunity to champion his cause:

> Never was a fairer field open to English seamen and adventurers to reap high renown and to keep our country in the vanguard of geographical discovery; and I cannot believe that that spirit which was awakened under the great Elizabeth can have passed away in the reign of Queen Victoria; but fervently trust, if our Government shrinks from its undoubted duty, that private individuals will secure to us the glory of being the first nation to have traversed the Polar Sea, as we have been foremost in all that is great and glorious in so many parts of the earth.[1]

One interesting occurrence of Albert Markham's voyage was his encounter with the rescued crew of the disastrous *Polaris* expedition.

American Charles Hall had left his home and his family in 1860 and made his own pilgrimage to the Arctic to find Franklin. He explored the area around Frobisher Bay for several years. He returned to the Arctic in 1864 and spent 5 years exploring by sled, recovering various Franklin relics, and living with and learning from the Inuit.

In 1871, funded by the US government, he set sail again, attempting the North Pole. Vastly different from his previous solo expeditions, this time he was commanding a tough whaling captain and crew. He also had a fractious group of German scientists aboard. The expedition mirrored many polar expeditions, both north and south, failing in its objective but rich in tragedy, deprivation and remarkable survival.

Hall reached 83° North by sled, but shortly after he became ill and died. The detailed inquiry following the expedition delivered a finding of apoplexy. A century later historian Chauncey Loomis exhumed Hall's remarkably preserved body. Tests found that Hall had high traces of arsenic which could well have been the cause of death.[2] The arsenic may have been self-administered or given to him by another member of the expedition.

The voyage had, to that time, been marked by discord and personal animosity. Hall had no experience or skill at leading such a party of men, and several showed little remorse at his death. After some desultory sledging attempts *Polaris* sailed for home.

The journey had been grim, but it was to get much grimmer. The ship was caught in heavy ice. Stores were placed on an icefloe in anticipation of the ship's imminent demise, but she broke away and sailed off leaving the Inuit hunters, wives, and children, (including a baby) and some crew, stranded. Amazingly this group survived, travelling on the disintegrating ice floes for over six months before being picked up by the whaler *Tigress*.

Their erstwhile crew mates remaining aboard the ship survived too. They ran an increasingly unseaworthy *Polaris* ashore and continued in the whale boats and were eventually picked up by *Ravenscraig*, a Scottish whaler. Markham's ship took half the crew when they encountered *Ravenscraig*. Before heading for home they took on the remaining survivors also to allow *Ravenscraig* to pursue more whales.

For Albert Markham it was an opportunity to learn from the *Polaris* crew's experiences. The man he conversed with most was German scientist Emil Bessel, one of the men who has been theorised as Hall's murderer. Bessel advised that 'no man should go north without some Esquimaux for hunting and dog driving'.[3] The *Polaris* expedition, though, was a disaster. Poorly lead by the inexperienced Hall, with disparate aims, and strong-willed scientists and crew unwilling to submit to Hall's authority, it was lucky that the entire expedition wasn't lost.

In 1873 the Royal Society and Royal Geographical Society, formed a joint committee to outline the scientific benefits of an expedition. The presidents of the two societies, Henry Rawlinson (RGS) and Joseph Hooker (RS) together with Sherard Osborn, met with Prime Minister Disraeli in August 1874, and, in a letter dated 17 November 1874, Disraeli advised Rawlinson that

> having carefully weighed the reasons set forth in support of such an expedition, the scientific advantages to be derived from it, its chances of success, as well as the importance of encouraging that spirit of maritime enterprise which has ever distinguished the English people, Her Majesty's Government have determined to lose no time in organizing a suitable expedition for the purposes in view.[4]

George Nares, captain of *Challenger*, was recalled in November 1874 to take charge of the British Arctic Expedition. The ships *Alert* and *Discovery* sailed on 29 May 1875, accompanied by the supply ship *Valorous*. Clements Markham journeyed with the voyage as far as Disko Island. On 6 July the three ships rendezvoused and *Valorous* transferred her supplies. She then returned south. On board were Gwyn Jeffreys and Phillip Carpenter. William Carpenter had again secured permission for the Royal Navy's co-operation with the program of dredging.

Meanwhile *Alert* and *Discovery* headed north. *Alert* reached 82°N finally eclipsing Parry's 1827 voyage with *Hecla*. The two ships and crew settled in for the winter. When the sun returned preparations were made for further exploration and on 3 April 1876 sledging parties were sent out. While Albert Markham's party reached a new furthest north of 83°20'26", all the sledging parties were greatly affected by scurvy. Their desperate return to the ships was heroic, but some men died and Nares quickly (and sensibly) retreated from the enclosing ice.

Nares had returned to England a year early and while he was initially feted he also faced disappointment and disapproval. Subsequently Clements Markham tried to paint a positive picture, but Nares was generally considered as having been at fault despite his prompt escape from the ice that may have avoided another Franklin like disaster. There was an enquiry into the outbreak of scurvy that had undermined the voyage but given the lack of knowledge of what scurvy was, and what caused it, the conclusions were inevitably speculative. Nares was blamed for varying from recommendations of the Medical General in not requiring the sledging parties to take lime juice for their journey. Nares had not considered these recommendations mandatory and there were scurvy cases aboard the two ships despite daily lime juice. The ensuing debate overwhelmed the positives of the voyage and undermined future attempts by Markham and others to raise interest in polar exploration. The British Medical Journal was damning.

> In framing false medical theories, and in assuming the responsibility of refusing to act upon his medical instructions, Sir George Nares brought disaster upon this expedition. He assumes the full responsibility of it, and we fear it must weigh heavily upon his shoulders.[5]

Although the same journal, some years later, published the Royal Society Food (War) Committee findings that

> West Indian lime juice, as ordinarily prepared, is useless for the prevention of scurvy ... Nare's expedition of 1875, notorious for the serious outbreaks of scurvy encountered, was the first to be provisioned with 'lime juice' prepared from the West Indies.[6]

Markham's view was that 'the outbreak of scurvy ... was not an unmixed evil. It has taught lessons which will be of great value hereafter ...'[7] The men of the expedition probably drew no comfort from this. Neither they would from the rather romantic view taken by a writer in the *Quarterly Review* (quoted by Markham, and sounding very Markhamish), who felt that

> surely nothing finer was ever recorded than this advance of three sledges, one to the north, another to the east, a third to the west, laden down with sick and dying men, in obedience to an order to do their best in their separate directions.[8]

In seeking reasons to mitigate any sense of failure of the expedition, Clements

Markham may have inadvertently identified a major weakness in the subsequent approach taken with Scott's Antarctic explorations. He suggested that a serious disadvantage in 1876 was the numerical weakness of the latter, as compared with the two previous expeditions under Austin and Belcher.

> While the latter had an effective force of one hundred and eighty men, the work of the late Expedition was more restricted, owing to its being seriously under-manned in comparison. It only had one hundred and twenty men, including chaplains.[9]

It is surprising he would consider Austin and particularly Belcher's voyages as successful, but the large British Antarctic expeditions under Scott indicated that neither he, nor the Admiralty, had heeded the lessons of John Ross's expedition aboard *Victory*. John Ross's party survived four years stranded in the Arctic (1829–33), including the loss of their ship, partly because they were lucky but also because they were few in number. McClintock's final successful search for Franklin was similarly small. Both also were private, organised without the expertise of the Royal Societies or the Admiralty, and were small mainly because funds didn't allow a large expedition. As Amundsen was to prove much to Clements Markham's chagrin, in polar exploration, small and streamlined is more effective than big and unwieldy. The more men there are, the more there are to feed and keep healthy, the more supplies need to be transported, and the more problems will be multiplied. The lessons of Franklin had not been heeded. Markham also pointed proudly to the fact that 'the sledge equipments and the clothing were identical, and the provisions were equally good'[10] to those of 20 years before. In other words the planning was rooted in that past of the Franklin searches and had not been updated by any subsequent experience of any non-British expeditions, or the Arctic Inuit.

The outcome was that the achievements of the expedition were overshadowed by the mysterious spectre of scurvy and death and the journey was considered a disappointment that further disinclined British governments from funding speculative polar exploration. It was left to a zealous few, led by Clements Markham, to try and revive interest. The final quarter of the century proved a barren period for Markham and his colleagues and the flame of Antarctic exploration was kept flickering elsewhere, primarily in the enthusiastic and ambitious colony of Victoria, Australia.

Chapter Eight

The Australian Antarctic Exploration Committee: The new champions of Antarctic exploration

In his letters of 1860 and 1861 Commander Maury, the pioneering American oceanographer, had identified Melbourne as a likely base for launching an Antarctic expedition.

> There is Melbourne, your great commercial mart, that is already, in amount of shipping, a rival of Liverpool. It is within two weeks run by steamer from the borders of this unknown region.[1]

The following year he was even more optimistic and had halved the travelling time.

> The gold of Australia has built up among the antipodes of Europe one of the most extensive shipping ports in the world. By steam, it is within less than a week's sailing distance of the Antarctic Circle.[2]

In the decade following the discovery of gold in 1851, Melbourne's population increased five-fold. The district of Port Phillip had initially been subject to a brief and unsuccessful attempt at European settlement in 1803. David Collins, a Royal Navy officer who had travelled to Australia initially as deputy judge advocate with the First Fleet, was appointed as Lieutenant-Governor of the proposed settlement. His subjects being the ragbag of soldiers and convicts that accompanied him. They had set up camp at Sullivan's Bay near current day Sorrento. Lack of water drove them to abandon the site, less a few convicts who wandered off to take their chances in the alien and unrelenting bush. What happened to most of these absconders is unknown, but one, William Buckley, walked around Port Phillip Bay to the opposite side near current day Point Lonsdale and was hospitably accepted by the local Aboriginal clans.

Collins sailed further south to establish the rather more lasting settlement of Hobart in Tasmania. Amongst their number was John Pascoe Fawkner, who was travelling with his convict father. Fawkner became one of the original European settlers in Hobart Town and then one of the key figures in the European settlement of Melbourne. In 1835 a party led by John Batman crossed Bass Strait from Tasmania to claim vast swathes of the Port Phillip District. They were surprised when escaped convict Buckley wandered into their camp.

A few months after Batman's party staked their claim, a party organised by John Pascoe Fawkner arrived in Port Phillip and set up camp on the banks of the Yarra River.

Whalers and sealers had worked parts of the Victorian coast around Portland, Wilsons Promontory and Phillip Island since the turn of the century and the Henty family had established themselves in 1834 in the fertile lands to the west near the magnificent deep-water harbour that is now Portland.

By the late 1830s Port Phillip was in the process of being transformed into a vast farm by the advance of adventurous squatters. This restless, rough, boisterous little settlement was administered from Sydney as a southern outpost of New South Wales. As Port Phillip grew, its denizens became ever more resentful of having to take direction from the distant mandarins of Sydney. In 1851 their noisy agitation paid off when Port Phillip became the colony of Victoria. At almost that exact moment gold was discovered north of Melbourne near Ballarat and Bendigo setting off one of the world's great gold rushes. In a trice the ports were bursting with arrivals from all over the world impatient to head to the goldfields to make their fortune. Many would be disappointed but Melbourne, despite some severe hiccups and a boom-and-bust roller coaster development, didn't look back. Phenomenal amounts of gold was mined, and verdant, vast farming lands were opened up, pushing aside the indigenous inhabitants with scant regard.

Georg von Neumayer

One visitor to the goldfields was a young man from Bavaria, Georg von Neumayer, who had worked his way from Europe aboard the ship *Reiherstieg*. He was an acolyte of the oceanographic theories of Matthew Maury and had a great interest in the science of magnetism and in the Antarctic. He found his way to the Bendigo goldfields and his success at the diggings enabled him to travel to the Murray River and South Australia. Neumayer returned to Europe, sailing from Melbourne in late January 1854. In Germany he used the knowledge he had built up about the colonies to deliver a series of lectures in the main German cities.

He published a paper on the advancement of physical geography which came to the notice of Baron von Liebig and through him, the King of Bavaria. With such powerful patrons and with funds from the King he set out once more for Australia, this time to Melbourne with a view to seeking government support for his research into terrestrial magnetism. He arrived on 27 January 1857 aboard *La Rochelle* out of Hamburg.

Despite opposition from some scientists who feared precious funds would be channelled to Neumayer at their expense, he was able to gain the ear of many of the influential decision makers of the Colony.

His proposals for a Melbourne Observatory were placed before the Legislative Assembly by Dr Greeves (formerly a minister but now in opposition) to consider funding. After debate the proposal was rejected which raised the ire of the major Melbourne daily, the *Argus*.

> ... It is inconceivable that Captain Clarke, the President of the Philosophical Institute, and the Government, should have opposed Professor Neumayer's proposal. It could not, we think, have been from any well founded objection to that proposal. Was it because it came from the Opposition benches?[3]

A few months later the editorial disdain for Neumayer's opponents was more strident.

> Between two and three months ago our legislators, and certain of our wise men, were engaged in pooh – poohing Professor Neumayer's proposals for the establishment of a Magnetic Observatory in this colony, and were temporarily successful in their gracious endeavours to thwart that gentleman, and to gain for us a reputation for gothic ignorance, and disregard of the cause of science.[4]

Philosophical Institute president Clarke expressed concern at scientific funding going to 'the employment of an itinerating scientific man' at the expense of 'the claims of those long resident in the country, who had worked without reward for a series of years'.[5] The attitude of the local scientists is hardly mysterious. Scientific funding is always competitive and sought after.

Neumayer also received strong support from the local German community. Otto Neuhauss wrote to the *Argus* pledging £100 if the observatory could not get government support. On 19 August a meeting of 70 or so German residents had been held at the Criterion Hotel where a subscription was enthusiastically endorsed to support Neumayer's observatory. £250 was pledged that night including £100 from Otto Neuhauss.[6]

After the initial loud debate, Parliament, rather quietly, did provide funding. On 16 December 1857 Hansard reported that the vote had carried £600 towards the magnetic survey.[7] Having won this battle, Neumayer, in the following December, commenced the first of 15 field trips to map Victoria's magnetic nature.

He had a lifelong commitment to Antarctic exploration and delivered a series of lectures to the German community in Melbourne in 1862. These were illustrated by another German immigrant, John Henning, at that time early in his celebrated career as a scenic artist in theatre. In 1864 Neumayer left Melbourne to return to Germany, with the good wishes of his many friends in the German and scientific community to send him on his way. At one of his farewell speeches he gave voice to his Antarctic ambitions.

> It would be a glorious moment in the next period of my career if I could seek the Antarctic regions in a German ship, and perhaps sometime you will see me return to these shores accompanied by the pick of the youth of all German races, bound on a voyage to the South Pole.[8]

True to his promise, in Germany he worked tirelessly towards a German expedition. He remained in contact with friends in Melbourne and was interested in their attempts to mount an Australian Antarctic expedition.

Neumayer was to suffer a series of disappointments before, in old age, observing the German South Polar (Gauss) Expedition of 1901–03. He was the first president of the International Polar Commission and was then chairman of the German Polar Commission, organising the German expeditions for the First International Polar Year (1882–83). Neumayer had passionately advocated a co-ordinated approach to Antarctic exploration at the Sixth International Geographical Congress held in London in 1895.

As a tribute to his dedication to promoting polar exploration and research his name is commemorated in both the Arctic and Antarctic.

Maury had identified Melbourne as a base for exploring the Antarctic, and Neumayer had looked hopefully south while conducting his magnetic surveys around Victoria and continued glancing more steadily in that direction even as he headed north back to Germany.

There continued to be a bubble of interest in Antarctic exploration. In 1868 the Melbourne *Argus* referred to the proposed British expedition to the Arctic (Nares British Arctic Expedition) suggesting the funds would be better used to support further exploration of the Antarctic.

> The growth of the Australian Colonies and the spread of settlement in New Zealand since the date of James Ross's voyage should of themselves be sufficient reasons why, if another exploring expedition is to be fitted out in England, its destination should be the Southern Ocean and not the Northwestern Passage ...[9]

In 1874 experienced Arctic whaling skippers David and John Gray published a brief pamphlet – *Report on new whaling grounds in the Southern Seas*. This was the only detailed publication assessing the potential of Antarctic whaling. Much of the content was sourced from Ross' voyages (1839–43). The Gray's suggested the area around the Weddell Sea from the Greenwich Meridian (just west of Bouvet Island) to Longitude 90° (the vicinity of Peter 1 Oy). The attraction of this area was that the Falklands Island (estimated in the pamphlet as 10 days sailing from the whaling fields) could be a staging post. However, despite predicting a £49,500 profit, the pamphlet had not elicited enough enthusiasm to result in an expedition. The pamphlet mainly indicates how little exploration had taken place in the Antarctic over those years since Ross's voyage.

In May 1878 C.W. Purnell delivered an address to the Otago Institute, urging:

> The despatch of an expedition, at joint expense of the Australian and New Zealand Governments, for the purpose of either following up Ross' discoveries, or examining any other part of the Antarctic regions which might be deemed more suitable.[10]

Purnell followed up with further articles. His piece printed in the *Melbourne Review* ended with a demand for the redirection of funds from public works 'which are at best luxuries' and added that 'money flows from their exchequers like water',[11] neither point likely to gain favour or funding from relevant governments.

By the 1880s Melbourne had grown from a few shanties on the banks of the Yarra, inhabited by the squabbling Fawkner and Batman camps, to a thriving, wealthy and ambitious metropolis. Successful men built vast English style mansions to exhibit their wealth, or perhaps their confidence in the seemingly endless economic boom and the ever-extending credit available. It was a vibrant, ambitious place. English journalist George Augustus Sala described Melbourne as 'magnificent and marvellous'.[12] Geographically Melburnians were no less ambitious, not for them to limit their aims to the horizons of their own colony or even the colonial continent, some of the leading citizens had eyes also for the large, frozen continent to the south. In January 1885 the *Leader* published an article regarding a rumour of Adolf Nordenskiöld preparing an assault of the south. The author points out that 'nearly all the information we possess about the Antarctic regions' comes from expeditions nearly 50 years past.

> This is not as it should be, Australians must bestir themselves. It is part of their destiny to explore these southern solitudes. Being a matter of Imperial interest England would of course join in supporting any well directed scheme formulated by the Australian Colonies for Antarctic discovery.[13]

The key step in Melbourne's pursuit of Antarctic exploration fell to another German immigrant, Ferdinand von Mueller, father of the Melbourne botanic gardens, also as president of the RS and RGS a key figure in the city's scientific community.

In 1854 The Philosophical Society of Victoria and the Victorian Institute for the Advancement of Science were both formed. They amalgamated to form the Philosophical Institute of Victoria and in 1859 were renamed the Royal Society of Victoria.

New South Wales had established a separate geographical society. In the middle of 1883, the Administrative Council of the NSW Geographical Society of Australasia (GSA) communicated with various Melbourne notables raising the idea of establishing a Victorian branch. At a meeting on 22 October 1883 two motions were discussed, the first that a Victorian branch of the GSA be formed. A second conflicting motion asked that 'that the gentlemen present cast in their lot with the Royal Society …'[14] The equal vote went to the Chairman Thomas Bride (Chief Librarian of the Melbourne Public Library (State Library Victoria)), who cast his decider for the formation of a Victorian Branch of the GSA. On 1 April 1884 the Committee set the inaugural meeting for 18 April 1884. Mueller had been appointed vice president and prepared a speech, in part lauding the goal of Antarctic exploration. Unfortunately he was unwell and unable to attend so his address was read by the secretary Alexander Macdonald. Outlining the benefits and challenges of Antarctic exploration Mueller noted that here was 'vast importance for science as well as commerce, and to no other people can research connected with the Antarctic regions be of that value which it must ever have for the Australian Colonies'.[15]

This speech could be seen as the beginning of more than a decade of earnest attempts to establish an expedition to Antarctica. Mueller, himself, felt his address had influenced the establishment in England of a high-powered Antarctic Committee reporting to the British Association for the Advancement of Science – 'It seems that my remarks in last year's address led to the appointment of Hooker, M'Klintock and Nares as an Antarctic Exploration Committee'.[16]

British Antarctic Committee

The British committee was established in October 1885 in response to a paper presented by Eramus Ommanney on 'Antarctic Research' at the September 1885 meeting of the British Association for the Advancement of Science. The committee was an impressive group including: Sir Joseph Hooker, botanist on Ross' expedition over 40 years previously; Admiral Leopold McClintock, a veteran of Arctic expeditions and the man who ultimately solved the Franklin mystery (to the degree that it has been solved) ; Sir George Nares, master of the *Challenger* and then the Arctic expedition of 1875/6 (see above); John Murray (*Challenger*); Clements Markham, who as a youngster had been a midshipman on Ommanney's *Assistance* as part of the search for Franklin, and who became the driving force that led, eventually, to the British Antarctic expeditions at the start of the new century; General John T. Walker, a cousin of Markham who spent a distinguished military career in India as a surveyor with the Royal Engineers, he saw action in the Indian Mutiny and other smaller conflicts and was a superintendent of the Great Trigonometrical Survey of India for two decades; and Admiral Erasmus Ommanney, navy veteran, captain of one of the many relief ships sent searching for Franklin (see above) and a close ally of Markham in the quest to head south.

Despite the power and experience of the names, the committee achieved little, perhaps this reflected the level of antipathy to an Antarctic expedition in official circles in England. 12 months after their appointment at the September 1886 meeting of the British Association at Birmingham, the committee reported that they had nothing to report.

> ... Your committee deem it desirable to defer making their report, with a view to giving more definition to the objects sought to be obtained and to the best means of obtaining them, as also to expand this Committee, in order to elicit to the fullest extent the opinions and to secure the support from those conversant with the various branches of science which are to be investigated during an exploration which, from its very important and serious nature, eminently merits the favourable consideration of the great and enterprising maritime nation.[17]

This appears a long-winded way of reporting that nothing worth mentioning had happened in the preceding 12 months.

Antarctic Exploration Committee

Meanwhile in Australia the idea of Antarctic exploration was being enthusiastically pursued. At the RGS (Vic) meeting 27 January 1886 George Griffiths read his paper *South Polar problems or objects and values of Antarctic Research*.[18] There followed discussion around sending or assisting with an Antarctic expedition. David Harrison referred to an article he wrote for the Melbourne *Leader* some years previously and noted the British Antarctic committee, remarking 'Australia cannot afford to be left out of such an enterprise'.[19]

In fact Victorian parliamentarian John Gavan Duffy had raised the matter of setting aside funding for Antarctic Research in the Assembly in 1885. He gave notice of motion 19 November 1885. His efforts were met with derision and disinterest by his colleagues.

> Loud laughter greeted the hon. member's announcement that he did not mean to press the vote on this occasion, but would certainly, if in the House,

take it up again next session. 'And in the meantime pay the Antarctic regions a visit,' was Mr Laurens' jokelet.[20]

This interest in Antarctic exploration found practical expression at a Special Meeting of Council of Royal Geographical Society of Australasia (Victorian Branch) (RGSA (Vic)) held on 19 May 1886. President von Mueller suggested 3 RGSA (Vic) members meet with 3 members from the Royal Society of Victoria (RSV) on the subject of Antarctic exploration. Crawford Pasco, ex Royal Navy, was nominated as President of this joint committee.

Eminent Gentlemen

The gentlemen who formed the inaugural Antarctic Exploration Committee (AEC) were eminent figures in Melbourne. They were well connected and able to get the ear of the Premier and to use the press to promote their cause.

The president, Captain Crawford Pasco (1818–98) had followed the family tradition and joined the Royal Navy as a 12-year-old. During his time in the navy he spent a considerable period in Australian waters. In 1852 he came to Victoria. He resigned from the navy and became a police magistrate. He was a founding member of the Royal Geographical Society of Victoria.

The committee representatives from the Royal Society of Victoria were Professor William C. Kernot (1845–1909) (President RSV). Kernot emigrated with his family from England to Geelong in 1851. Kernot studied engineering at Melbourne University graduating in 1866. He worked with various Government departments until 1875 when he lectured at Melbourne University becoming Professor of Engineering in 1883. He was president of the Royal Society 1885 to 1900.

Robert L.J. Ellery (1827–1908) arrived in Melbourne from England in 1853. He became the inaugural director of the Williamstown observatory and held this position for 42 years. From 1863 he acted as government astronomer and meteorologist. From 1866 to 1884 he was President of the Royal Society of Victoria.

George S. Griffiths (1847–1906) was born in British Guiana and came to Australia with his parents in 1851. He was a stockbroker by profession with a strong interest in scientific matters. He was on the council of the Royal Society of Victoria from 1885–96 and a Fellow of the Royal Geographical Society.

Representing the RGSA (Vic) were Baron Ferdinand von Mueller (1825–96) who was born in Rostock, Mecklenburg-Schwerin (Germany). He emigrated to Australia in 1847 and became government botanist in Melbourne in 1853. In 1855 he was botanist on the Northwest Australia Expedition which travelled for 16 months from Victoria River to Moreton Bay. In 1857 he became director of the Royal Botanic Gardens in Melbourne, a position he held for the next 20 years. He was president of the Royal Society of Victoria in 1859 and later was also the first president of the Royal Geographical Society (Victoria).

Irish-born Dr Thomas F. Bride (1849–1927) came to Melbourne with his parents as a child. He graduated from Melbourne University and became librarian at Melbourne Public Library (State Library of Victoria) in 1881. In 1895 he left the Library to take up the post of curator of Intestate Estates, retiring in 1909. He was active in public life, standing unsuccessfully for Parliament in 1880 and acting on the councils of Melbourne University and the Working Men's College together with his membership of the RGS and AEC.

J. Gavan Duffy (1844–1917) was also born in Ireland he came to Victoria in 1859. His father Charles Gavan Duffy was an Irish Nationalist who emigrated to Victoria in 1855 (after being acquitted of treason in Ireland) and became a notable politician and Premier of Victoria. Duffy followed his father into politics, sitting in the Legislative Assembly for 30 years. He first raised the issue of Antarctic exploration in parliament in 1885.

Dr John. J. Wild (1828–1900) was born in Zurich, Switzerland and gained a PhD from the University of Berne. He was artist and secretary for the *Challenger* Expedition which undertook major oceangraphic study around the world (including the Antarctic region) from 1872–76. He came to Australia in 1881 and held the position of examiner in French and German at Melbourne University for some years. He was the only member of the AEC to have been to the Antarctic.

There were also appointed three secretaries. Alexander Cameron Macdonald (1828–1917) (from RGSA (V)) was a notable citizen of Victoria, especially in the Geelong area, was variously an accountant, surveyor, company director and real estate entrepreneur, he made a significant contribution to the study of the geography and history of Victoria and served various roles at the RGSA (V) for 23 years.

Australia born George W. Selby (1857–1949), (from RSV) was the son of notable earlier pastoralist George senior, Selby was a pioneer experimenter in wireless telegraphy. He worked as an auditor for BHP from 1886.

Henry Keylock Rusden (1826–1910), (from RSV) was born in England arriving in New South Wales as a child. The gold rush brought him to Victoria but he left the diggings to become a career public servant, working as an accountant with the Police. His was a radical and an atheist, with strong views and wide interests.

At the first meeting of the AEC, held on 8 June 1886, George Griffiths presented a paper outlining 3 possible courses of action:

1. Despatch of purely Australian expedition
2. Establish an Observation station on an island in high southern latitudes.
3. Co-operate with other colonies and Imperial Government and British Antarctic Committee regarding Imperial Expedition.

On 28 June 1886 the committee published a *Memorandum of the Objects to be served by Antarctic research*. These objects reflected various issues raised in Griffith's paper – geographical discovery; whale trade; geology; fossils; climatology; South magnetic pole; auroras. It was hoped that committees be established in each of the colonies; to promote interest through lectures; seek government help from each colony; 'approach the English Committee with a contribution which would justify it in asking that Australasia might be associated with the mother country in carrying through this great undertaking'.[21]

The AEC pursued their objectives with great zeal. Following the publication of the 'objects' the AEC distributed copies to the Premier of Victoria, the governments and scientific societies of the other colonies, the secretary of the British Association Antarctic Committee, and other interested and influential people. On 4 August 1886 the AEC met with Premier and this set in motion a flurry of activity. The AEC recognised that funding a purely scientific expedition was unlikely and so promoted the commercial opportunities of the Antarctic. An expedition would aim to survey the whaling potential (and possibly pursue whales) but also carry scientists to undertake a scientific program.

On 13 August 1886 Premier Gillies distributed a circular to other

Australasian colonies asking for co-operation, (meaning contributing financially). This was enormously important as the entire endeavour would rise (and more importantly fall) on the funding. Just as importantly on 19 August 1886 he forwarded a telegram to the Victorian Agent General in London.

> Gillies received deputation learned societies urging Antarctic exploration, represented remunerative enterprise whaling, but asked Government encourage. Gillies replied willing give subsidy scientific discovery, ask other colonies join, meantime Agent General to inquire if steam whalers disposed embark enterprise and what subsidy required.[22]

Victoria's Agent General at that time was Graham Berry, a former premier of Victoria and a grand and controversial figure in the combative politics of the colony. He was quick to act on Gillies's request. Almost immediately the interest from the colony of Victoria had aroused the interest of the London press with the *London Observer* suggesting, sarcastically, that Britain should lend an RN ship.

> Undeterred by the sorrowful record of Arctic adventure which Englishmen have contributed to the annals of science, our Australian kinsmen are ambitious of reproducing, as nearly as may be, at the Antipodes, our melancholy experiences in the cruel 'White North' that holds the bones of Franklin and many another gallant and high hearted voyager ... it might be a graceful act if the British Admiralty were to offer to lend the Colonial expedition a ship, for after the lamentable fiasco of Sir George Nares scurvy-stricken expedition we do not suppose the Australians would desire to man an Antarctic expedition from the Royal Navy.[23]

Meanwhile in Melbourne from the outset the *Argus* saw no reason to encourage the project.

> Considering that the object of the excursion is to make scientific observations, and catch whales, the inducements are not overpowering to the general run of mankind. Scientific observations will not determine how to avoid the next drought, and a whale is scarcely the sort of creature in which everybody takes delight.[24]

The newspaper followed a few days later with a valid and oft-repeated criticism of the venture, the combination of a commercial and scientific enterprise.

> The dual nature of the scheme renders it of doubtful validity ... It would probably be found impossible to serve the oil trade and science in one expedition.[25]

Amongst the British geographic and scientific societies, the AEC initiative was applauded, partly as it seemed to have an energy and will that was lacking in Britain. It was seen though as an initiative that could contribute to a large, expensive British expedition.

> 'The spirited action of the Australian Society is in every way commendable, and deserves energetic support', said John Murray (of Challenger) 'Should the Australian Governments be induced to vote, say, £10,000 each towards the outfit of an Antarctic expedition, on the condition that the Imperial Parliament vote the remainder of the necessary £150,000 the success of the undertaking is almost assured ...'[26]

The apparently incompatible dual aims meant the cost was much less than that of a purely scientific expedition, but the North Sea whaling captains, their traditional grounds yielding less and less, were interested in a subsidised voyage to gauge the potential profits in the South without taking the risk of the substantial loss a voyage returning with empty oil barrels might entail. The science was likely to be merely an inconvenience when there were whales to be caught.

Chapter Nine

Northern whalemen and the London Agent General for Victoria

Graham Berry was quick off the mark and there was no shortage of whaling skippers interested in a subsidised reconnaissance of whaling fields in the Antarctic. On 27 August 1886 David Bruce and Co of 3 Fenchurch Ave London wrote offering sale or hire of the steam whalers *Esquimaux* and *Polynia*. At the time of writing the ships were still away seeking whales in the Davis Strait, between Baffin Island and Greenland.

There followed a succession of offers. Graham Berry had piqued the interest of some of the most successful and famous whaling captains and managers in Britain and Norway. The reason for the eager response was summed up by Captain James Fairweather of Dundee who noted in a letter of 28 September 1886. 'I am of the opinion that our trade here is fast dying out on account of the continued catching and decadence of the whale in our northern waters.'[1]

Fairweather made a successful career as an Arctic whaler. He skippered *Aurora* (later famous in the 'heroic' age of Antarctic exploration) from 1883 to 1888 venturing to the far north in search of whale and seal. Certainly at the time of his correspondence with the Graham Berry he was well qualified to master a ship bound for icy waters. Nothing came of his offer, although he was one of several notable Arctic captains who put their name forward.

A letter dated 30 September 1886 was received from Christen Christensen, a ship builder and owner from Sandefjord, Norway, offering a choice of 4 steamships *Jason*, *Hertha Elida* and *Fortuna*. Christensen's view was that whaling and science were incompatible. He offered them for hire for 12 months at prices ranging from £3500 to £6500 (including captain and crew) and assumed that any scientific expedition would be overwintering in the Antarctic. It was an interesting offer and did provide an opportunity for a strictly scientific voyage, at vastly less cost than the estimates of the British Association Antarctic Committee. The AEC, though, saw the commercial opportunities presented by whaling as defraying cost and being attractive to colonial governments, suggesting a new and lucrative industry that the colonies were geographically well placed to exploit.

In Melbourne, despite the offer of Christensen, it was clear that a full independent overwintering scientific expedition was unattainable. In October 1886 George Griffiths read an address on Antarctic Exploration. He outlined two schemes, the Imperial scheme – 2 ships for 3 years at £150,000 cost which was too great for the colonies and 'must therefore be left to the mother country ... our scheme is more modest, but we believe that its observations will prepare the way for the other ...' This is the whalers with observers' scheme. The expedition had coalesced to a flying summer reconnaissance as a prelude to a large, ambitious, and expensive Imperial endeavour.[2]

On 6 October 1886 Captain David Gray from Peterhead, whose 1874 pamphlet, co-written with his brother, was the basis for much of the interest in Antarctic whaling, himself offered the ships *Erik*, *Hope*, and *Eclipse*. He had never followed up he and his brother's ideas regarding Antarctic whaling as his ships were still successful in the north. He was strongly against the idea of an expedition trying to serve science and commerce.

> I do not like the idea expressed in your letter, of intending to combine exploration with fishing, collecting guano and other commercial products, I think if you do so you are sure to fail. Your commander's mind will be too much divided, and will be apt to leave one thing and go after another, especially if things are not getting on so well as he would like. I know this plan has never succeeded hither too and it is not likely to succeed in your case. Send your ships out to explore if you like, but let it be exploration only, and if you decide on a whaling voyage, confine your master's attention to that only and I have little doubt you will succeed beyond your expectations.[3]

His brother, John, followed up with a letter on 3 February 1887; in part he had

> no doubt that if a favourable offer were made by the Victorian Government two or three steamers could be secured to test the desirability of establishing a whale fishery in the Antarctic Seas.[4]

The Gray's interest in the whaling prospects remained strong despite nothing coming of the correspondence with the AEC.

On 19 November 1886 Berry met with Sir Allen Young and discussed the possibility of Young himself leading an expedition to the Antarctic. Allen Young was again an eminently qualified leader. A notable Arctic explorer and merchant captain he commanded the troopship *Adelaide* during the Crimean War. In 1857 he was appointed navigator of the ship *Fox* for Lady Franklin's privately funded expedition under McClintock. Young, from a wealthy brewing family, contributed £500 to the expedition's cost. Away for two years, McClintock and his men went further than any other in unravelling the mystery of Franklin's lost men. Young, himself, made several notable sled journeys during the search.

In 1860 he commanded *Fox* for the North Atlantic Telegraph Expedition surveying the route above Scotland through the Faeroe Islands, Iceland and Greenland. He purchased *Pandora* and in June 1875, in another attempt on the Northwest Passage, was thwarted by impenetrable ice in Peel Strait.

The following year he sailed north again to assist the Nares Arctic expedition. The expedition returned a year early and Young's encounter with them took place when he sighted their ships in the Atlantic on the way home. In 1882 Young was prevailed on to command *Hope*, a whaler hired for the relief of the Benjamin Leigh Smith expedition to Franz Josef Land. Smith was another intrepid Arctic explorer and adventurer from a wealthy family. He set out on four voyages to the Spitsbergen region in the 1870s.

In 1880 he sailed north in his newly built brigantine *Eira* continuing his exploratory work in the Spitsbergen region. In 1881 again he returned. *Eira* though was crushed. His party wintered at Cape Flora on coastal islands off Franz Josef Land. They then boarded the whale boats and made their way to Novaya Zemlya where they were duly rescued by Allen Young.

At his meeting with Graham Berry, Young suggested he might lead an expedition if underwritten for losses (if the whaling was unsuccessful) at £10,000 or at least £8,000. With his considerable experience, skill and means he would have been a notable expedition leader, however a substantial offer didn't follow the interview.

By the end of 1886 the AEC had taken substantial steps forward. Though nothing concrete had occurred, the Premier was assisting them through his London Agent General and was seeking support from the other Australasian colonies. A number of notable Arctic whaling veterans had responded quickly to the initial idea, and there was positive support from such respected veterans of the ice and the ocean as Admiral Ommanney and John Murray.

James Fairweather wrote again in the New Year on 29 January 1887. This time he advised that 'it would be a very difficult business to get the owners of any of the steam whalers to move in the adventure from this quarter so long as they have any hope of procuring fair cargoes in the Arctic Seas.' He went on to suggest building 'two powerful Steam whalers of 600 to 700 tons … fitted with the most approved appliances for Ice Navigation …'[5]

This could be done, he reckoned, for £40,000 with an additional £10,000 for wages and expenses.

He suggested an alternative option of one purpose built steamer accompanied by SS *Alert*, a ship used in Nares 1874–1875 Arctic expedition, and more recently lent to the United States of America to assist with the relief of the Greely expedition. The AEC would need to convince the Admiralty and Imperial Government of the soundness of such a plan. This plan seemed most attractive to Northern whalers rather than colonial scientists. The AEC were bearing the large expense in effect to subsidise a speculative voyage by northern whalemen, looking for new whale grounds having so depleted the waters of the Arctic.

The AEC were keen to maintain the momentum and on 8 February 1887 made ambitious recommendations to the Premier. There were 23 conditions, stipulations and aims. They suggested £10,000 be placed on estimates for bonuses, equipment and staff, and that tenders be invited from suitably experienced Arctic captains and chief mates. They also required free passage for two scientific staff and accommodation for scientists, and co-operation afforded for their scientific pursuits as long as it didn't interfere with the work or safety of the ship. This seemed almost certain to cause conflict. The further expectations of the AEC were rather grand and unrealistic.

> The services desired are as follows: viz:- A flying survey of any coast lines lying within the Antarctic Circle, and not now laid down upon the Admiralty Charts. The discovery of new waterways leading towards the South Pole, and of harbours suitable for wintering in. Opportunities to be afforded to

the scientific staff to add to our knowledge of Meteorology, Oceanography, Terrestrial Magnetism, Natural History, and Geology of the region …

This was a substantial list of aims. They wished bonuses for each degree attained from 70°S. Further bonuses were suggested for the establishment of observing stations. 'The government should pay for only one such station every 120 miles.' There was also to be bonuses for every 60 miles attained by shore parties. Finally the ships were required to be ready to commence from Port Phillip Bay on 15 October. The covering letter suggested that balloons 'would be for Polar Exploration a new and probably an extremely useful appliance …' and it would be 'a means of effecting an extended survey of long distances beyond inaccessible points like the Ice barrier …'[6]

The AEC's proposals were not endorsed by the Victorian Government however interested parties in Britain and Norway continued to contact the Agent General. On 9 February 1887 Charles Tod, a Peterhead ship owner who had met with the Agent General in August 1886 and initially forwarded the Gray's 1874 pamphlet regarding the potential for whaling in the Antarctic, was again the intermediary for another Peterhead native, William Baxter, offering Screw Whaler *Windward* for £3,000.[7]

On 21 February 1887 a rather more detailed proposal was sent by H.F. Dessen offering the Tönsberg steam whaler *Westye Egeberg* (formerly *Michelle Selchan*). This was by far the most substantial proposal received. It laid out the most complete description of the ship and then addressed issues of mixing science and commercial whaling. The proposal acknowledges the precedence of the charterers – the captain 'shall consequently be bound to proceed with the vessel wherever the senior of the gentlemen sent by the charterers may require within the Antarctic or adjacent regions'.

Furthermore, the accommodation would be quite adequate.

> The ship's saloon, 4 berths and all the accommodation aft, excepting the Chief Officer's cabin, shall be at the disposal of the Australian gentlemen and a further 2 berths shall be provided elsewhere if necessary.

Mr Dessen expected that *Westye Egeberg*, having spent the northern summer in the Arctic, could arrive in Melbourne in early October, and be ready to sail south in late October. The aim was to return by 1 April 1888. The cost of the charter was £6500 for that period. With regard to whaling, the document proposes it be permitted 'so far as it does not interfere with the objects of the expedition'. It is also suggested that their undertaking of the expedition would allow them at some 'future time be accorded the same privileges and exemptions as subjects of the Colony themselves, in case they should wish to carry on whaling or sealing enterprise there'.[8]

The proposal ran to 16 pages and went as far as to stipulate who would be responsible for bedclothes (the scientists 'must bring their own'). While written in ignorance of the AEC's expansive 23 points of early February it was certainly a proposal that in retrospect seems one of the most likely to succeed. However, as with all of the AEC's actions, their ambitions were thwarted because the money they needed didn't ever become available. With funding from each colony and the Imperial Treasury, and from public subscription, a summer survey of the Ross Sea, focussed on science and geography, would have been possible. But the offer of Mr Dessen wasn't taken up.

Queried on their consideration of this offer, the AEC's rather testy response to the Premier, not written until 23 June 1887, stated that

> the Committee did not feel itself in a position to entertain Mr Dessen's offer for two reasons; 1st, it was not based on the conditions recommended by the Committee as a basis for inviting tenders, and 2ndly, the Committee, being entirely in the dark as to the probabilities of funds being provided for the purpose, felt disabled from dealing with it, and from even framing a recommendation respecting it. If a subsidy of £10,000 could reasonably be reckoned upon, the Committee could only have recommended that Mr Dessen be requested to modify his offer in accordance with the conditions recommended. The Committee would be greatly obliged if you could kindly let it know the position in which it stands, as it is at present at a loss how even to reply to its correspondents.[9]

On 26 March 1887, Crawford Pasco wrote again to the Premier acknowledging the receipt of copies of correspondence from William Baxter and Captain John Gray (as above) and suggesting a London approval committee to assess European offers. The AEC meeting on 25 March 1887 had suggested various eminent explorers currently serving on the Antarctic Committee of the British Association for the Advancement of Science, such as M'Clintock, Nares and Murray, with Captain Allen Young, and M.P and shipowner Henry Green. This was sensible but the AEC's enthusiasm was dampened by the Premier's response through his secretary on 30 March 1887 advising tenders wouldn't go ahead pending further communication with other the other colonies ... 'the action of this Government must necessarily depend upon that of the other Colonial Governments'.[10]

Vincennes in Disappointment Bay. C.A. Jewell from a sketch by Charles Wilkes (Wilkes, 1849)

View of the Antarctic Continent. C.A. Jewell from a sketch by Charles Wilkes (Wilkes, 1849)

Beaufort Island and Mount Erebus discovered, 28 January 1841. J.E. Davis, lithographer R. Carrick (Ross, 1847)

Coulman Island discovered, 17 January 1841. J.E. Davis, lithographer T. Picken (Ross, 1847)

The Midnight Sun – Balleny Island. *Illustrated Australian News*, 1 April 1895, p. 22 (State Library Victoria)

Balleny Island. *Illustrated Australian News*, 1 April 1895, p. 21 (State Library Victoria)

Sealers at work in the mist. W.G. Murdoch (Bull, 1896)

The 'Antarctic' among the icebergs. W.L. Wyllie (Bull 1896, frontispiece)

Cape Adare, First Landing on the Mainland. *Illustrated Australian News*, 1 April 1895, p. 21 (SLV)

Mount Adare. *Illustrated Australian News*, 1 April 1895, p. 22 (SLV)

C.E. Borchgrevink & H.J. Bull. Johnstone & O'Shannassy carte de visite. (Courtesy Warrnambool Library)

Crawford Pasco, President of the AEC. J.W. Lindt (SLV Accession H12989)

Hanson's grave. Borchgrevink, 1901 (SLV)

Chapter Ten

Lords of the Imperial Treasury

The previously sceptical and dismissive Melbourne *Argus* suddenly decided there was urgency in mounting an expedition and strongly suggested an approach to the Imperial Treasury.

> If, however, some action is not taken by the Victorian Government in the course of the next few days, the season of 1887–88 will be lost, and then, in all probability, the honour of opening up the mysterious region round the South Pole will be secured by other than British or Victorian navigators … The estimated cost of such an expedition is £10,000 – an amount which Mr Gillies is not likely to see his way clear to provide; and no help is to be expected from the other colonies.
>
> There is, however, one course open, which we strongly recommend Mr Gilles to adopt, and that is to promptly telegraph to the agent-general, instructing him to communicate with Mr Goschen, the Chancellor of the Exchequer (a practical and far seeing statesman), and offer £5,000 if the British Government will contribute the other moiety of the expenses of the expedition … and we venture to predict that only a very insignificant minority of the House of Commons would be opposed to it. … In conclusion we would remind Mr Gillies that this is Jubilee year. It would be by no means the least glorious event of Her Majesty's reign if, during it, the British flag could be hoisted on the eternal ice at a higher southern latitude than has ever previously been reached by man.[1]

A week later, on 11 July 1887, the Premier sent a telegram to Agent General Berry requesting that he enquire whether the Chancellor of the Exchequer would place on the Estimates the sum of £5,000 'in the event of the Australian Colonies advancing the same sum towards the project'.[2]

This was a notable step and one that if successful, would likely be the catalyst to the AEC being able to sponsor a summer expedition to Antarctica. If the Imperial Treasury provided £5,000, it would be an utter humiliation if the Australasian colonies couldn't, between them, provide the balance of £5,000. On 29 July 1887, A/G Berry duly wrote to the Colonial Office on behalf of the Premier. On 6 August 1887, the Under Secretary for the Colonial Office forwarded the request to the Board of Trade and The Admiralty to ascertain their views. Graham Berry also sought support from Admiral Ommanney.

Admiral Ommanney duly and unequivocally offered his support in a letter of 17 September 1887. He regretted that the British Association had held its annual meeting and 'just at this season it would be impracticable to secure a meeting of the Committee'.[3] The committee certainly seemed unfussed by urgency in matters of promoting Antarctic exploration.

On 5 October 1887 *The Times* reported the Victorian Government's request for a contribution from the Imperial government. The article discussed Antarctic exploration at some length and ended with endorsement and hope that

> Her Majesty's Government will be able to see their way to comply with the request placed before them by Sir Graham Berry ... But the great matter now is to decide whether Australia and England can co-operate in an important undertaking which will bring credit, and mayhap profit, to both.[4]

On 25 October 1887 the secretary of the Royal Colonial Institute penned a letter on behalf of the Institute's Council expressing strong support for the AEC plan.

> The Council earnestly hope that Her Majesty's Government will avail themselves of this opportunity for cordial co-operation with the Colonies in this noble scientific work, and accede to a request which will not only show that there exists between the Mother Country and the Colonies a unanimity of feeling in the promotion of this and similar objects, but also that the British spirit of enterprise is unaffected by change of latitude or clime.[5]

This rousing endorsement was forwarded to the Prime Minister, the Chancellor of the Exchequer, the First Lord of the Treasury and the Secretary of State for Colonial Office.

This was followed on 16 November 1887 by a letter from Richard Strachey, Vice-President of the Royal Geographical Society, to the Secretary of State, Colonial Office, giving strong support to the AEC proposal.

> The Council of our Society having given due consideration to the character of the information that might be acquired through such an exploration, unanimously recognised its probable great value and importance from many scientific points of view, apart from any possible economical utility it might have ...[6]

Strachey also wrote to Berry on the same day:

> ... it affords the Council of our Society very great gratifications to find that the Royal Geographical Society of Vic has contemplated such an expedition as that now proposed, thereby indicating the desire, and no doubt the ability of the cultivators of science in the Australian Colonies to extend the field of original research on which they have already entered.[7]

On 17 November 1887 a substantial piece appeared in *The Times*. While favouring a much more substantial (and expensive) expedition they acknowledged the probable benefits of a 'preliminary expedition, a sort of reconnaissance to prepare the way for a serious attack'. They went on further to predict that 'the enthusiasm on the other side of the world will become universal ...'[8]

At the November meeting of the Royal Society, the AEC reported that Allen Young was willing to contribute £2,000 and lead the expedition. They were hopeful that 'during the summer of 1888 Allen Young will be actively engaged in carrying out the proposed exploration within the Antarctic Circle'.[9]

On 30 November 1887 Michael Foster, secretary of the Royal Society London, responded to the Secretary of State for the Colonies. The Society had developed the reply after careful consideration 'by the President and Council with the assistance of a Committee consisting of Fellows of the Society specially qualified to form a judgement on the matter'.[10] Additionally to the President Professor Stokes and Secretary Dr Foster, the committee consisted of the treasurer Dr John Evans, Lord Rayleigh, Professor Williamson, William Christie, Sir Joseph Hooker, Professor Huxley, Admiral Richards, General Strachey and General John T. Walker.

This was a high-powered group. Aside from Hooker and Walker mentioned above, mathematician George Stokes, physiologist Michael Foster and physicist Lord Rayleigh all held professorships at Cambridge University. While Alexander Wilson was professor of chemistry at University College

London, John Evans was a notable archaeologist, General George Richards had been Hydrographer to the Admiralty, meteorologist General Richard Strachey went on to the presidency of the RGS 1888–1890, William Christie was Astronomer-Royal, famous biologist Thomas Huxley was one of the great names of British 19th Century science and a close colleague and supporter of Charles Darwin.

In their response the Royal Society committee laid out optimum outcomes:

> 1. Hydrographical observations. 2. Meteorological observations 3. Magnetic observations 4. Temperature. 5. Soundings / dredgings 6. Marine fauna/ flora 7. New land.

They conceded this was far beyond the scope of the proposed expedition, however they felt that a

> small pioneer expedition, which, while avowedly not designed to undertake an exhaustive enquiry would be able, under competent direction to make careful survey of the northern boundary of the circumpolar ice region, to determine approximately the distribution of open water and the direction of oceanic currents, to take magnetical and meteorological observations, and, by means of the tow net and the dredge, used at moderate depths, to collect pelagic animals and plants. The results of such a general survey, even though not wholly complete, would not only of themselves be of great interest and value, but also be of paramount importance in guiding a decision as to the desirability, or the contrary, of sending out in the future, expeditions more thoroughly equipped …
>
> The President and the Council will regard that decision [by the British government to provide the £5,000 requested by the Victorian Premier] with great satisfaction.[11]

On 12 December 1887 the Under Secretary of State, Colonial Office, John Bramston, penned a letter to the Secretary of the Treasury recommending the scheme to the Lords of Treasury. He highlighted the various groups in favour of the scheme and dismissed the concerns of the Board of Trade.

> The Board of Trade do not however seem to have regarded the probability of a considerable trade in sperm oil and other products of whale and of other products of whale fishing arising in the future, or the importance of the expedition for scientific purposes.

The Under Secretary went on to emphasise his department's strong endorsement for the funding proposal:

> Sir H [Henry] Holland trusts that their Lordships will give their favourable consideration to this application on behalf of the government of Victoria and consent to the contribution of the sum of £5,000 toward the scientific objects of the expedition. It would seem undesirable for Her Majesty's government to take any direct share in the equipment or management of the expedition.[12]

Unfortunately, despite the strong representations of the Colonial Institute, the Royal Society, the Royal Geographical Society, and the Colonial Office, the Lords of Treasury did not look favourably on the request.

On 3 January a letter was drafted by Treasury citing the Board of Trade's assessment that there would be little commercial benefit and 'that the scale contemplated could do very little in the way of scientific investigation' as their reasons for refusing the rather paltry amount. This rather harsh assessment was followed by a dismissive suggestion that

> my lords may be allowed to regard the present proposal as an indication that, if any like expedition be undertaken by the Imperial Government, some of the British Colonies more closely interested in it might not be unwilling to contribute to the costs.[13]

So they had turned a request for funding from the colonies into an offer by the colonies to fund Imperial Britain's Antarctic adventures.

On 25 January 1888 the AEC were informed of the decision of the Lords of Treasury. This must have been a bitter disappointment. The Imperial subsidy would almost certainly have put the colonial governments in a position of obligation regarding their own contributions, and Imperial endorsement would likely lead to private subscriptions from colonial citizens made good and keen to support a project with the mother country's imprimatur of approval. At the beginning of 1888, the looming financial crash of the 1890s was still sufficiently distant to not unduly effect fund raising as it would a few years later.

Two years after the decision of the Imperial Treasury, in an article related to the further endeavours of the AEC, *The Times* voiced the surprise and disappointment felt at the decision:

> It was widely considered in certain circles a pity that this opportunity for co-operation in an important undertaking between the mother country and the great section of the Empire in the Southern hemisphere had not been welcomed.[14]

The AEC, though, adopted a stoic public position regarding this latest disappointment. On 22 February 1888 Secretary Rusden wrote on behalf of the Committee to the Premier acknowledging receipt of the news of the Chancellor of the Exchequers decision. The letter recorded the AEC's gratitude to Premier Gillies and Agent-General Berry and went on to comment

> that it was not expected that the British Government would entertain the proposal at once, without considerable pressure from without; and for this time and opportunity for operating on public opinion are indispensable. Experience proves that it takes several years to move the Home Government to enter upon such an undertaking and that patience and perseverance are the main desiderata in agitating for any enterprise ...[15]

The letter ended optimistically noting that at their conference, Australian Natives Association delegates had unanimously passed a resolution of support for the AEC's Antarctic aims.

By July the mood was rather sombre. Captain Pasco's at the 31 July 1888 meeting of the RGSA Victoria, acknowledged that

> ... the desire to federate with the sister colonies in the financial responsibility, has, unfortunately, well-nigh brought us to a deadlock, unless we can take comfort in the truism that 'the darkest hour of night is just before the dawn'; for the sad unforseen calls on the Treasury for railway disasters, &c, darkened all hopes of Victoria being able, single-handed, to grasp the south polar prize as a fitting crowning jewel ...[16]

In September 1888 an old friend of many members of the AEC, and a great champion of Antarctic exploration, Georg von Neumayer, wrote in answer to a letter from Crawford Pasco. He detailed his own recent attempts in his long quest to raise a German expedition to the Antarctic. Henry Villard, a German made good in the United States, (he was president of the North Pacific Railway Company), offered to underwrite half of the estimated £120,000 to fund the expedition. Unfortunately, the German government declined to contribute the other half and the expedition didn't go ahead. This was a far more ambitious and expensive plan than the AEC's and Neumayer, like the AEC, was left to continue the long and frustrating process of trying to raise funds and interest in the benefits of a scientific expedition to the Antarctic.[17]

The report of the AEC 28 August 1889 outlined the promising initiatives of the committee over the previous 3 years. Concluding that

> these encouraging proposals, early in 1888, amply justified the sanguine hope of the Committee, that by the southern spring of 1888 we might have witnessed the departure of the expedition from this port in time to return with whale and sea products wherewith to furnish an Antarctic Court in the recent Centennial Exhibition. That such was not realised is the misfortune of this Committee, but not its fault.[18]

Bemoaning the lack of funding from the Imperial Government, the report concluded that 'as Geographers, we will not fail to welcome and co-operate with any nationality that will contribute to our knowledge of any terra incognita'.[19]

As it happened there were more opportunities just around the corner, and they were not British.

In September 1889, the Consul for Sweden and Norway in Victoria, Hans Gundersen, forwarded a translation of a letter noted Norwegian whaler Svend Foyn had sent to Graham Berry, asking for details of whales in the Southern Ocean.

Born the son of a master mariner into comfortable surroundings in Tønsberg in 1809, Svend Foyn lost his father to the sea in 1813. After that, life was harsh with his mother battling poverty to keep the family together. The struggle of his childhood after his father's death helped shape an austere, plain Christian man with a fierce work ethic.

Foyn qualified as a master mariner in 1824 and set about methodically building a fortune through the sea. Initially he transported timber. By the 1840s he was a sealing captain and businessman. By the 1860s successful sealing seasons became more sporadic and Foyn turned his mind to developing more effective ways of whaling.

He poured the profits from his sealing business into building a ship designed specifically for whaling and began to work on a more effective method of catching whales than a harpoon hurled from a small boat. For more than a decade, through the vicissitudes of varied sealing and unsuccessful whaling seasons he painstakingly experimented with a harpoon gun. As he arrived at an effective model, and developed an onshore processing plant, he became concerned with competition (particularly Germans setting up in the same area) stealing his ideas (and the whales). He was an influential businessman in Norway and the King granted him a ten-year monopoly which enabled him to amass a vast fortune as his new whaling methods proved finally decisive.

Ever the hard-nosed businessman, in his correspondence with the AEC Foyn wanted £6,000 regardless of results and advised that his ships would not be ready to leave Norway until at least September 1890. His covering letter to Gundersen contained a postscript:

> I hear that there are no, or only very few, whales in the Antarctic Ocean, which explains that there are so few whaling vessels in the south. If this be the case, I think the idea is scarcely practicable.[20]

As it happened experience would bear out these fears, but at the time it may merely have been a way of pushing for subsidies. The AEC undertook to get further information on whale numbers and types.

Chapter Eleven

The Swedish Offer

Just as their efforts seem to have lost all momentum the new year of 1890 brought with it new hope for the Antarctic Exploration Committee (AEC). By the start of 1890 the idea of a joint commercial and scientific expedition was to a great extent abandoned due to lack of realistic offers from prospective parties and the lack of real financial commitment from Victoria and the other colonial governments.

Depending on the colonial governments for subsidies, that none of those governments could finally commit to, had paralysed the Committee in every way from the start. It was never in a position to make an offer of any kind and was even unable to respond effectively to any offer received. The Committee was restricted to commending its opinion to the consideration of the Victorian Government and without overwhelming public interest in the matter (or genuine prospect of commitment from the other colonial governments) it became evident that the Victorian Government, however courteously and even kindly disposed, could not be expected to even propose a vote to Parliament or place subsidies in the estimates.

At the far end of the world, though, the work of the AEC had not gone unnoticed by Adolf Nordenskiöld. Busy with publishing the results of his traverse of the Northeast Passage when the AEC had previously been in contact, Nordenskiöld was now of a mind to mount another expedition. There had been sporadic rumours that Nordenskiöld and Fridtjof Nansen were considering a joint expedition to the Antarctic. While these rumours of a joint expedition didn't come to fruition, at the start of 1890 Nordenskiöld was looking southward. In fact the AEC had been corresponding with Nansen in the hope that he would come to Australia for a lecture tour. On 23 April

1890 Fridtjof Nansen had written a gracious letter to Mueller advising that he wouldn't be able to undertake such a tour.[1]

Prior to this, on 8 January 1890, Nordenskiöld made a significant address to the Swedish Royal Academy of Sciences. In part he recalled the AEC's approach to him in 1887. He advised that he and Baron Dickson had recently received a letter from the Foreign Minister (sent by the Melbourne Consul for Sweden and Norway, Hans Gundersen) enclosing Ferdinand von Mueller's speech to the RGSA (Victorian Branch) on 2 September 1889 indicating an ongoing commitment to Antarctic exploration. Mueller in fact emphasised the advantages of tying any expedition to commercial whaling and mentions the recent Foyn offer. Mueller introduces his topic however in a rather desultory manner.

> Turning now to Antarctic exploration … all we can claim as being attained is having in a more prominent and lasting manner than heretofore impressed the practical advantages of such exploits on the public mind.[2]

Nordenskiöld also referred to Gundersen's letter intimating that a funding of £5,000 might be available for a suitable expedition and saw the situation of the AEC as an opportunity.

> I therefore thought that the present occasion which here offered itself to get together a Swedish Antarctic expedition ought to be made use of.[3]

With Dickson's financial backing of £5,000 and expecting the same amount from Australia, Nordenskiöld committed to the expedition. This was passed by (Daniel) Georg Lindhagen, noted astronomer and Academy Secretary, to the Swedish Foreign Minister, who in turn forwarded it to Gundersen. Georg Lindhagen's covering letter advised that Baron Nordenskiöld, with Baron Dickson's backing, was 'willing to fit out an expedition such as proposed and also to procure a suitable Swedish vessel, provided that the above-named subscription [£5,000] from the Australian society be placed at their disposal for the purpose'. This showed great confidence in the Australian financial commitment which was, in fact, an aspiration rather than an actuality.

The letter went on to outline the aims of the expedition.

> The object of the expedition which should have to start from Sweden during the course of the year 1891, is, 1st, to commence a thorough exploration from a natural history point of view of the Antarctic regions and seas; 2nd,

to make geographical investigations concerning the extension and nature of the regions surrounding the South Pole; third, to investigate whether any valuable fishing and shooting is to be found in those parts of the Antarctic Ocean which the expedition is intended to explore.[4]

This broadly met the criteria of the AEC. In this plan the commercial element was secondary whereas all the offers from northern whalers had it as primary. There was, though, no mention of Australian participation beyond finances, an issue that from the AEC's point of view, contributed to the inability of both parties to launch the expedition.

It was reported that Captain Pasco had acknowledged the receipt of the offer on 27 February 1890[5] and the offer was discussed at the AEC meeting of 4 March 1890.

However this exciting development of Nordenskiöld's offer was surprisingly omitted from the AEC progress report, written by Pasco and delivered by Griffiths at the RGSA (Vic) general meeting on 21 March 1890. (Despite the report referring to rumours of a joint Nordenskiöld /Nansen expedition to the Antarctic) Perhaps Nordenskiöld's offer wasn't mentioned as the AEC hadn't formulated an official response. The report stated that the AEC

> ... do not intend to relax our endeavours in the future. ... Suitable vessels are available both in Scotland and in Scandinavia, their owners and officers are willing to embark in the adventure. Unfortunately the owners are not spirited enough to undertake it without liberal payments, which we cannot make unless the United Colonies will assist us ...[6]

Thus forever the bind. European shipowners were only interested if subsidised and each colony only willing if the others were. This at a time when the Colony of Victoria's economic boom bubble was bursting towards the grim depression of the 1890s.

Hans Gundersen wrote to Mueller on 24 March about the offer. Gunderson concedes:

> it will yet take some considerable time before the RGSA can give a definite answer. ... Although it is nowhere expressly said, I am strongly under the impression that the Swedish now calculate upon this subsidy as a matter of course and are already commencing their preparations for the Antarctic Expedition ...[7]

Gundersen was right, things did not move particularly speedily from that point. On 30 July 1890 the AEC met to consider action on the Nordenskiöld offer. It was decided that 'an appeal should be made to the public for support …'[8] in order to help raise the £5,000 that the Swedes assumed was already available. It was decided that George Griffiths upcoming address to the Banker's Institute would be a good opportunity to promote their appeal.

The previous Norwegian and British offers were to provide both ships and crews for ample bonuses but irrespective of results, and with a clear aim of seeing the AEC as an opportunity to subsidise reconnaissance of potential whaling grounds. The new offer had the immense advantage of being primarily for scientific purposes, to be led by Adolf Nordenskiöld, the most notable Arctic explorer of the time, half the funding was guaranteed by Baron Dickson, and the expedition had far superior prospects of success in every practical way.

The AEC met at the Observatory on the Tuesday morning, 29 July 1890 and formally accepted the offer and resolved 'to appeal to general public throughout the Australasian colonies for subscriptions towards the movement'.[9] The meeting further decided to try and solicit co-operation from the other colonial chapters of the RGSA. Consul Gundersen attended the meeting and undertook to communicate the meeting resolutions to Nordenskiöld and Dickson.

On 15 August 1890 the AEC sent a cablegram to Sweden advising that 'The Antarctic Exploration Committee collecting five thousand pounds. Is Baron Dickson's offer still open?' The Swedish Academy was rather prompter with their response and on 22 August confirmed their commitment to the expedition 'with pleasure'.[10]

On 27 August 1890, George Griffiths delivered his lecture to the Bankers Institute of Australia at the Melbourne Athenaeum. The lecture was titled *South Polar Problems; Or, the Objects and Values of Antarctic Research*. The Victorian governor, the Earl of Hopetoun, was in attendance. This was a notable lecture garnering publicity for the AEC as the Nordenskiöld offer was being discussed in the local press. Griffith's lecture was published internationally in both *Science* and *Nature* and received substantial comment in *The Times*.[11]

On 5 October 1890 the AEC wrote to the Swedish Academy, emphasising:

> we wish in any case to make it quite clear that our means are still prospective,

though much more hopeful than when we were depending solely upon Government assistance. We are only commencing, and in the present absorbed state of the public mind here, from extensive labour strikes, we can scarcely attempt to make much progress just now, but we shall at once circulate our subscription lists, and introduce the subject before the public by occasional lectures ...[12]

It seems very likely that the Swedish Academy thought that £5,000 was just sitting waiting for the right project. The AEC response could hardly have been more honest, but for the Swedes it was rather disconcerting.

On 18 November 1890 Georg Lindhagen, Secretary of the Swedish Academy of Science, wrote to the AEC advising that

> when the money question is definitely settled, Baron Nordenskiöld will send you a detailed memorandum on the equipment of the expedition, selecting of the ship and the scientific staff, plan for the first summer campaign, for selecting the winter harbour &c.[13]

The letter went on to point out that because of the limited funds for the expedition a maximum of two Australian scientists could be included in the party. The letter also acknowledged that because of delays in the Australian funding the expedition was unlikely to commence before 1893.

Meanwhile Admiral Ommanney was labouring in vain in England to raise interest in an expedition from the mother country. He wrote to the Crawford Pasco on 13 October 1890, lauding the progress in Victoria and despairing of disinterest in England:

> I have seen with infinite satisfaction that the matter of exploring the Antarctic Sea has again been revived in Victoria; I do most fully hope that your efforts may succeed ... I deplore that the initiation which I took toward arousing public attention to this important enterprise in the British Association met with little or no encouragement.[14]

Again because of the vagaries of 19th century communication, this letter was not tabled at an AEC meeting until February 1891, by which stage reports from overseas were sounding more ominous.

The ongoing stumbling block of government financial support was again a key issue in the AEC's inability to guarantee the £5,000 required for the expedition. On 20 November the Melbourne *Age* reported that it would appear there is but little prospect of the proposed Antarctic expedition receiving monetary assistance from the Australian governments. Baron von Mueller who is taking, with other scientists, a very great interest in the matter, forwarded a communication to the Premier, in which he suggested that the Government should contribute towards the expense of fitting out the expedition. Before committing himself to any promise, Mr Munro communicated with the Governments of the other colonies on the subject, and in each instance received an unfavourable response. In these circumstance Mr Munro was constrained to inform Baron von Mueller that the Government is not prepared to bear the whole burden of fitting out the expedition.[15]

The major fund raising activity for the AEC was the Grand White Character and Plain Dress Ball held on 19 December 1890 at the Royal Exhibition Buildings. Admission was 15 shillings for gentlemen and 10 shillings and sixpence for ladies and the organisers were hopeful of many guests attending in costumes consistent with the icy regions.

The Ball was not a great success and Melbourne *Table Talk* found the whole event rather amusing:

> Readers of E.A.Poe's imaginary 'Journey to the South Pole ... will remember the eerie feeling of passing for ever, apparently, by the white walls and through the vast and silent sea spaces ... [At the White Ball] doubtless something of the same eerie feeling came over them [the guests] from the ghastly immensity of the building, which would require about 3,000 dancers to make it look cheerfully filled, whereas, on this occasion, only about one sixth of that number were present.

The author was warming to his task:

> Against the closed doors of the concert hall rose an 'Antarctic' stage ... with a few stuffed dodos, seals and walruses, and two 'moving' Esquimaux, who looked extremely uncomfortable with all their furs ... By the bye, does the expedition expect to find Esquimaux at South Victoria! ... The Antarctic efforts of the promoters of the ball were but feebly seconded however by those who attended, for though there might be a majority of white dresses amongst the ladies, there were few indeed amongst the gentlemen, and the costumes, either striking, novel or appropriate were 'far between'.[16]

While attendance didn't nearly fill the cavernous Royal Exhibition Building, notables from Melbourne's society, led by the Governor and the Mayor, were there.

The Australasian Association for the Advancement of Science met in Christchurch in January 1891, and this provided another forum for promoting the proposed Nordenskiöld expedition, with AEC being strongly represented on various committees. Mueller, Griffiths and Ellery were part of the Antarctic Exploration committee. George Griffiths was also president of the Geography section and spoke in detail about the potential value of Antarctic research.

> ... any reference to this subject is sure to be met with the query, Cui bono? What good can it do? ... let me observe that it would indeed be strange if an unexplored region, eight million square miles in area – twice the size of Europe– and grouped around the axis of rotation and the magnetic pole, could fail to yield to investigators some novel and valuable information.[17]

Griffiths concluded with the grand claim that

> I feel assured that nothing could bring to us greater distinction in the eyes of the whole civilised world than such an expedition, judiciously planned and skilfully carried out.[18]

Also at the meeting Charles Purnell read a paper on Antarctic Exploration. He had been publicly advocating the importance of an expedition since presenting a paper to the Otago Institute in 1878. He, rather heretically (and prophetically), cast doubt on the likelihood of the Nordenskiöld expedition going ahead. He ended too by exhorting the Australasian colonies to 'engage in a patriotic enterprise worthy of the traditions of a maritime nation, and which would make the names of Australia and New Zealand respected throughout the civilised world'.[19]

Purnell's doubts on the Nordenskiöld expedition may have had a sound basis. In February 1891 *The Times* reported a conversation with Baron Dickson, commenting that the joint expedition

> 'seems to be hanging fire' and stating that Baron Dickson 'naturally expresses surprise at the conduct of the Australasian Geographical Society ... if the Australians come up with the moderate sum of £5,000, Baron Dickson is willing to be responsible for the balance ...'
>
> ... From Australia 'nothing more substantial than words has been

forthcoming. True, a bazaar or a ball has been talked of ... surely the last humiliating refuge for a wealthy country like Australia ...'[20]

Dickson and Nordenskiöld had aimed to embark in 1891 so the uncertainty of funding was placing the expedition in jeopardy, although the pomposity of the journalist is a bit rich given Britain's previous lack of material support.

Attempts to further raise awareness of the expedition and generate funding from across the colonies, continued. On 28 April 1891 John James Wild, an original member of the AEC, and a member of the famous *Challenger* expedition, delivered a lecture on Antarctic Exploration, illustrated by limelight views and delivered in the vestibule of Sydney Town Hall to the RGSA NSW.

He focussed on his experiences aboard *Challenger* and outlined briefly the history of Antarctic exploration and the opportunities for further discoveries from a new expedition. His paper was then delivered in August 1891, by E. Delmar Morgan, (Congress delegate of the NSW Branch of the RGSA), to the fifth International Geographical Congress held in Berne.

Crawford Pasco and William Potter had gone to Sydney for the Federal convention, attended by Premiers of the Australian colonies, and lobbied for funding with apparently some success. Queensland reportedly agreed to place £1,000 on Estimates and the AEC understood that NSW Premier Henry Parkes promised to provide £1366 should the NSW RGSA raise £684 although as with all attempts for government funding, promised amounts usually failed to materialise as genuine budget items.

Mueller wrote to Parkes regarding his reported offer. He asked that the government funds be forthcoming even if the agreed amount had not been raised by public subscription and exhorted Parkes to use his influence with the Victorian government.[21] Further Mueller wrote to his RGSA colleagues in South Australia urging them to lobby their government for support. Unfortunately

> ... the government were of the opinion that South Australia would not be benefited by the expedition, ... If the Governments of the other colonies were unanimously supporting the expedition ... he [the Premier] would be pleased to join them but under the present circumstances the Cabinet had decided that it could not place the sum on the Estimates for the purpose named.[22]

Elder's Offer

At the meeting of the RGSA (Vic) held on 22 August 1890, Baron von Mueller had tabled a letter from Thomas Elder, offering to cover the cost of a further exploration to Central Australia. This led to the Elder Scientific Exploring Expedition (1891–92).

Elder was a self-made man who had accumulated a fortune through the development of vast pastoral properties in South Australia. He was a generous philanthropist, with a great interest in exploration. He provided funds for a number of expeditions to map western and central Australia – Warburton (1872–73), Giles (1875), Ross (1874), and Lewis (1875). He also provided significant endowments to the University of Adelaide and his will allowed for generous bequests to hospitals and religious groups amongst others. He was a good man to know for any worthy cause or endeavour seeking financial backing. This latest exploring expedition was entirely financed by Elder. The expedition aimed to travel through areas of Western Australia unexplored by previous Elder funded explorations. Baron von Mueller together with the South Australian Branch of the Royal Geographical Society of Australasia (RGSA) were involved in the planning of the expedition. David Lindsay was chosen as leader and the party left Adelaide in several groups in late April, rendezvousing at Warrina on 29 April 1891. While the expedition mapped a vast uncharted area, it ended abruptly in acrimony when Streich, the geologist, Helms the naturalist, Elliot the medical officer and Ramsay an assistant, all resigned on 31 December 1891. David Lindsay journeyed to Geraldton and exchanged various telegrams with the expedition committee. The upshot was that he was recalled and on 1 February 1892 he was explaining his position to Thomas Elder over lunch in Adelaide. In early March the four disgruntled scientists outlined their grievances to the RGSA (SA) with Lindsay in attendance. On 14 March 1892, Thomas Elder wrote to the Society giving his view that the main impediment to the success of the party was the 'unfavourable character of the season' and concluded generously that 'I have not lost confidence in Mr Lindsay's management, and still think he was beaten by the season, I propose to give him what I consider fair compensation for loss of office'.[23]

David Lindsay later wrote to Baron von Mueller apologising for the disappointing end to the expedition but pointing out that 'we have travelled about 2250 miles in new country and mapped down about 80,000 square miles so that the results of the expedition are by no means insignificant'.[24] This expedition was a very real example of Elder's willingness to support ambitious exploring projects and to judge their success or failure fairly and without rancour. Thomas Elder, wealthy, astute, and a generous supporter of science and exploration, was exactly the sort of benefactor with the money and potentially the interest to ensure the Nordenskiöld expedition went ahead. In short he could be Australia's Baron Dickson.

At the November 1891 meeting of the RSV the possibility of securing funds from Thomas Elder was raised

> ... but more was expected from persons in position like that of Sir Thomas Elder, who had offered £5,000 towards Central Australian Exploration, and, if the cablegrams could be relied on, had since offered a like sum to Antarctic Exploration ...[25]

On 5 June 1891, Thomas Elder answered Baron von Mueller's 'urgent appeal for help' writing that he was 'quite prepared to do what Baron Dickson has done in subscribing £5,000 to the Antarctic Expedition'.[26] His initial offer was predicated on the condition that the total expedition cost did not exceed £15,000, and that he would work through the RGS (SA) rather than directly with the AEC in Melbourne.

On 11 June 1891 Hans Gundersen telegraphed the Foreign Office in Stockholm on behalf of the AEC to confirm that the expedition's total cost did not exceed the £15,000 stipulated by Elder. On 17 June 1891 the Swedish Minister for Foreign Affairs Carl Lewenhaupt confirmed that £15,000 was 'amply sufficient'. This exchange though then created some confusion between the two country's regarding their respective commitments. Minister Lewenhaupt continued 'five thousand are found here, please inform me if you mean to say that ten thousand have been found in Australia ...' Gundersen for the AEC replied '£7700 secured. Ten probable.'[27]

At the meeting of the RGSA (Vic) on 3 July 1891 the AEC report noted that Baron von Mueller had secured a promise of £5,000 from Thomas Elder.

> ... it was owing to his (Baron von Mueller's) indomitable energy that such a grand donation had been promised by Sir Thomas Elder. Baron von Mueller wrote to Thomas Elder, asking him if he would give £5,000 towards the

exploration, as Baron Dickson had done in Sweden, and the answer came back that he would.

The report spoke with extreme, understandable (and subsequently misplaced) optimism claiming that a total of £10,000 was virtually raised.

> We are therefore in a position to congratulate our fellow colonists upon the successful issue of our five years labour, for the balance still wanting to ensure the starting of the expedition next year is so small that we feel certain of obtaining it.[28]

The Antarctic Exploration Committee thought that £20,000 might be raised 'so as to allow of a margin, and to carry out the expedition in the best style'. Kernot, Ellery and Rusden, in answer to a question from Professor Spencer, all confirmed that it was the understanding of the AEC that Baron Nordenskiöld himself would lead the expedition despite his advancing years. Rusden added that Professor Spencer and Mr Wragge were likely scientific candidates to accompany the expedition. He further suggested that 'Australia should be entitled to send no fewer than four scientists, as its contribution was double that originally proposed'.[29]

However this optimism waned as the year ended. In January 1892, Baron von Mueller travelled to Adelaide 'to consult personally with Sir Thomas Elder about measures yet required for the forthcoming south-polar expedition of Baron Nordenskiöld'.[30]

The meeting with Elder did not go well. On 28 January 1892, Mueller reported that Elder had attached specific conditions to his offer:

1. That the expedition must consist of two whaling ships, so that something remunerative might come out of the expedition.
2. The ships must be in Australian waters next year.
3. That the expedition must touch at Adelaide.
4. That the £5,000 would be ready to be paid when the vessels reached Adelaide.

These conditions had not been anticipated and were untenable for the AEC, and 'all subsequent efforts of the Committee to produce a change in Sir Thomas's mind proved unavailing'.[31] This was a huge blow to the already fraught process of raising the necessary funds.

The AEC Progress Report read at the RGSA Vic meeting of 19 February

1892, claimed that £9094 had been 'raised' in Australasia. This amount was mainly promises and assumptions of funding. The figure included, rather optimistically, the £5,000 pledge from Elder, £1,000 from Robert Reid, £500 from the Tasmanian Government and £1,334 from NSW (despite the fact that the RGSA NSW contribution was listed as £260, well short of the amount of £684 required before the NSW government would honour its' offer). The £1,000 to be placed on estimates in Queensland had been voted down, although the AEC remained optimistic.

In March 1892 the NSW legislature became the only colony to commit government funds to the expedition by placing the £1366 on the estimates if the RGSA NSW raised half that figure.

Then, on 25 May 1892, the *Argus* carried a telegram from London stating that because the Australasian colonies had failed to provide the agreed funds that the expedition had been abandoned. George Griffiths responded immediately to the newspaper. He claimed that the AEC were waiting for a promised 'written scheme of operations' from Baron Nordenskiöld. Lindhagen's letter of 18 November 1890, though, on behalf of Nordenskiöld (see above) indicated that such a plan could not be furnished until the money issue was settled. Griffiths ploughed on '… we were surprised to get a later letter from Sweden asking us to make our contribution £10,000'.[32]

This latter claim seems to have arisen as a result of the flurry of telegrams in June 1891 (see above) regarding Thomas Elder's requirement that the total cost not exceed £15,000, and was contradicted by AEC secretary Henry Rusden in a letter of 6 June advising that

> no such request ever reached the committee from Sweden. The committee, having received through Baron von Mueller from Sir Thomas Elder a promise of £5,000, spontaneously determined unasked, to add that amount to the £5,000 that it was engaged in collecting for the expedition.[33]

At the AEC meeting of 15 June, a letter was tabled from the Swedish Minister of Foreign Affairs, Carl Lewenhaupt, written on 25 April 1892 and forwarded in translation by Hans Gundersen (dated 1 June 1892).

It explicitly stated that the Swedes were withdrawing from the expedition due to the unavailability of the promised Australian funds by 1 January 1892. The AEC claimed that no such date had been agreed to, however the funds were still not available two years after the original expedition proposal. It seems clear that the Swedes understood the money to be sitting waiting for a suitable expedition, and not made up of half promises and hopes as proved to be the case.

The AEC lost no time in moving on. At the meeting of 22 July, a letter was sent to the Swedish Academy of Sciences and a sub-committee was formed to promote a British–Australian expedition.

Their renewed enthusiasm may have been driven by correspondence relating to two notable British mariners. In February 1892 a Mr Tweedle forwarded some correspondence he had received from Joseph Wiggins making an offer to lead an Antarctic expedition funded for the magical amount of £5,000. There is little doubt that Wiggins would have been an excellent expedition leader. He was a notable explorer having made a number of voyages in the Kara Sea and Yenisey River (like Nordenskiöld) with a hope to opening commercial routes in Arctic Siberia. Commenting on the proposed Nordenskiöld expedition he remarked. 'What! Cannot your brave mariners find one in your Greater Britain to uphold the flag that has braved a thousand years in their frigid zones. If not are there none to be found in Old England?'[34]

The offer came to nothing although again it is probably testament to the belief amongst northern mariners that there was a £5,000 subsidy waiting to be claimed. Over 60 years old, Wiggins was certainly not ready for retirement and in 1893 he led a group of ships delivering rails for the Trans-Siberian Railway. He crossed the Kara Sea to the Yenisei River. The two British ships, *Orestes* and *Blencathra*, returned home but Wiggins accompanied the Russian ships (commissioned as river vessels by the Russian government and built in England) up the river to Yeniseysk to deliver the rails. He made several further trips to the Siberian Arctic with mixed commercial results. He remained involved in the shipping trade in that area until his death in 1905.

On 23 March 1892 the AEC received a letter from David Gray, requesting co-operation on an expedition. As previously outlined, Captain Gray and his brother John were very experienced and respected Arctic whalers whose advice had been sought by the AEC when plans were first being developed in 1886. At that time the Grays had been interested in visiting the Antarctic if a subsidy was available. On this occasion David Gray was struggling to finance an Antarctic expedition with two ships. The AEC, still believing the Nordenskiöld plan would go ahead, declined his request. Ironically it had been reported that Nordenskiöld's son was to travel with Gray. It was intended that two ships be sent south but the expedition didn't go ahead as adequate finance couldn't be raised.

At this time Crawford Pasco left Australia for Europe, according to George Griffiths, Pasco had 'gone to Stockholm to endeavour to smooth over the difficulties which have arisen there, and which threaten to upset our plans',[35] While in Britain Pasco witnessed the despatch of the Dundee whaling venture to the Antarctic in September 1892, which was accompanied by William Speirs Bruce. Pasco arrived back in Melbourne on 4 February 1893.

In the end it seems that the Swedish Academy wanted to send a Swedish expedition to the Antarctic and saw the AEC as a suitable partner to provide finance. The AEC, despite their optimism at various points, had received a number of promises and possibilities of finance, but few actual pounds. As enthusiastic and determined as the committee was, the finances needed to send even a modest expedition didn't ever materialise.

Chapter Twelve

The NSW government subsidy

While there followed a quiet time for the AEC, they did attempt to secure the NSW Government funding of £1366 (contingent on the NSW RGSA raising £684). The RGSA (NSW) were well short of the required sum to trigger the government funds, but the AEC were determined to claim the subsidy.

On 23 October 1891 the NSW Antarctic Exploration Committee met for the first time since 31 March 1891 (the scheduled meeting of 15 May 1891 lapsed due to the lack of a quorum). They met specifically to endorse the stance of the RGSA NSW and passed the following resolution:

> That owing to the apathy of the public in subscribing to the Antarctic Expedition, and the change of government which dispenses with previous engagements to place any sum of money on the estimates, this Committee regrets that it cannot at present quarantine a further sum than the actual amount of £225 now in hand towards the fund of the Swedish Antarctic Expedition.[1]

Soon after, on 10 November 1891 there was another meeting of the NSW committee to discuss correspondence from the AEC in Melbourne. The AEC (Melbourne) wanted to use £400 from Robert Reid's donation, to boost the NSW contribution close the amount required to obtain the subsidy. The AEC (Melbourne) didn't endear themselves to their NSW colleagues by also writing directly to the NSW Premier. This was deemed 'somewhat premature' by the NSW committee.

This was an unsatisfactory situation for all involved. The AEC though were determined to extract the funding they understood the NSW Government to be offering.

George Dibbs took over from Parkes as Premier of NSW in October 1891. In November 1891 the RGSA (NSW) reported that John Mann had visited Dibbs on behalf of the Society. Dibbs had confirmed his commitment to Parkes undertaking. In the NSW Legislative Assembly on 24 November 1891, Dibbs was asked 'is it the intention of the Government to place a sum of money upon the estimates as a contribution to the cost of the proposed expedition to the Antarctic Sea?'

Dibbs responded: 'I find that the late government entered into an arrangement ... and agreed to place £1500 on the estimates for next year'.[2] The new premier was confirming a commitment to place the amount on the estimates, this was not a commitment that the funding would go ahead, but it was a greater commitment than had been received from any of the other colonial governments.

Three months later, on 25 February, again in the NSW Legislative Assembly, in answer to a question by Dr Andrew Ross as to whether 'it is the intention of the Government to place on the supplementary estimates a special grant ... in aid of the Royal Geographical Society of Australasia towards Antarctic exploration?' Dibbs responded '£1500 has been placed upon the estimates in chief'.[3]

In December 1892, six months after the confirmation that the Swedish-Australian Expedition had been abandoned, William Potter visited Sydney to try and convince his NSW colleagues to accept part of Robert Reid's contribution and thereby reach the amount required to claim the subsidy offered by Henry Parkes and confirmed in parliament by his successor George Dibbs.

Potter met with his NSW counterpart William Crummer on 6 December 1892 and attended a meeting of the NSW committee on 7 December. Potter confided to Mueller that the idea was challenged by William Crummer who felt it constituted 'sharp practice and deceiving the Government to take Mr Reid's money ...' Crummer also 'spoke bitterly against what he called Victorian interference, as if they in Sydney were not able to manage their own affairs'.[4]

Unbowed Potter attended the Committee meeting on 13 December. He told the NSW Committee that he had met with NSW Premier George Dibbs who again had undertaken to honour Parkes promise if the RGSA NSW could raise their agreed share. At the committee meeting Potter reiterated the AEC plan to use some of Robert Reid's money to boost the NSW contribution to the amount required to get the subsidy.

One of the attendees was Frederick Eccleston Du Faur. Du Faur was a notable figure, a member of the Royal Society of NSW since 1873, member of the RGS (London) and founder and first chairman of the Geographical Society of Australasia. He lived long enough to observe the great terrestrial explorations of the Antarctic in the first decade of the new century and was on a committee to raise funds for Mawson's expedition, a great Australian venture more ambitious than anything dreamed of by the AEC.

On that December evening in 1892 Du Faur was distinctly unimpressed and he

> considered that Baron Dickson and Nordenskiöld had acted very properly in limiting the time required for collecting these monies, and it would be unreasonable to suppose that anyone would keep such an offer open for unlimited time … Mr Du Faur most emphatically objected to adopt Mr Potter's scheme … asking for this sum of £1,500 under existing circumstances would be unconstitutional and objectionable and was a course which he could not countenance.[The references to the amount varies between this and £1,366.][5]

The meeting resolved not to approach the government seeking the subsidy, much to the disappointment of Rev. Potter who returned to Melbourne the next day.

Thus finally ended actions related to the Swedish-Australian Antarctic Expedition. This was probably the closest the AEC got to achieving their aims and was the last time they were involved with planning an expedition.

At the 5th Meeting of Australasian Association for the Advancement of Science, held in Adelaide in 1893, the President of the Geography section, and one of the AEC secretaries, Alexander MacDonald, advanced the AEC's view of the reasons for the collapse of the proposed Swedish Australian Antarctic Expedition.

> Owing, however, to the severe commercial depression … only a small portion of the Australasian subscriptions were paid into the Antarctic Committee by the end of 1892, and consequently Barons Dickson and Nordenskiöld withdrew their offer of co-operation, and the project of a purely scientific expedition has had to be abandoned.[6]

MacDonald went on to outline the efforts of the AEC, claiming some credit for the *Balaena* whaling expedition, (Bruce).

> This action of the committee [offering inducements to whalers] it was, no doubt, that led to the commercial enterprise of the Balaena and other vessels which last year sailed from Europe for the Antarctic upon American meridians, all of which vessels returned this year richly laden with seal oil and seal skins …

MacDonald was still hopeful that 'With the revival of commercial prosperity, the Antarctic Committee may hope to succeed in raising the necessary funds for an expedition …'[7]

Despite the disappointments of the previous 8 years the AEC did, though, take great interest in the next foray to the deep south from Melbourne, the voyage of the *Antarctic*, managed by Henrik Bull, who had lived in Melbourne for almost the whole period that the AEC was active, and took great interest in their progress.

Chapter Thirteen

Henrik Johan Bull and an accidental triumph

On the last day of the 1886, Norwegian Henrik Johan Bull arrived in Melbourne aboard the *Professor Johnson*. A native of the notable fishing and whaling centre of Tønsberg, Norway, he had tried his hand in the fishing industry with mixed results. He arrived in Melbourne with nothing. He had left his wife and children behind in Norway hoping to make a success in the bustling new city of Melbourne and to restore the family fortunes.

Bull was born on 18 October 1844 in Vestfold. As a young man, with strong familial connections to many of the notable and successful families in Tønsberg, his entrepreneurial skills in the fishing industry made him an early success. By his own admission in the boom times of the 1870s in Tønsberg he developed a taste for the high life.

> Parties and friends became the most important. Business and home came as number two and number three. The results were then also as usual: a gradual decline in income, loss of trust, and in short, after sixteen years had gone by, all that I had owned, including the essential part of my wife's estate, had completely disappeared.[1]

There had been unlucky speculations. In 1884–85 he equipped a cod fishing expedition to Iceland, but it failed due to bad weather. Bull, though, mainly blamed himself for neglecting his business. He chose to travel almost as far from his home as it was possible to go, resolving to 'conquer the compulsive passion which had got control over me at home, or else I would go under in a fight ...'[2]

He doesn't make this destructive 'passion' explicit but it related to his hectic social life and the temptations it presented.

He landed in Melbourne at a propitious time for a man ambitious and experienced in commercial fishing, but it was a little while before he contributed his views to the AEC's attempts to mount an expedition. Melbourne was a brash, wealthy, burgeoning town in the midst of the mad expansion, speculation and over extension of the 1880s, but Bull had a tough time of it initially. In fact his first five years were a 'life on a knife's edge, with loneliness, poverty and deprivation'.[3]

In his mid-40s, having lived an affluent life as a young man, he found himself reduced to the brutal physical labour of timber felling and digging. He had, though, a clear and unshakeable faith in the commercial prospects of Antarctic whaling and sealing. He became aware of the endeavours of the AEC. Like the Gray brothers and his countryman Christen Christensen (a Norwegian pioneer of factory whaling ships in the Antarctic), he had read James Ross' accounts of all those whales in the Antarctic waters directly below Australia and New Zealand. Bull could see the opportunity to restore his fortunes and his dignity. With few friends or connections he turned to the press to publicise his ideas.

In June 1890, he wrote to the short-lived Melbourne evening newspaper the *Evening Standard*:

> I am aware that through the Geographical Society of Melbourne efforts are being made to engage some ship or ships with the view to proceed towards the Antarctic to explore those regions for scientific as well as for more material purposes; but I am also told that the above named honourable society at present at least, have very limited funds at their disposal to defray cost and expense of such an expedition. If, however, I look upon the matter from a pure business point of view, I should think that there is full encouragement for some of the enterprising men of Melbourne to equip a suitable vessel for sealing and whaling purposes in these regions, giving at the same time some scientific men the opportunity of accompanying the vessel.[4]

While he didn't receive any written replies to his letter, he did attract the attention of Baron von Mueller who invited him to the annual meeting of the Geographical Society. At last things were looking up. In October 1891 finally he was able to obtain a position in the great metropolis with shipping agents Trapp, Blair and Co, in William Street, Melbourne, just near the Customs House. This was a business he knew, and in Mr Trapp he found a man interested and encouraging of his dream of managing a commercial expedition to the south.

At the time there was regular news in the press regarding the plans of the AEC and Bull took great interest in their activities. In November 1891 he had another letter published in the press, this time in the Melbourne *Argus*. This detailed various sightings of large numbers of whales by James Ross in 1840–41. He professed that

> to myself and other countrymen, as well as Scotchmen residing in Australia, who know what wealth and riches annually are brought home from the icy regions of the north, it is only natural to be surprised that the vast fields of the Antarctic are still left untouched by the enterprising business men of these colonies.[5]

He acknowledged the then current planning for the Swedish-Australian expedition but added rather presciently:

> But it seems, however, to be somewhat uncertain when that expedition is going to start, and many years may elapse before further knowledge is acquired about the Antarctic unless some enterprising business men will give the whaling and sealing a fair trial.[6]

The letter created some interest with several correspondents responding positively.

Mr Lyon of Ballarat recommended Dundee whalers Messrs Stephens and Sons. He identified their ship *Terra Nova* as 'by far the best steamer afloat for whaling purposes, both as regards construction and power'. He added 'Perhaps something might yet be done to try our waters for such a mighty remunerative business'.[7]

Prominent Melbourne timber merchant Otto Romcke joined with Bull 'in a hearty wish in seeing an enterprise as suggested started in this colony'.[8] Romcke, too, was a Norwegian, and had achieved the level of business success Bull aspired to. Romcke had married in Melbourne and lived in a grand mansion in Canterbury. On land he owned opposite his house, he established a park and planted a wide variety of trees. He donated the park to the local council. It is still maintained as a public park, many of Romcke's trees have now passed their century. The park bears the name he gave his house – Norway. He remained a supporter of Bull and offered to purchase shares if Bull was able to develop a viable whaling and sealing enterprise.

Henrik Bull had high hopes for creating a company to undertake whaling and sealing in the Antarctic. He was encouraged by the zeal with which the AEC had promoted Antarctic exploration, highlighting as they did both the scientific and commercial benefits. However the 1890s was a period of severe recession following the wild speculation and fiscal excess of the previous decade.

> Through the support which my then employer gave to my advocacy of the Antarctic as a commercial field of operation, I had at one time fair prospects in Melbourne of floating a company for whaling and sealing purposes; but the financial crack of 1892 intervening, effectually destroyed for the time being all hopes of success in Australia of any enterprise of such a nature.[9]

Bull had support and offers of investment from his employer Trapp, and Otto Romcke. But as the colony slipped deeper into a crippling financial depression he realised, much as the AEC did at that time, that the chances for raising adequate funds to mount an Antarctic expedition from Melbourne were remote. With encouragement from Trapp, Bull returned to Tønsberg, Norway, in February 1893 in the hope that he may have more fortune in attracting interest for his plans. He knew Svend Foyn. In fact he had delivered a lecture on him at the Scandinavian Church in Melbourne in 1892. In Tønsberg, he paid him a courtesy visit. Bull found that Foyn 'was aware of my newspaper articles in Melbourne, and my correspondence with Norwegian whalers, and I had scarcely been with him for five minutes when he started off on the Antarctic subject'.[10] Within 15 minutes, Foyn had agreed to finance the voyage.

The ship Foyn chose for the expedition was a retired sealer, a small 226-ton steamship built in 1872 and named *Cap Nor*. In need of a refit, she was rechristened *Antarctic*. The skipper originally appointed, a Mr Sanne, had a falling out with Svend Foyn and was replaced by Leonard Kristensen. Bull's role as expedition manager was never clearly defined and he and Kristensen rarely saw eye to eye. This was one obstacle to the success of the expedition.

Both Foyn and Bull, well versed in the attempts of the AEC to convince the colonial governments to support a polar expedition, were keen to claim any possible subsidy. On 7 June 1893 Bull wrote to Baron von Mueller, renewing his acquaintance and informing him of Bull's plans. He added that

Svend Foyn

> expects that the Australian Governments – or the Victorian Government only – will grant him a bonus for thus striving to open up a new source of wealth, from which the colonies no doubt in particular will reap the best benefit; and, at the same time, Commander Foyn declares his willingness to let one or two of your scientific men follow the vessel if your Government or the Geographical Society should choose to do so, it being, however, distinctly understood that the presence on board of these representatives of science must not interfere with the expedition as a commercial enterprise on which basis only Commander Foyn is prepared to send his vessel. At the same time you may easily conclude that there will be a number of opportunities for those scientists to make valuable observations, soundings,&c, and they may be sure that on board they will meet with all due consideration and assistance ...[11]

Finally, the ship was ready and sailed from Tønsberg on 20 September 1893. There had been wildly differing views of the cost of outfitting an expedition, and the proposed Swedish–Australian expedition had been expected to cost at least £10,000. British estimates had been up to 15 times that, albeit for a far more ambitious overwintering expedition. Bull detailed the budget for his enterprise at about £5,000. This included the cost of the ship and refit (£2,000 and £500). Apart from a small investment by Bull (representing all his savings) and £550 from Thomas Johannes Heftye and Sons of Christiana (Oslo), Svend Foyn bore all the costs.

The AEC made representations to the Government regarding Foyn's request for a subsidy, but predictably with no positive response. The AEC reported to the Royal Society (Victoria) on 16 November 1893 that the voyage of the *Antarctic* had commenced. For want of a Victorian subsidy she was expected to call at Newcastle or Sydney rather than Melbourne. George Griffiths took the opportunity to

> congratulate the Society upon the efforts made by the joint Committee during the past seven years, as they have resulted in the re-opening of the Antarctic Seas, after fifty years of absolute neglect.[12]

At the RGSA Vic Council meeting held a week later it was reported that W.G. Burn Murdoch (artist in the *Balaena* expedition) had expressed interest in joining any Australian Antarctic expedition.

Given Henrik Bull's apparent intention of calling at Sydney and Hobart en route in response to the Victorian Government's decision not to offer a subsidy, George Griffiths was deputed to proceed to Sydney to welcome him on behalf of the AEC.

Whether Bull actually intended to take his expedition via Sydney, Newcastle, Hobart or Melbourne is not clear. It was easy for him to announce any of these cities as his intended destination in Australia in order to force the issue of a subsidy. In the end no colonial government offered a subsidy and Bull did come to his old home of Melbourne.

Henrik Bull's expedition proceeded slowly, taking on coal at Las Palmas, Grand Canary on 21 October 1893. On 25 November they made port at remote Tristan da Cunha, situated 1,500 miles from the nearest habitation, deep in the South Atlantic.

At the time of Bull's visit, Tristan da Cunha was inhabited by about 100 people, an assortment of shipwrecked sailors, women from St Helena and others, it is one of the smallest and most far-flung parts of the British Empire. While there Bull spoke to a man he named as Captain Higgins, an inhabitant for 45 years who advised that he had caught Right whales south of the Tristan da Cunha group. At the time of year he predicted some success for whaling further south, around the Prince Edward, Crozet, Kerguelen and Heard Islands. 'Captain Higgins' actually appears to have been Andrew Hagan, an American who arrived there in 1849, married and settled.

The *Antarctic* sailed on 27 November on a course for Prince Edward Island. On 4 December they encountered their first iceberg. They sighted Marion and then Prince Edward Island on 12 December, and Possession and East Island on 15 December. They sailed on towards the Kerguelen Islands. Arriving on 19 December the ship cautiously entered Greenland Harbour, at the south-east end of the main island. At 2.00 a.m. the following morning the crew commenced the brutal business of killing sea elephants, and in two days shot 350 of these creatures. While Henrik Bull saw the commercial advantage of such an enterprise, the actuality of it he found less palatable.

> The details of seal hunting are so particularly nauseating that I will spare my readers an exhaustive description. The elephant must die that we may live. This can be our only excuse for the slaughter of a particularly innocent and defenceless animal ... The sportsman can find nothing attractive in the

capture of the kind of seals we met with. They generally look on with quiet curiosity and interest at preparations for their own execution by rifle bullet or pickaxe.[13]

After a couple of days off for Christmas, they sailed from Greenland Harbour a short distance north, arriving at Royal Sound on 27 December 1893 where they took 190 seals. For the next few weeks they continued searching the bays of the Kerguelen's for seal colonies. On 3 February 1894, they set a course for southern Australia having taken 1,600 seals. *Antarctic* anchored in Hobson's Bay, Williamstown, Melbourne on 23 February 1894.

Henrik Bull was concerned at how his expedition might be received in Melbourne. He need not have worried. The reception from both the scientific community and the press was effusive.

> The colonial enthusiasm for our expedition …. was an agreeable surprise to us, as we had been afraid that our nationality might have given rise to a natural jealousy. As a matter of fact we saw no evidence whatever of any such feeling, whilst the scientific bodies of Australia were also earnestly anxious to assist, and enable us to collect useful scientific data during our prospective voyage.[14]

On 6 January 1894, prior to *Antarctic's* arrival, the Melbourne daily, the *Age*, had published a substantial article specifically about the Bull expedition, and the great commercial windfall such a journey would almost certainly achieve. The newspaper, despite the Norwegian crew, ship and funding, saw it as a Melbourne venture, sponsored primarily by Henrik Bull's Melbourne employer Mr Trapp. It is likely Trapp was substantially the source of the article.

> The transplanting of such an important industry to this portion of the globe, with Victoria as its headquarters, is not at all haphazard even. It is the result of several years of energy and toil on the part of a Victorian. Mr Trapp, of Messrs Trapp, Blair and co, William Street, Melbourne, was first induced to give serious attention to the project by contact with a Mr Bull, a relation of Mr Foyn, who casually mentioned some of the particulars narrated above. Mr Trapp being a shrewd man at once realised the great importance of such an industry to the colonies, and he accordingly set about taking steps to secure it as a monopoly for Victoria.

The article goes on to rather optimistically declare 'Success for this project is pretty much assured'. The writer also addresses the issues of government subsidy, declaring that Premier Patterson

> ... could not see the force of paying out moneys of the State as a reward for demonstrating a fact about which there can be no doubt, viz, the existence in those waters of baleen whales and fur seals ... But when he [Patterson] realises that scientific investigations are necessary for the promotion and success of commercial enterprises, and two such objects can be made to work together without much expense and to their mutual advantage, he will doubtless be willing to assist proposals of a practical character ...[15]

This proved rather wishful thinking, as no government subsidies were forthcoming, and the whaling expedition was utterly unsuccessful commercially. But at the point of the arrival of *Antarctic* there was great optimism amongst elements of both the scientific and commercial communities in Melbourne. Much as Mr Trapp saw his own hand behind the commercial side of the venture, the AEC were excited by the scientific possibilities and saw the expedition as a culmination of their endeavours, and various members of the Chamber of Manufactures viewed the expedition as the forerunner of a new industry. The Press too gave much coverage to the expedition.

On 26 February 1894 a substantial article appeared in the *Age*:

> When next November, the expedition is attempted to the Antarctic circle, arrangements will be made, if desired, to take scientific men on board, so that besides attending to commercial pursuits geographical and ethnological progress may also be consulted.[16]

On 9 March 1894, the AEC and the Councils of the RS (V) and the RGSA (V) held a conversazione at the Royal Society rooms. Henrik Bull, Captain Kristensen, and the ship's officers were feted by the scientific establishment of Melbourne. Henrik Bull received rousing applause and was cheered when he rose to speak. He was followed by Consul Gundersen, then AEC representatives Baron von Mueller, George Griffiths, Alexander Macdonald, and Dr Wild, and then Frank Scarr, a founding member of the Geographical Society.

At the end of the evening Captain Kristensen issued an open invitation to visit the ship, and the next afternoon a large group of ladies and gentlemen took up his offer. Mr Bull had ordered a flag be made for the journey that incorporated the Union Jack and the Southern Cross and had it flying for the visit.

A few days prior, on 7 March, the ship was also visited by members of the Chamber of Manufactures. Politician Dr Louis Lawrence Smith MLA, was amongst the group and he

> expressed the hope that the whaling industry would shortly be established on a permanent and satisfactory basis, so as to become a new source of wealth for Victoria.[17]

So sincerely did Dr Smith hold this view that he burst into that evening's Chamber of Manufacturers meeting, accompanied by Bull, Gundersen and an armful of sealskins and proceeded to talk at length about the commercial prospects of whaling and sealing, much to the chagrin of J.H. Knipe who had been just about to deliver his presentation on 'Go-ahead Australia'. Smith spoke for over an hour, and Mr Knipe's talk was postponed to the next meeting.

Bull, the AEC and local commercial interests all still hoped for some government assistance. To this end AEC president Crawford Pasco and Rev. Potter visited the Victorian Premier Patterson and request that he 'do whatever he can to assist and encourage' the voyage of the *Antarctic*.

> This is the first vessel and if well received here, others will doubtless follow and a valuable trade may be established. If not well received here [they] may go to another colony next time.[18]

In fact Bull had suggested earlier that the expedition might choose to dock at Sydney rather than Melbourne. But in the depths of Victoria's 1890's financial depression the Premier was unmoved. He forwarded the request on to the Commissioner of Trade and Customs on 7 March 1894, and nothing more was heard of it.

Such was local interest in the expedition that when the *Argus* reported that the *Antarctic* was to be in for an overhaul, crowds flocked to the graving dock in Williamstown for a close up view of the ship.

While local entrepreneurs were tempted by the potential profits of whaling and sealing, the evidence of Bull's endeavours thus far were not promising. His haul of seal skins and oil proved far less lucrative than he had hoped.

He sold the 95 tons of oil rendered from the seal blubber for £1775. He felt though, for the seal skins that he could do better than the colonial offers.

He had already recognised that they weren't premium quality. 'They are of inferior quality, and therefore their skins could not be made up for ladies jackets. For making harness, saddles, leather belting, &c, they are very suitable.'[19]

The skins proved worse than this though:

> As time went on, however, the inferior quality of the hides became distressingly apparent. The animals were undoubtedly out of sorts at the time of our visit: the hairs were moulting, and the skins themselves of little strength; in many cases they also exhibited hairless scurvy patches ... A pair of shoes made from a piece of tanned hide felt and looked perfection, but after only a fortnight's wear dissolution of sole and uppers set in so rapidly that an early and discreet funeral became necessary. My great pride and boasting at their debut led to many embarrassing inquiries on their sudden disappearance.[20]

Bull sent the skins to London where they were sold for £200, most of which went in freight costs. Local businessmen though were still keen on the venture and made an offer of £5,000 to buy out Svend Foyn. Foyn, in one of his less successful business decisions, demanded £10,000 and Bull's Melbourne friends declined the venture at that price.

The triumphant arrival of the expedition in Melbourne had been soured slightly by the disappointing financial returns of the seal skins. However, this was to prove the commercial highpoint of the expedition. The ship was readied for a winter cruise amongst New Zealand's sub-Antarctic Campbell and Auckland Islands in the hopes of catching whales. The relationship between Bull and Captain Kristensen was already strained. Bull was the expedition manager, but Kristensen was in charge at sea, and the muddied chain of responsibility between two men with little in common led to tension and general disfunction in the aims and approaches of the expedition.

Bull recognised the 'anomalous' position the two men were in – 'as the manager aboard I had great powers but did not feel that they justified me in interfering in the actual direction in what any capable skipper would justly consider his domain'. However he claimed that 'My scrupulous observance of this self-imposed restriction did not, in my opinion, meet with similar consideration on the part of the Captain'.[21] Bull stayed in Melbourne to attend to business and there was a sense of foreboding on his part as he watched the ship set sail on 12 April 1894.

The ship cruised along the Tasmanian coast for a few days, hoping to find whales. When none were sighted Kristensen set a course for the Campbell Islands. The next Bull heard of his ship was when he received the following telegram:

> Antarctic left wrecked at Campbell, having struck Terror Shoal. Main mast sprung, loss of anchor, etc., requiring seventy tons of coals and immediate assistance.[22]

From Tasmania the ship had actually sailed first to the Auckland Islands. The New Zealand government was interested in their movements as sealing season was closed until 1 July. *Hinemoa*, under command of Captain Fairchild, was despatched to make sure the Norwegians both understood and were adhering to the closed season and were not taking seals.

On 1 May 1894 Fairchild sighted *Antarctic* at Port Ross, Enderby Island (one of the Auckland group). They informed him of the closed season and the serious fines for breaching the seasonal ban on sealing. Captain Fairchild was suspicious of Kristensen's intentions with some cause. He reported the Norwegian as remarking – 'If you want your seals protected, you will have to send a man-of-war down to do it'.[23] It appears though, that Kristensen heeded Fairchild's warnings, and didn't take seals but rather cruised the islands for whales, many of which were sighted but only one was captured.

With seal season closed and whales proving elusive, Kristensen sailed on to the Campbell Islands. Arriving in foul weather on 14 May 1894, Kristensen manoeuvred his ship into Perseverance Harbour, but there was little protection from the fierce gale and *Antarctic* was dragged onto Terror Reef. It took several days to get free of the reef. The topsail was torn to shreds and the anchor was lost. On 12 June a New Zealand ketch *Gratitude* under Captain Brown entered Perseverance Harbour. Kristensen explained his predicament and he commissioned Captain Brown to return to Bluff (New Zealand) and bring back coal, anchors and other supplies. Brown was sufficiently suspicious of Kristensen's intentions that he left 5 crew on the Campbell islands to ensure there was no illegal sealing. The telegram received by Bull had been sent by Joseph Hatch the owner of *Gratitude*. It made the situation seem rather more dramatic than it was. When Captain Brown returned to the Campbell's on 12 July, he couldn't find *Antarctic*. He then sailed on to the Auckland Islands, locating Kristensen's ship on 18 July.

Kristensen had dispatched a letter with Captain Brown, which was duly posted at the time the telegram was sent. In Melbourne Bull received the letter many days after the telegram. The letter, while requesting coal and an anchor, had none of the urgency suggested in the telegram. Bull, though, had already acted on receipt of the telegram. Had Bull been aware that the situation was not as dire or immediate as the telegram suggested, arrangements could have been made to resupply *Antarctic* at lower cost. This muddle of communications proved another wedge between captain and manager.

Kristensen for his part was

> very much annoyed at a letter he received from his Melbourne agents [Bull] reporting that until Mr Hatch's vessel [*Gratitude*] had arrived they had received no intelligence whatever of his whereabouts, but a report from New Zealand that he had insulted the captain of the Government SS *Hinemoa*.[24]

Bull blamed Kristensen for the failure of this winter voyage and in his turn Kristensen didn't want advice from a man 'who knows little about whaling, either in Southern or any waters'.[25]

The return of *Antarctic* to Melbourne on 21 August 1894 was greeted by a melancholy Henrik Bull.

> Now our vessel steams in bearing signs of defeat and failure in her patched-up mast and generally crippled appearance, every heart oppressed with sullen gloom …[26]

Enthusiasm for the expedition amongst Melburnians was not diminished though. The Geographical Society loaned Bull charts and books, offered instruments, and were keen to place a scientist on board. AEC member John James Wild visited Bull with a collection of sketches and charts he had made of the Kerguelen Islands during the *Challenger* expedition.

After years of promise and disappointment, the AEC were keen to have an Australian scientist accompany *Antarctic* on the southern voyage. Foyn had suggested several times he might take some scientists with the expedition in exchange for a subsidy. Griffiths referred to the possibly of sending a scientist with the voyage at the meeting of the RSV on 16 November 1893.

> Efforts should be made to secure a passage for a scientific observer, whose work need not impede the work of the voyage while it should be of greatest scientific value.[27]

At the RSV Council meeting of 6 September 1894, the matter had still not been resolved. Griffiths had suggested that the physicist and RSV Honorary Secretary, E.F.J. Love (1861–1929) might go, but Love declined. The society undertook to set up a small committee, but there was very little time. In the preceding year they had not found a scientist suitable and willing to join the expedition so it was unlikely to be achieved in the final few weeks. One view was that 'The Melbourne scientists thought it too rough on board Antarctic, and preferred to remain on shore'.[28]

There were, though, other well qualified men keen to accompany the voyage. William Speirs Bruce (1867–1921), who had previously accompanied Dundee whalers to the Antarctic, and would later lead the Scottish National Antarctic Expedition, received Foyn's permission to join the voyage, as did Eivind Astrup (1871–1895). Astrup, despite his youth, was famous in his native Norway for explorations in Greenland where he had travelled with Robert Peary. Neither man was able to reach Melbourne in time to join the expedition. Eivind Astrup, only 25 years old, died the following year in an apparent suicide near Hjerkinn, Norway. Bull subsequently lamented the limited scientific results 'through the deplorable failure of Mr Bruce to reach us before our start from Melbourne'.[29]

Finding additional space to accommodate scientists on the voyage was a problem. Bull claimed: 'It is true that we had intended to build an extra cabin for the explorers above referred to, and for the colonial men of science who at one time contemplated joining us.'[30] The ship's captain Kristensen, in a letter to *The Times* of London, stated:

> ... there was at one time under consideration the possibility of taking with us two scientific men under the auspices of the Geographical Society in Melbourne. These negotiations stranded on several reasons – first, the cabin on board had to be altogether altered to make sufficient room; secondly, there was not sufficient time left them for their preparations.[31]

The inability of either Bruce or Astrup to get to Melbourne in time, and the failure of the AEC to propose a qualified and willing scientist to accompany the expedition, left the way open for another Norwegian, Carsten Egeberg Borchgrevink.

Borchgrevink had been living in Australia over the previous six years. He had participated in land surveys in outback Queensland and had taught in New South Wales probably at Coerwull Academy, Bowenfels near Lithgow NSW, and at St Andrew's College, Sydney. He told Bull that he had been a student at Christiana University, he later claimed to be a friend of Nansen while attending Gjertsen College.

Borchgrevink received some local fame in July 1890 when he and Edwin Villiers-Brown climbed Mt Lindesay in the McPherson Range, Southern Queensland. They claimed it to be the first ascent by Europeans, but it turned out that a confirmed ascent occurred in 1872, and there were several other probable ascents before then.

Bull knew of Borchgrevink's family and took him on over the objections of Captain Kristensen. He was signed on, in fact, as a 'generally useful hand'[32] with an understanding, with Bull at least, that he could devote his spare time to scientific work. When *Antarctic* docked in Hobart on the voyage south, Bull introduced him as the expert scientist of the voyage. Borchgrevink's background remains obscure. He appears desperately ambitious, with an ability to alienate colleagues. But the appointment, despite his lack of any genuine scientific training, led directly to the first over-wintering on the Antarctic continent.

After the disappointing sale of the seal skins, and the unsuccessful winter voyage, coupled with the worsening relations between Manager Bull and Captain Kristensen, one further ill portent occurred a month prior to sailing. Crewman Frederick Andersen, returning to the ship late on Monday 27 August 1894, was drowned in the Yarra River. An inquest found it to be accidental death. On 26 September 1894 *Antarctic* left Melbourne on their southern journey.

Bull allowed himself a moment of optimism. 'Shall we meet the schools and shoals of Right whales described by him, and return with a full cargo and the just elation of the successful pioneer?'[33] A number of the original Norwegian crew had left the ship and the crew now included Danes, Swedes, Poles and Englishmen with the remnants of the Norwegian crew. In Hobart the ship was received with great interest and locals were invited aboard. Bull stated that

'When the vessel gets to a town of any importance the men "clear"'.[34] In fact two thirds of the crew that signed on in Norway had since left the ship and been replaced. Bull went on to spruik the potential of whaling.

They sighted the Campbell Islands on 25 October, to find that the sealing season ended on 1 November. They managed a paltry haul of about ten seals over the next few days, but also lost one of the ship's boats which was smashed against rocks. Fortunately, the three crewmen escaped drowning.

On 7 November 1894, more ill fortune attended the voyage when the propeller was damaged. The engineer confided to Bull that he had been concerned about the propeller since the grounding on the winter trip to the Campbell Islands. Kristensen had dismissed his concern. Now, facing the possibility of having to turn back for repairs, Bull had more reason to doubt his captain. Kristensen thought the problem serious, but was loathe to turn back:

> Not to have use of the propeller was a very serious matter for us – its value in the pack-ice is easily understood. Certainly we had sails to depend on, and my own mind was to continue southward as well as we could without the aid of the engine, but finding the majority against me, the other alternative, a return to the nearest city for repairs was decided on.[35]

With the latest setback morale on the ship was poor. On leaving Melbourne Bull had described the crew as a 'really fine set of men, the majority entering thoroughly into the spirit of the venture',[36] two months later, it was much different. Bull now felt a 'sullen and ill-boding spirit' among the crew and didn't believe 'that a single contented or happy being is found on board'.[37]

They arrived at Port Chalmers (NZ) on 18 November.[38] Two sailors swam to shore that night. A further 6 sailors and the steward also refused to head south again. Regarding these desertions Kristensen wryly observed: 'I believe the icebergs and the cold weather had so much satisfied them that they did not care for another trip'.[39] The ship sailed as quickly as possible to avoid losing any more crew. They made a brief stop at Stewart Island to engage four more men to help cover the desertions and proceeded south again. In the early hours of 3 December 1894, they sighted two icebergs.

As they encountered more ice floes they sighted and took a number of seals. Bull, while he hoped to make his fortune on the cruise, found the seal hunt as ugly as he had at the Kerguelen's:

The sealing in Antarctic waters offers no more excitement to the sportsman than at Kerguelen; the seals on approach are either found in a state of peaceful slumber, or look on with mild curiosity as the rifle is levelled. The killing is therefore particularly repugnant even to the hardened sealer.[40]

On 14 December Young Island, one of the Balleny group, was sighted.[41] They crossed the Antarctic Circle on Christmas Day, and on Boxing Day were able to vary their monotonous diet with the flesh of a small Mincke whale they had caught. On 27 December Augustus Johannessen, the chief engineer, was badly injured when his leg was smashed by an iron bar used to adjust the wings of the propeller. The unfortunate Mr Johannessen received rudimentary treatment from the second officer. The leg was set as best they could manage, and he spent 7 weeks bed bound below decks.

Their hopes of successfully catching whales remained unfulfilled and they had to be satisfied with killing small groups of unsuspecting seals, basking on ice floes. On 18 January a group including Captain Kristensen and Carsten Borchgrevink were able to make a landing on Possession Island, just off Cape Adare. It was here that Borchgrevink made his notable discovery of lichen growing. With fair weather and open water the ship then sailed easily to 74°10' South. The conditions beckoned them to sail further, but Kristensen was mindful of the commercial imperatives of the voyage, thus far not met, and with an element of reluctance the ship turned north once more.

They passed very close to Cape Adare, and at 1:00am on 24 January 1895, a boat was lowered and a party including Kristensen, Borchgrevink and Bull, rowed towards the beach. Amidst the disappointments of the voyage this was the notable, albeit incidental, achievement. They made the first recorded landing on the Antarctic mainland. Despite subsequent evidence coming to light many years later about some possible landings on the west of the continent, and landfalls in the vicinity of the Antarctic Peninsula, this landing was the first publicly recorded and confirmed. As such it had an immediate influence and was a catalyst for the race to terrestrial exploration.

The ever-ambitious Borchgrevink claimed vehemently to be the first ashore, but Captain Kristensen said he was at the bow of the boat and had the honour of the first to step ashore. Bull's droll opinion was that

> The sensation of being the first men who had set foot on the real Antarctic mainland was both strange and pleasurable, although Mr Foyn would no

doubt have preferred to exchange this pleasing sensation on our part for a Right whale even of small dimensions.[42]

In keeping with the expedition's record of ill-luck and misjudgement, the triumphant group, having just made the first recorded landing on the Antarctic continent, were almost lost on the relatively routine return to the ship. No-one on the ship noticed them returning, despite instructions to keep a keen lookout. 'We thus had the pleasure of seeing the ship working in towards the land in one direction, whilst we were compelled by ice to take the opposite one.'[43]

Captain Kristensen fastened the boat flag to a 14-foot pole in a desperate attempt to attract attention:

> Not till they heard our shouts close by did anybody notice us. It must indeed be said to that man's praise who had the lookout from the crow's nest, that he had proved himself very clever, because on the chief officer's question if he could see us, he had answered - 'Yes; now I can see them go into the boat.' Very likely it was penguins he had seen moving, because by that time we had left land long ago. Which end of the telescope he had out to his eye I never got to know, but he was candid enough to declare to me that he had never seen through a telescope before.[44]

The mood of the expedition was not lightened by this historic landing. Henrik Bull, a naturally gregarious man, considered himself a 'raconteur amongst philistines ... it is no insult to my good shipmates to confess that I never met a less humorous set of men in my life'.[45]

He took

> ... some credit to myself for having at rare intervals even conquered the whole of our glum company in the cabin and set them laughing heartily. At other times the atmosphere was beyond clearing; as you reel off a good story, grim or contemptuous silence chills you ... you end by leaving the company to their own melancholia, swearing that you will never cast pearls before Norwegian sailors again.[46]

Bull though, found some humour in his self-proclaimed skill as a raconteur, citing a story he told of a mix-up with some monkeys ordered as a gift by a ships' captain for a son's birthday. His telling was received in stony silence by his companions. He noted that

... this story has never been told by me without bringing down the house and its shipwreck in the cabin of the *Antarctic* constitutes, to my mind, a crime beyond forgiveness.[47]

Bull admitted that with this story

if your victim is at your mercy, say in an express train stopping nowhere for hours, or on board a vessel in the Arctic or Antarctic seas, the variations and expansions are without any other limit than your victim's patience, nay, even beyond the latter.[48]

By 2 February 1895, the ship emerged from the ice. On 5 February 1895, they sighted Young Island, one of the Balleny group, but fierce weather conditions made a landing impossible. As they approached southern Tasmania they sighted whales and finally they managed to capture a small specimen that took all night to land. Other whales were seen but by this stage 'every soul on board was sick of the expedition, and to a great extent of each other, and the vessel was therefore kept going towards good old Melbourne'.[49]

As a whaling enterprise, the voyage was an abject failure. The vast numbers of black or Right whales sighted by James Ross in the early 1840s were nowhere to be found, and the ship did not have the equipment to be able to take the many blue whales sighted. Bull thought that the indiscriminate plunder of Right whales over the previous fifty years meant that there were few left to migrate to the Ross Sea.

Antarctic entered Port Phillip Heads in Victoria on 11 March 1895 and docked in Hobson's Bay, Williamstown (Melbourne) the next day. Despite the disappointing commercial outcome, there was enormous interest in the voyage, particularly with regard to the landing on the Antarctic mainland. The major Melbourne newspapers all ran stories and the AEC and both Royal Societies organised major receptions. Foyn had died in late 1894 so was spared the news of the financial loss, as was Bull spared having to relay such news.

The initial newspaper reports focused on the poor commercial results. *The Age* headline was 'The Whaler Antarctic – a barren cruise'[50], while the equivalent in *The Argus* was 'An unsuccessful cruise'.[51] However the first reception, organised by the AEC with both Royal Societies and held at

Melbourne Town Hall on 19 March 1895, heralded a triumphant return. Both Borchgrevink and Bull addressed the meeting. In view of subsequent events, Borchgrevink delivered a modest speech, generous to his colleagues and self-deprecating regarding his own role. He made no claim at this time to have been the first ashore at Cape Adare, a point of unseemly contention a little later, and he described his own scientific work as 'extremely meagre', though also suggesting

> the hope that [this work] will form one of the stepping stones to push on a new expedition on merely scientific principles, and that we may see such an expedition started at an early date.[52]

Henrik Bull commenced his address by outlining the disappointment of the voyage:

> Our cruise in the Antarctic Sea is now completed, and, as you already know, we have, in many respects, been sorely disappointed, our hopes, or rather almost certainty at the start, to lay the foundation for a future big Antarctic trade, have been largely baffled. …. When I say that, in many respects, we have been sorely disappointed, I must explain that contrary to what we were led to believe from previous expeditions to the Antarctic Seas, we did not meet with one single Right whale, and as our enterprise was almost entirely based on the suppositions of finding this valuable kind of whale in great numbers and not being in any way prepared to tackle those large whales of the finned tribe that we actually did see in considerable numbers, it is easily explained that our expedition, financially, necessarily must prove a failure.[53]

Bull, though, was characteristically optimistic about the future commercial prospects of Antarctic expeditions.

> Notwithstanding the serious loss experienced by the *Antarctic*'s voyages, I do not consider the money misspent or the time wasted, and if Captain Foyn had been still amongst the living he might, and probably would, with his usual perseverance, have utilised the experiences now gained, and recouped his loss.[54]

He reiterated these views in a letter to *The Times* later in the year theorising that perhaps

> an error has been made by Sir James Ross in mistaking for Right whales the large finned variety known in Norway by the name of 'blue' whale, with

which kind the Antarctic seas abound ... Another explanation why none of the late expeditions have encountered the Right whales may be found in the fact that since Sir James Ross visited the Antarctic large numbers of these whales have been killed in the Southern hemisphere.

Bull was similarly optimistic about the viability of an Antarctic whaling industry with equipment suitable to capturing blue whales.

There is no doubt whatever that if we had been provided with a small steamer, as above referred to, we should have returned with a full ship of blue whale blubber from the Antarctic.[55]

He acknowledged that while Norwegian whalers were successful in hunting blue whales closer to home, any such industry would need to be based in Australia. Bull didn't ever give up his dream and both he and Borchgrevink were thinking ahead to new expeditions. In moving a vote of thanks Professor Kernot stated that he 'considered this an historical voyage as one little vessel had penetrated nearly as far south as Sir James Ross' large and well-equipped expedition'.[56]

Borchgrevink and Bull each wrote substantial illustrated accounts of the expedition in the weekly illustrated newspapers.[57]

It was a busy time for both men. On 2 April they attended a meeting of the Royal Geographical Society, where George Griffiths delivered a paper *Comments upon results of the Cruise of the Antarctic Whaler*.

At the meeting Professor Kernot gave full reign to hyperbole:

There were ... very few people in the history of the world who could say they were the first to place foot on a new continent. Now to follow, Captain Kristensen, Messrs Bull and Borchgrevink, the Columbus' of the South, 1895 repeated 1492, the last of the great continents ... In conclusion he again congratulated these gentlemen whose names would never be forgotten in history as the pioneers of the Antarctic.[58]

On 8 April, Borchgrevink attended a meeting of the Field Naturalists Club with Baron von Mueller. In his address Borchgrevink surmised that James Ross had mistaken finned whales for Right whales. He also disagreed with Ross regarding significant scars observed on many seals. Ross believed the scars were inflicted by fights amongst the seals. Borchgrevink stated that he had no doubt 'that a large animal, hitherto undiscovered, exists on the

Antarctic Continent' and was likely responsible for attacks on the seals. Borchgrevink went on to describe the birdlife. He finished by advising that he was going immediately to London to urge a land expedition of which he aimed to be part, citing his ability with the Norwegian snowshoe as being of great benefit.[59]

The next day an illustrated public lecture was held at the Athenaeum Theatre on 9 April 1895 again with both Bull and Borchgrevink speaking and the acting governor John Madden chairing the event.

Kristensen had been ordered to return the ship to Norway as soon as possible but Bull and Borchgrevink next went to Sydney where they delivered papers at Centenary Hall. Bull met several New South Wales politicians including the Premier George Reid. Despite much interest, 'no substantial support could be found in the Colonies for a new venture, and it became necessary to contemplate a canvass in Europe'.[60]

Chapter Fourteen

Borchgrevink's ambition

It was in Sydney that Bull and Borchgrevink had a dispute and went their separate ways. According to Bull the cause was 'the way in which he aggregated to himself the chief, if not the whole, credit and honour of the results of the expedition ...'[1] This proved to be not an isolated view.

Borchgrevink, for his part, was determined to make the most of his voyage on *Antarctic*. Uninvited, he set off to the International Geographical Congress (IGC) held in London in July 1895. The librarian of the Royal Geographical Society at the time was Hugh Robert Mill. He remembered Borchgrevink:

> a determined young man ... who had not previously offered a paper, insistently demanded a place in the programme ... No one liked Borchgrevink very much at that time, but he had a dynamic quality and a set purpose to get out again to the unknown South that struck some of us as boding well for exploration.[2]

Certainly, that was the case. Borchgrevink's dynamic determination enabled him to organise the first wintering on the Antarctic continent, but he was no great leader of men. His paper delivered to the IGC on 1 August 1895, was a modest account admitting that 'the scientific results of this expedition have been few'.[3] Neither the captain of the vessel nor the manager of the expedition is mentioned. But his paper received a positive response. In the discussion following its delivery, Admiral Erasmus Ommanney, a veteran of the Franklin search and such a key figure in British attempts to mount an Antarctic expedition, commented:

> I rejoice to have lived long enough to shake hands with the first man, as far as we know, who has set foot upon and come back safely from the great continent that exists near the South Pole.[4]

Adolphus Greely was another attendee at the IGC. Greely was a US army officer, and amongst a distinguished career he had led the harrowing US expedition to Lady Franklin Bay, Ellesmere Island during the first International Polar Year 1882–83. This expedition is mentioned in more detail previously. Suffice to say, his relief stores ship was crushed, another relief ship was blocked by ice. In October 1883 Greely led his team south hoping to rendezvous with the relief ships, or at least find stores that may have been left. Neither occurred and the expedition was forced to build a rough shelter on Pim Island and try and survive on meagre rations. When relief finally arrived in June 1884 only seven men of the original party of 25, had survived, with one of them dying on the return voyage. Greely knew the worst of Polar regions, yet Borchgrevink's modest landing on the Antarctic mainland resonated with him too.

> Among the hundreds of delegates and scores of speakers at the Sixth International Geographical Congress, held in London in July last, there were three men whose appearance and utterances created unusual interest. These men – Slatin Pasha, Borchgrevink, and Andrée – may be said to be representative of the past, the present, and the future.[5]

The Antarctic was the predominant theme of the Congress. Borchgrevink's

> appearance before the congress was in the nature of a surprise, and a hum of appreciative expectation filled the great Institute Hall when his presence was announced … Whether Borchgrevink will return to the Antarctic regions or not, there is no doubt that his experiences have greatly stimulated interest in this work.

While Greely found Borchgrevink to have a 'modest mien …' and 'an impersonal and retiring disposition'[6] a rather different side of Borchgrevink's personality revealed itself shortly after in a shrill exchange of correspondence with former shipmates in *The Times*.

The voyage of *Antarctic* had been tense. Kristensen seems not to have had good relations with either Bull or Borchgrevink, and the latter two, while friendly enough on the voyage, fell out in Australia. Simmering tension between Borchgrevink and Kristensen boiled over on the minor point of who stepped ashore first at Cape Adare. A third 'claimant' for the honour was Alexander von Tunzelman, a Stewart Islander, who 'quietly maintained to his dying day that he was actually first ashore'.[7] However, Kristensen did not include him in his list of the eight men who made the landing.

In the paper he delivered in March 1895 in Melbourne, Borchgrevink merely recorded 'on the 23rd we were again at Cape Adare, and successfully effected a landing, being the first human creatures who ever put foot on the mainland'.[8] According to Bull, it was actually the early hours of 24 January.[9] In his IGC paper, Borchgrevink again records the landing without indicating who was first from the boat. In Kristensen's account, dated 19 May 1895, he claimed 'I was sitting in the boat, and jumped ashore as the boat struck, saying "I have then the honour of being the first man who ever put foot on South Victoria Land"'.[10]

There followed a rather childish exchange of correspondence in the pages of *The Times*. On 6 September 1895, Borchgrevink, in the afterglow of his successful IGC appearance, had a long article promoting his ideas on Antarctic exploration. On the same page appeared a letter from Kristensen expressing his anger at Borchgrevink's paper to the IGC. Given that the paper seems reasonably inoffensive, Kristensen's reaction probably reflects the long-standing problems between the two men. Kristensen also suspected that Borchgrevink had used his journals without acknowledgement. In this regard Kristensen thought him 'highly wanting both in tact and consideration'.[11] Again such a view of Borchgrevink seemed commonly held by those who had an association with him.

The following day an irate letter from Borchgrevink was published. In it were contained 7 'declarations' regarding Kristensen's poor treatment of him, signed by the first and second mate and a crewman. He further quotes from the Hobart *Mercury* article of October 1894 and threatens Kristensen with legal action 'if the captain persists in his insulting writings against me'.[12]

In his letter, Kristensen had mentioned that his journals were to be forwarded by the AEC to the IGC (and RGS) president Clements Markham. Markham responded advising that he had received the journal and accompanying charts, but that they had not arrived until after the conclusion of the congress. He went on to praise Kristensen on his expedition.[13]

Clements Markham also wrote a journal article at this time praising the achievements of the voyage. He considered that the commercial loss 'was money well spent from a practical and scientific point of view'.[14] In the article Markham quoted Kristensen's account of the Cape Adare landing. This prompted another lengthy letter to *The Times* from Borchgrevink proclaiming 'I was the first man to put foot on the South Victoria Continent'.[15]

Later, he was quite adamant as to who was out of the boat first.

> I jumped over the side of the boat. I thus killed two birds with one stone, being the first man on shore, and relieving the boat of my weight, thus enabling her to approach land near enough to let the captain jump ashore dry-shod.[16]

He also claimed that Kristensen's account was substantially written by Reverend William Potter, the Honorary Secretary of the AEC. *The Times* then published a further letter, this time signed by the director of the whaling and sealing firm, Svend Foyn at Tønsberg. The letter may not have been written by Bull but it certainly is expressing his point of view, deploring the conflict between Kristensen and Borchgrevink and indicating that Bull's kindness to Borchgrevink was repaid 'in a very unkind manner'.[17]

In Australia, Reverend Potter was understandably appalled at Borchgrevink's accusations and wrote to *The Times* to refute them emphatically. His letter dated 21 November 1895 was published on 6 January 1896. This was followed by another letter from Potter quoting a resolution from the AEC meeting of 2 December 1895 affirming Potter's version.[18]

Borchgrevink would not desist and immediately wrote again to *The Times*. This time he chose to claim all the scientific work as his own, but Potter had not disputed that.[19]

This was an unedifying postscript to the voyage. Bull and Kristensen had not related well as Bull makes clear in his book. Bull, as manager of the voyage often gave advice, while Kristensen as captain, was not interested in interference from the man he nearly always referred to as the 'supercargo.' The exchange of letters indicates the level of antipathy between Borchgrevink and Kristensen, and while Borchgrevink got on well with Bull during the voyage they clearly had a major dispute in Sydney, and it became necessary to 'cut the painter'.[20]

For his part, Borchgrevink was not about to let the ill feeling subside. He and William Speirs Bruce had some subsequent discussion regarding a possible joint expedition. But, as Bruce was also having discussions with Bull, Borchgrevink wrote 'I see that you already have made arrangements with Mr H.J. Bull and regret therefore that we cannot co-operate'.[21]

Borchgrevink was determined to lead his own expedition back to Cape Adare and pursued financial backing for a return expedition to the Antarctic with utter single mindedness, promoting himself and his ambitions on both sides of the Atlantic.

In December 1895 *The Times* reported that 'a syndicate had been formed in London for the purpose of sending out an expedition to the Antarctic with a view to carrying on whaling and seal fishing'.

In keeping with Bull's theories it was proposed that 'two whaling vessels of 300 or 400 tons and … one or more of the smaller steamboats which are used by the Norwegians for the capture of the blue whale …'[22] This proposal had no association with Bull though, but Borchgrevink hoped to have a small scientific team taken out with the whaling ships and be landed at Cape Adare, to be collected by the whaling ships the following year.

In January 1896, *The Times* further reported that Mr T. Gilbert Bowick, chairman of the expedition's executive committee, was seeking subscriptions to fund Borchgrevink's party which was expected to reach the Antarctic in November 1896 with primarily scientific goals.[23] The commercial enterprise claimed to have access to £100,000 to underwrite the venture. It didn't go ahead and Borchgrevink expressed doubts as to the company's intentions. He had received £4,000 for assisting the company in getting the government concession to guano deposits on Cape Adare. While he complained that his name was omitted from the concession, the guano deposits were never commercially exploited (or viable), so the £4,000 payment was somewhat of a bonus.

In February 1896 Borchgrevink could be found in New York, as part of a lecture tour. Interviewed by the *New York Times* he confidently reiterated his aim to launch his expedition in 1896.[24] He received favourable, and not entirely accurate, press coverage in the United States.

A syndicated interview with journalist Frank Carpenter described Borchgrevink as the 'great Antarctic explorer'.[25] In another article he became 'Professor' Borchgrevink.[26] The *Los Angeles Herald* referred to him as 'one of Dr Nansen's most intimate friends, an associate and confidant in all his plans for polar explorations'.[27] There is no evidence of a close friendship between the two, Nansen was stuck in the Arctic at that time in his audacious bid to float with the ice to the North Pole so was removed from any opportunity to contradict Borchgrevink. Roland Huntford, in his biography of Nansen, states that Borchgrevink had asked Nansen for help, 'but Nansen, who unfairly disparaged him as a fraud, for some reason declined to give it'.[28]

While journalistic hyperbole could account for some of the exaggeration in reporting of Borchgrevink's achievements and qualifications, there is little doubt that Borchgrevink considerably inflated his own reputation.

In mid-January 1897 Borchgrevink arrived in Adelaide from London, travelling across Australia, lecturing and trying to attract funds for his proposed expedition. While his lectures attracted interest, there were no funds forthcoming. He was better known in Australia and the reporting was not as fanciful. He sailed back to London from Melbourne via Adelaide at the end of June.[29]

Back in England he laid his scheme before the wealthy English publisher George Newnes. He had been introduced to Newnes in 1896. In 1898 Newnes agreed to fund Borchgrevink's British Antarctic Expedition. While Borchgrevink was a difficult man with an overbearing and grasping personality that alienated many, his determination was admirable and he obtained substantial financial backing to mount a scientific expedition to the Antarctic that would attempt the first overwintering on the continent, at a time when several more powerful and well-connected syndicates were struggling to realise their plans.

Chapter Fifteen

A minor journey

While Borchgrevink was preparing his expedition, Hans Gundersen, The Melbourne Consul for Sweden and Norway, so active in effecting communications between the AEC and Adolf Nordenskiöld, financed his own modest expedition to the sub-Antarctic. While minor it is not without interest.

Hans Gundersen was born in 1850, at sea, aboard his grandfather's barque *Minerva* under the command of his father. He grew up in Trondheim, Norway. Trained as a lawyer, as a young man he travelled widely and in 1879 he was appointed Vice-Consul for Sweden and Norway in Bordeaux, France. In February 1886 he was appointed Secretary to the Consulate-General in London. In September 1887 he was appointed consul in Victoria.

During the 1880s most of his savings were lost in shipping speculations. The remnant was lost in Victoria with the collapse of the Land Credit Bank, one of the early speculation scandals that ended the boom times and heralded the 1890s economic collapse of the Victorian economy.[1] Much like his countryman Henrik Bull, Gundersen remained undaunted by these setbacks. He set about investing in, and accompanying, a sealing voyage to the sub-Antarctic. It was less ambitious than Bull's expedition, but more successful. Gundersen owned a small brig (251 tons) *Edward*. The crew included Gundersen's cousin as second mate. Gundersen, together with Robert Hall, a noted naturalist, and Hugh Evans also travelled. The ship's master was John Steenson. Evans was a cousin of Charles Rowland who provided finance for the journey.

Later Evans joined Borchgrevink's first Antarctic over-wintering expedition and lived beyond his 100th year. Through his connections specimens taken by Robert Hall ended up with eccentric collector Lionel Rothschild at his Tring Museum.

Edward sailed from Melbourne on 27 October 1897, destined for the Kerguelen Islands. The trip successfully combined commerce and science in a way that Bull's more ambitious voyage didn't manage to do. Some 900 skins and 19,000 gallons of oil were brought back. *The Argus* newspaper wrote that from a financial standpoint the expedition was 'not gratifying as the value of the "take" … is barely expected to cover' costs.[2] Hugh Evans though declared 'the catch was excellent' and 'profitable to all concerned'.[3]

Robert Hall returned with a range of specimens and delivered papers on his findings to the Victorian Naturalist Society and also published the results of his observations in the British Ornithologists' Union journal, *Ibis*. Hall noted that he saw his work as supplementary to that of expeditions in 1874 to observe the Transit of Venus, and the *Challenger* expedition. Various nations had sent ships to various parts of the sub-Antarctic to observe the transit. British, German and US scientists all observed the Transit from Kerguelen. *Challenger* visited later in 1874.

Robert Hall was an adventurous ornithologist. In 1903, he travelled, with his assistant Ernie Trebilcock, to Siberia where they collected 400 birds. They journeyed through the country between Vladivostok and Lake Baikal, and then north to the Arctic Ocean. They did pioneering work in the vast Lena River valley.

On the same journey the two men also travelled through Japan and Korea collecting birds and sold many bird skins to Rothschild's natural history museum at Tring. The Korean specimens, gathered in the Wonsan area in what is now North Korea, have remained of particular interest because of the ongoing paucity of research and difficulty of access in that region.

Baron Rothschild suffered severe financial setbacks in the mid-1930s and sold most of his vast bird collection to the American Natural History Museum where Hall's specimens are now located.

Chapter Sixteen

The First Overwintering

By the time the modest sealing expedition of the *Edward* returned to Melbourne, Borchgrevink was preparing to lead the first expedition aimed at overwintering on the continent. The powerful RGS president Clements Markham, had, with Erasmus Ommanney and various other influential gentlemen, been lobbying for a British expedition. So it was much to his chagrin that the brash Norwegian, Borchgrevink, succeeded in launching the first expedition to overwinter on the Antarctic continent.

While Borchgrevink was preparing his expedition, another a multinational expedition under a Belgian flag and a Belgian commander, Adrian de Gerlache, was setting forth. The expedition contained two men, Roald Amundsen and Frederick Cook, who would become famous as explorers for very different reasons.[1] *Belgica* became beset by ice and was stranded for an Antarctic winter. This was not a planned overwintering and was on a ship in sea ice, not a settlement on the continent.

With backing from English publishing magnate George Newnes, Borchgrevink's Antarctic ambitions were able to become a reality. His British Antarctic Expedition used a Norwegian sealing ship, *Pollux*, refitted and appropriately renamed *Southern Cross*. The crew were Norwegian, the Captain was Bernhard Jensen, who had been second mate on *Antarctic*. The scientific staff were mixed. William Colbeck, an English Royal Navy Reservist, was taken as magnetic observer. Nicolai Hanson was a young Norwegian zoologist, very highly regarded in his field. Hugh Evans, recently returned from Gundersen's sub-Antarctic sealing venture, where he had worked closely with ornithologist Robert Hall, was appointed assistant zoologist. Physicist Louis Bernacchi grew up in Tasmania and had most recently worked at the Melbourne's astronomical observatory. He volunteered successfully for the *Belgica* expedition. It was planned that *Belgica* would sail from the Antarctic to winter in Melbourne, where Bernacchi would join the expedition for a second Antarctic season. *Belgica*, though, became trapped in ice in the Bellingshausen Sea south of Peter 1 Island, not escaping until the following summer, and consequently didn't reach Melbourne. Frustrated at this lost opportunity, the ever adventurous Bernacchi jumped at the chance to join Borchgrevink's expedition. Herlof Kløvstad, a Norwegian, was the expedition doctor. Anton Fougner, another Norwegian, was taken on as a general scientific assistant. His added qualifications were that he was an experienced sailor and experienced in snow. Interestingly, Borchgrevink also took two Sami (then known as Laplanders) Ole Must and Persen Savio.

Borchgrevink had displayed indomitable determination in successfully pursuing funds for the expedition, particularly in competition with the powerful men in England attempting to fund a national expedition at that time. Borchgrevink's ability to manage the logistics of such an undertaking is also impressive. He was a difficult man though. He quarrelled easily, had a keen sense of injustice if it affected himself and was prone to self-aggrandisement. He had no leadership experience and had not been trained as a leader in either the army or the navy. His claims to scientific knowledge seemed spurious to the expeditioners in the scientific team. The conditions of the Antarctic winter would test the most charismatic leader and Borchgrevink was far from that.

The expedition embarked from St Katharine's dock on the Thames, on 22 August 1898. They docked at Madeira and then St. Vincent in the Cape Verde Islands. Unfortunately several crew members became very ill from water drawn from the wells at St. Vincent. Nicolai Hanson was the worst affected, and it is likely that this illness was the catalyst for his untimely demise less than a year later.

On 28 November 1898 they reached Hobart receiving an enthusiastic welcome and warm hospitality during their stay there. Bernacchi, Borchgrevink and Klövstad made a quick trip to Melbourne and on 9 December 1898, attending another reception there, under the auspices of the RGSA (Vic). They sailed from Hobart on 17 December 1898. They had a difficult time penetrating the pack ice and finally landed at Cape Adare on 17 February 1899, five and a half months after they had set sail from London. Unloading the stores proved challenging due to the ferocious weather. A few days after that first landing 7 men were stranded on shore in a storm. Fortunately, the two Sami had their tent. Men and dogs piled in, thankful for such uncomfortable warmth. The two prefabricated huts were erected. These 5 x 5 metre huts were very cleverly designed.

> Numbered 160 x 85mm interlocking boards of 40–50 year old Norway spruce (picea abies) had steel rods inserted vertically through them to make them rigid.[2]

Over a century after they were erected, utterly exposed to the worst winds and storms the Antarctic can summon, they still stand.

Southern Cross set sail for New Zealand on 1 March 1899, leaving ten men to begin the first overwintering on the continent. This expedition was a leap into the unknown. The men were utterly marooned, with no recourse if their huts failed to endure the unknown extremes of an Antarctic winter, and utterly reliant on the return of their ship the following year. Being part of the shore party required an adventurous spirit and impressive courage. Under an inexperienced and abrasive leader, stranded on a particularly exposed beach, enclosed by cliffs that severely hampered any exploration, it proved to be a difficult year.

Relations between Borchgrevink and his crew quickly deteriorated. As the ice set in Robertson's Bay, Borchgrevink determined to explore their surroundings. He took Fougner, Savio and Bernacchi, and a dog team. It soon became apparent that the ice was dangerously thin. They found a small niche beneath the forbidding cliffs where they could pitch a tent. In his diary entries Bernacchi refers to Borchgrevink as 'the individual' and is very critical of the leader's behaviour. During the night the men scrambled from their tent as waves crashed into their camp. According to Bernacchi, Borchgrevink fled to higher ground, leaving it to the others to save the tent, sleds and dogs. Bernacchi thought him a 'thoroughly incompetent and a miserable coward', who sought his own safety, provided no leadership and left everything to be done by others. 'His prime objective was his own personal safety.'[3]

Fougner and Savio attempted to get back to the camp across the sea in a canvas canoe, but the sludgy ice halted them and they struggled back to Borchgrevink and Bernacchi. On seeing them Bernacchi exchanged harsh words with his leader about the need to hastily try and assist the other two men who they could see approaching.

> high words ensued and he [Borchgrevink] made use of some coarse ill-bred remarks – language of the gutter – and made some certain threats that I requested him to carry out. He abstained ...[4]

The men managed to struggle across the cliffs back to the huts. Most of their abandoned dog team, though worse for wear, found their own way back with only two losses.[5] The fractious exchange between Borchgrevink and Bernacchi, reflect the deterioration of Borchgrevink's relationship with his men. In such conditions, in complete isolation, there was bound to be friction. However, most of the tension appears not to be generally amongst the men, but between Borchgrevink and the men. He had none of the training and rigid Royal Navy structure that Scott could rely on, or the charisma and intuitive leadership of Shackleton, or the experience and efficiency of Amundsen, or the natural, austere authority of Mawson.

None of these leaders could have been accused of cowardice either, and they all had the luxury of having men with them who they knew and trusted. For the men of this British Antarctic Expedition it was going to be a long, difficult winter. At various other times in his diary Bernacchi refers to Borchgrevink as pusillanimous, a 'contemptible fool', a 'disreputable beggar', a 'numskull'.[6] Even allowing for the tension of disparate personalities being thrown together in such extreme circumstances, Bernacchi rarely criticises any other individuals except his leader.

Further to Bernacchi's general opinion of Borchgrevink, he was also scornful of Borchgrevink's understanding of basic scientific instruments. Again, there is little evidence of Borchgrevink having any significant scientific training, despite his own claims. According to Bernacchi one day Borchgrevink took it upon himself to bring down the thermograph. Unsurprisingly to Bernacchi, Borchgrevink's records were 'dirty valueless besmeared sheets' leaving a fortnight's gap in records that had previously been unbroken.[7]

In late August Colbeck was out on the ice and Borchgrevink was to take the meteorological readings. According to Bernacchi he made 'a frightful hash' of this task incorrectly recording the barometric readings, failing to set the maximum and minimum thermometers and missing hours of observations. The chronometer, which was keeping Greenwich time and had been assiduously maintained, was also forgotten by Borchgrevink and allowed to run down, despite careful instructions from Colbeck.[8] Hugh Evans related that 'Borchgrevink tried taxidermy, but the results looked like long necked wine bottles and were left at Cape Adare'.⁹

In the midst of the Antarctic darkness, Borchgrevink continued to alienate his men. In a famous incident he produced an edict, purportedly signed by 'Uchley Jones, Q.C., A Burreli Barrister, Geo. Newnes', which he read in Norwegian and then translated into English:

> That the following things would be considered mutiny: to oppose CEB [Carsten Egeberg Borchgrevink] or to induce others to do so, to speak ill of CEB, to ridicule Mr CEB or his work, to try and force CEB to alter contracts etc.

Bernacchi's view was that; 'My opinion that Borchgrevink is insane now confirmed. Really believe him to be insane.'[10] Later that day Borchgrevink handed Colbeck a letter advising him he was dismissed from the expedition. Nicolai Hanson's diary suggests this was an example of Borchgrevink's paranoia and suspicion that his men were out to undermine and replace him. The situation was awkwardly and unsatisfactorily settled a few weeks later with a stern discussion between the two men following a conciliatory gesture of sorts from Borchgrevink.

Through a range of actions Borchgrevink had managed to undermine his own leadership. His tenacity in successfully pursuing funds, and his organisational skills in mounting the expedition were admirable, but he was utterly unsuitable as a leader of men in these most alien and trying conditions.

The expedition, frustrated by their location, hemmed in by cliffs that thwarted substantial exploration, suffered several potentially disastrous incidents. On 25 May, Evans had to check the meteorological instruments during a ferocious storm and was almost lost. Blown down by the wind, with his lamp extinguished, he lost his bearings and was eventually found by Fougner and Ole Must. He suffered frostbite that later bothered him during his ranching days in Canada but was lucky to have been located.

In July Colbeck carelessly left a candle burning near his bunk. The wall caught fire and the room filled with thick smoke. Colbeck was able to extinguish the fire, but had the fire caught hold the result would have been disastrous. On 1 September 1899, several of the expeditioners almost suffocated from fumes from the coal fire still burning in the sealed room while they slept. Fortunately, one awoke and they were able to open the door.

On investigation they found the wind had blown down the stove flue and the fumes couldn't escape the room. Had they not been roused they would have died.

Zoologist Nicolai Hanson was an extremely popular member of the expedition. He had been one who had been very ill after leaving Cape Verde Islands. Initially he seemed to recover but his condition deteriorated during the winter. By early October the doctor held little hope. The zoologist had been anticipating the return of the Adelie penguins. On 14 October, the first Adelie penguins of the season appeared, and one was brought to the dying Hanson, who passed away 30 minutes later. Hanson was greatly respected and admired for his skills but also well liked for his constant, cheerful and unselfish personality. His death was a vast blow to an already demoralised expedition. Bernacchi, when told of Hanson's imminent demise, noted sadly that Hanson 'a man in the dawn of life, only married a few short months before leaving home, should be about to die, seemed a dreadful anomaly'.[11]

On 20 October Hanson was buried on the summit of Cape Adare, the first burial on the Antarctic continent, as lonely and remote a grave site imaginable.

As they approached the end of January 1900 the men were faced with the real prospect of being stranded for another year. Given the unhappiness of the party this would have been unendurable. On 28 January the sleeping men were awoken by the call of 'Post'. To the great relief of the party Captain Jensen had arrived. They sailed from Cape Adare on 2 February 1900. The ship penetrated the Ross Sea and made landings on Possession, Coulman and Ross islands. On 17 February the ship was able to land a small party led by Borchgrevink on low ice and they trekked south for several hours, reaching approximately 78° 50'S, surpassing James Ross' 60-year-old 'furthest south' record. On 19 February, another party, consisting of Bernacchi, Fougner, Evans and the ship's second engineer Julius Johanesen set off on another trek south. They too estimated that they had reached approximately 78° 50'S. They had travelled for 8 hours, the other party for 5. Which party went further south is impossible to say. Borchgrevink certainly claimed the record.

Southern Cross turned north again. Just in time as it turned out, with the ship having to crash through the ice that was rapidly forming. The ship struggled through severe weather and all were glad to sight the Auckland

Islands where the ship was able to harbour on 21 March. They stayed for a few days taking fresh water and cleaning up their battered vessel. On 31 March 1900 they arrived at Stewart Island (New Zealand). Borchgrevink crossed to Bluff on 1 April and sent a telegram to George Newnes to announce the party's return. Borchgrevink left for Hobart on 4 April aboard *Mokoia*, arriving in Hobart on 6 April.

Southern Cross reached Hobart on 18 April to a warm welcome. The local Royal Society organised a conversazione at the Town Hall on the same evening. Various of the Australian geographical and royal societies proffered hearty congratulations. Clements Markham, as Royal Geographical Society president, offered 'Warmest congratulations', while Professor Neilson of Christiana University telegrammed 'congratulations – Your success creating a sensation'. Borchgrevink's contract with George Newnes publications meant that he was 'in a rather unfortunate position ... wishing to say much but obliged to say little'.[12]

When Borchgrevink arrived in London (on 29 May 1900) he was to be disappointed by his reception. There was little interest in his achievement, and he was not feted as he had been at his appearance at the International Geographical Congress after the rather more modest achievements of the *Antarctic* expedition. Following that expedition, on the basis of a hurried landing at Cape Adare and finding vegetation on the Possession Islands, Borchgrevink had been enthusiastically lauded by polar veterans Erasmus Ommanney, Adolphus Greely and various others.

In 1900 Clements Markham had finally succeeded in organising a British National Antarctic Expedition and found it easy to ignore the return of a difficult man like Borchgrevink who had forestalled Markham's ambition for a Royal Navy / Royal Geographical Society expedition to lead the exploration of this final unconquered continent. Borchgrevink was invited to read a paper on the results of the expedition. An eminent group had gathered, including George Nares, Erasmus Ommanney, Francis McLintock, Henry Stanley and Scott Keltie. On conclusion he was 'loudly cheered as he resumed his seat'. However, no honours were forthcoming from the RGS and beyond that paper his expedition and achievements seemed quickly to be overlooked.[13]

In May 1902 Borchgrevink was a member of a party sent by the United States National Geographic Society (NGS) to report on volcanic eruptions in Martinique and St Vincent. They arrived on 21 May, immediately after a violent eruption of Mt Pelée (which had also erupted on 8 May). In July 1902 Borchgrevink published an account of the eruptions in a 'Martinique Supplement' to *Frank Leslie's Monthly*. This populist piece was to be followed by a report to the NGS. No such report appears to have been published and Borchgrevink's piece for *Frank Leslie's Monthly* drew sharp criticism in a letter to *Science* magazine from Edmund Otis Hovey.

Hovey was curator of geology at the American Museum of Natural History, author of numerous scientific papers, an authority on volcanoes and a man who notably studied the Mt Pelée eruption. He was unimpressed by Borchgrevink's article.

> There are certain features of the article ... which are so inaccurate or misleading that they should be corrected ... It seems to the writer that Mr Borchgrevink should explain such very inaccurate statements as those cited regarding four important illustrations accompanying his article. These corrections are particularly important at the present time as Mr Borchgrevink is now trying to raise funds for another expedition to the Antarctic regions and the public should be satisfied as to the scientific accuracy of one who desires to undertake such enterprises.[14]

Further controversy, mainly of his own making, awaited Borchgrevink. It related to the work of the late zoologist Nicolai Hanson. Hanson's specimens were handed to the Natural History Museum and a report on the collections of natural history made in the Antarctic regions during the voyage of the *Southern Cross* was published in 1902, by the British Museum, edited by Ray Lankester, director of the Natural History Department of the British Museum. The publication included contributions by various members of staff and other naturalists. The report, though, was severely compromised because so much of Nicolai Hanson's written work was missing. The peremptory conclusion of expeditioner Hugh Evans was that Borchgrevink was very jealous of Hanson's expertise and had lost or destroyed notebooks Hanson had passed to him just prior to his death. Evans claimed that Borchgrevink had destroyed some of his own notes.[15]

The report included extracts from the diary of Nicolai Hanson with a footnote from Richard Bowdler Sharpe, Assistant Keeper in the Department of Zoology at the British Museum.

> His notebooks were handed to the Commander of the Expedition by the dying naturalist on the 14th of October, 1899 (Bernacchi *t.c.* p. 185). Mr Borchgrevink has published some observations from one of these books in his 'Appendix' (pp. 320–4), and has handed to me one other book, which contains a mere list of the Procellariidae collected during the voyage out, and details are also to be found on labels attached to the specimens themselves.[16]

Borchgrevink was outraged at what he saw as aspersions cast against him. As he had with his battle with Kristensen after the *Antarctic* expedition regarding who actually set foot on Cape Adare first, he took his grievance to the pages of *The Times*, opening an acrimonious correspondence by taking aim at Bowdler Sharpe:

> The tendency of the volume, as diverted by Dr. Bowdler Sharpe, is disloyal and spiteful towards myself and a reference is made to some notes lost, insinuating that I should have kept them away purposely.[17]

Ray Lankester responded on behalf of his staff:

> The collections when received at the Museum were, to a considerable extent, in a state of neglect and disorder. Nicolai Hanson's notebooks, which would undoubtedly have assisted us in the working out of the collections, were not handed to us by Mr Borchgrevink. In my opinion it was proper to mention these facts in relation to the natural history results of the voyage ... I am not able to state whether Mr Borchgrevink admits having received these notebooks or not; whether he still retains possession of them or has lost them.[18]

Of course, Borchgrevink responded. Having been chided by Lankester for referring to Hanson 'an accomplished zoologist ... erroneously spoken of in Mr Borchgrevink's letter in your column as "my taxidermist"'.[19] Borchgrevink, in his second letter continues to refer to Hanson as 'my taxidermist'.[20]

Lankester responded 'I am sure that it will be obvious to those who have read Mr Borchgrevink's letters to you that he is a person with whom one would gladly have no dealings ...'[21] Remarkably this ill-tempered exchange continued right through to September. No doubt Borchgrevink was feeling underappreciated in England. Out of his depth when dealing with experienced scientists, having had his authority challenged on the expedition and his lack of scientific training exposed, he was undermining any goodwill he may have had by so aggressively nit-picking over the issue of the notebooks, which had clearly disappeared. Further this concerned the work of Nicolai Hanson, greatly liked by the other expeditioners, respected by colleagues in both Norway and England, and tragically dead so very young. Borchgrevink's overwrought sense of personal injustice, together with his lack of tact or sensitivity in dealing with anyone else, ill served him. His reception after the *Antarctic* expedition greatly outweighed his achievements. Here it was the opposite.

In fact, Borchgrevink applied to the Royal Society for support for a second expedition but was turned down and attempts to raise another expedition didn't get anywhere. His poorly received observation on volcanic activity in Martinique and St Vincent was his last significant involvement with scientific expeditions.

He returned to Norway and lived a quiet life, maintaining a great sense of injustice at the lack of regard afforded him. Such lack of regard was partly his own doing. He exaggerated his own qualifications and expertise, and, as expedition leader, he alienated his men. However, managing to successfully organise and undertake an expedition to complete the first overwintering on the Antarctic was a significant achievement, and his disappointment at receiving approbation for his failures and indifference rather than credit for his achievements, is understandable.

He was an accidental explorer, taken on at the last minute for *Antarctic*'s trip south, and then fortunate that the ship was close enough to Cape Adare to make a landing, and to arrive back just in time to attend the International Geographical Congress. There he was feted as the first man on the Antarctic continent, at a time when the focus of the world's geographical and scientific societies was firmly towards uncovering the mysteries of the Antarctic.

Borchgrevink's good fortune and determination in joining the *Antarctic*, and his relentless promotion of his achievements on the expedition, enabled him to raise funds to undertake his own expedition. Despite his shortcomings as a leader, Borchgrevink's *Southern Cross* expedition did provide some lessons, not always heeded by subsequent expeditions. He used skis and dogs. His huts withstood the ferocious climate, and they still do. His team included two Sami from Lapland who had great knowledge of survival in such extreme conditions. He proved that men could survive and adequately over winter on the Antarctic continent.

Underrated at the time, his work was finally recognised by the Royal Geographical Society in London with the award of the Patron's Medal in 1930. In presenting the medal, the President, Colonel Sir Charles Close, admitted that

> when the Southern Cross returned, this Society was engaged in fitting out Captain Scott to the same region, from which expedition much was expected, and the magnitude of the difficulties overcome by Mr Borchgrevink were underestimated. It was only after the work of Scott's Northern Party on the second expedition of 1912, and when that was discussed in the Reports of the Terra Nova expedition, recently completed, that we were able to realize the improbability that any explorer could do more in the Cape Adare district than Mr Borchgrevink had accomplished.[22]

The latter part of his life appears not to have been easy. In 1930 his wife Constance wrote to the Royal Geographical Society seeking some financial support in recognition of the achievements of his expedition. None was forthcoming.

Borchgrevink died in Oslo on 21 April 1934. Despite his frailties as a leader, he achieved one of the great firsts of geography and exploration, organising and leading the first overwintering on the Antarctic continent.

Chapter Seventeen

Henrik Johan Bull's later life

During the tumult of Borchgrevink's activities, Henrik Bull retained a burning desire to organise another expedition to the South. His ambitions remained rather more commercial than scientific.

In 1907 in a paper delivered by Bull to the RGSA (V), he referred to Borchgrevink as being permitted to join the Antarctic voyage and stated that it was 'a permission for which he on many occasions and in different ways has pressed his gratitude to both Captain Kristensen and myself'. Clearly such gratitude was not apparent in the immediate aftermath of the voyage but perhaps Borchgrevink became more gracious with age, or perhaps Bull was simply being kind.[1]

Despite the great Australian interest in the voyage of *Antarctic*, Bull was unable to obtain financial backers for another expedition. He returned to Europe and spent some time in London writing a book about the voyage. He stayed with his cousin whose English wife was a great help with the text. In 1896, *The cruise of the 'Antarctic' to the south polar regions* was published. A Norwegian edition followed in 1898. It is a very readable account and Bull's knowledge of English was sufficient to enable him, subsequently, to translate Eivind Astrup's *With Peary near the pole* (1898) from the original Norwegian. He worked as a shipping agent in Tønsberg, Norway, still trying to obtain finance for another expedition. He was in correspondence with Bruce regarding a possible expedition but had trouble gathering sufficient funds.

Perhaps time helped heal the rifts, for Bull at least. He again worked with Kristensen, managing *Hekla*, an Arctic sealer, which was captained by Kristensen. After losses in sealing the owners sold the ship and eventually it was sold again to William Speirs Bruce and renamed *Scotia* for his Scottish National Expedition (1902–04), overwintering on the South Orkney Islands.

When Bruce was planning his expedition the ever-adventurous Bull asked for a place on board. While he could not do 'hard work' he felt he might be some use 'with my pen and otherwise with the outfit of the vessel'.[2] This offer was not accepted by Bruce. In June 1903, Bull returned to Melbourne still hoping to launch further Antarctic endeavours. He was 'not a moneyed man' and 'had many hard turns' raising finance,[3] but finally, back in Norway, friends sold him the small ship *Cathrine* (127 tons) on very favourable terms.*

Nearing his 62nd birthday, Bull joined the ship as manager and again headed southward. The ship's captain was Anders Harboe-Ree, a young Norwegian who had also invested in the expedition. Leaving Norway on 23 August 1906 they anchored in American Bay, Crozet Islands, on 25 November 1906, after an uneventful voyage. After the difficulties with Kristensen on the *Antarctic* voyage, Bull was delighted to find his captain such a congenial companion and

> within a very short time we became fast friends. The days spent on board the Catherine (sic), in his company, I shall always look back upon with feelings of unmixed pleasure.[4]

Bull, though, so desperate for this venture to succeed, so attuned to his plans coming to naught, was 'terribly nervous' and this irritated the crew. 'No, even with all his many good sides Bull does not fit in on board a hunting vessel,' opined the captain.[5] Despite misgivings about Bull's suitability on such a tough and demanding expedition, and his desperation for success, the captain reciprocated Bull's friendship with 'my splendid old comrade whom I am also thanking herewith for everything between us, which has only been good and enjoyable'.[6]

While the Crozet Islands fur seal population had been utterly decimated in the previous century, the shores they viewed were crowded with elephant seals. They immediately proceeded with the ugly harvest. Once killed the animals were skinned, the blubber cut, transported to the ship and boiled down in burners in the ship's hold. The skins then were heavily salted. It was hard, gruesome work but finally Henrik Bull could see the success that had, for so many frustrating years, eluded him.

In the midst of the manager and captain's plans of future expeditions with larger ships and more crew and great profits, the weather turned. After

---

* Spelled variously as Cathrine (Lloyds and Headland) or Catherine (Bull).

two days of battling ferocious gales, the ship was thrown onto a reef and abandoned on 4 December. The small crew managed to land on Possession Island and watched from the shore as their little ship was smashed to pieces on the reef.

This was disastrous for Bull. Beside the very real possibility of the men being stranded for a long time, with an equally real prospect of not surviving, it also meant that his dreams of success were again dashed. He had worked

> fully eleven years to try and head southward again ... Either it must succeed or all hope of being able to get something together again at the age of sixty-two would be totally extinguished.[7]

After the wreck, having finally come so close to a success, Bull stood on the beach consumed by a bitterness 'the likes of which I have never felt in my life'. It was directed against 'my God and Maker, against Him who in all these years not only preserved my life so amazingly, but ... had also let me keep my character from my youth ...' Despite this he did feel some justification in holding God responsible.

> But still I could not, and still cannot, understand the Lord's meaning in letting me get so far with my plans only just to *show* me the riches I wished for so much. It was like saying to me, Look, but don't touch ...[8]

As the captain noted 'Poor fellow. For him it was the worst. All his plans and all his work were stranded on Crozet Islands.'[9]

Captain Harboe-Ree had been cool and calm amidst the tumult of the storm with the ship at any moment likely to be wrecked on the rocks. Quite prepared to go down with his vessel he now was planning an open boat journey to find help for his companions. On 11 January 1907, he and two crewmates set out in one of the ship's boats hoping to sail the 7,300 km to Australia. This was a fearless attempt, and one with a very uncertain outcome. After eight days and 1,000 km* they were fortunate to be spotted by a passing ship *De Ruyter*. Their rescuer Captain Tuitjer drily remarked to Captain Harboe-Ree:

> It was a madman's undertaking, that one of yours, to try and sail from the Crozets to Australia, and you would never have reached land in that boat.[10]

---

* Captain Harboe-Ree, in the Christmas House article estimates the distance at 720 statute miles.

Three weeks later Captain Harboe-Ree and his two shipmates arrived in Melbourne.

The remaining eleven men were picked up by the passenger liner *Turakina* and were delivered to Hobart where several men were able to arrange passage back to Europe on a Danish ship. The remaining men including Henrik Bull then crossed to Melbourne. Bull was welcomed by old friends and invited to recount his adventure to the RGSA (V) March meeting, which he cheerfully did.

Castaway on the desolate Possession Island beach in the Crozet group, Henrik Bull had conceded 'I realise that I still cannot abandon the thought of regaining yet my independence through hunting in the South'.[11]

After investing so much of his life on the dream of successful sealing and whaling in the Antarctic the loss of *Cathrine* was devastating. Bull had seen it as his last chance. 'Either it must succeed or all hope of being able to get something together at the age of sixty-two would be totally extinguished.'[12] Bull, though, was an optimist, and having escaped the grim castaway life in the sub-Antarctic he was already planning a new expedition.

His son Ole Olsen Bull, who had come to Melbourne in 1891 to help his father and try to encourage him to return to his home, had become a successful businessman, establishing O.O. Bull & Co in Christiana (Oslo) in 1898. It was a trading company ranging widely from luxury objects such as silk hats and gold watches, to hardware and shipping. Early in the new century a partner, Ole Johannes Storm, came in. The business became Storm, Bull and Co and moved into steel, iron and building materials. Still anxious to help his father and impressed by his unfailing faith in the business potential of the deep south, Ole's company sponsored Henrik Bull's next expedition.

This time the ship was *Solglimt*, a much larger vessel of 1810 tons. It had a crew of seventy and was managed by Storm, Bull and Company. It was to be captained by Anders Harboe-Ree with Bull accompanying the voyage.

At last Henrik Bull was managing a really substantial venture. There was even room for two scientists, Ola Raknes and Dr Svindal. The voyage left in early October 1907 and this time the trip was uneventful and successful, returning 700 tons of blubber, a yield that would have been greater but for poor weather.

Bull, then approaching 64 years, chose not to join *Solglimt* for a sealing expedition in the next year. His misfortune with his Antarctic ventures struck again. The ship, again under Captain Harboe-Ree, left Durban on the 5 October 1908 for Marion Island. In mid-October sailing in what charts showed to be deep water, several miles from the shore *Solglimt*

> .... shuddered violently and listed as she scraped over a pinnacle of rock. Water gushed in through the torn plates and Ree had time only to race for the landing place and ram his bows on to the steeply-sloping beach before his ship filled and settled on the bottom.[13]

Again, all crew made it to land and they were able to retrieve much food and provisions before the ship broke up. Again, Harboe-Ree began to prepare for an open boat voyage to Australia, this time a distance of over 6,000 km. Again, he was fortunate. Before he could set off two Nova Scotia sealers, *Agnes G. Donohue* and *Beatrice L. Corcom* arrived. The two ships shared the seventy stranded sailors, but still had to leave behind several of their own men to be collected on their return. *Agnes G. Donohue* arrived in Durban on 30 November 1908 and *Beatrice L. Corcom* four days later.

Even this latest misfortune did not deter Bull. Following the loss of *Solglimt*, Storm, Bull and Company had even more ambitious plans to establish a permanent whaling station in the Kerguelen Islands. The French government had granted a concession for development of commercial enterprises on the island to René and Henry Bossière. The two brothers hadn't been able to raise capital to undertake any enterprises. In 1908 Storm, Bull and Company proposed a whaling station with a percentage of the profits going to the Bossière.

An agreement was struck giving the Company whaling and sealing rights at Kerguelen for 22 years. Storm, Bull and Company, presumably to limit their liability in case of failure, then created another company, the Kerguelen Whaling Company (or Aktieselskabet Kerguelen), and sought investors for their scheme. The prospectus was speculative, claiming that the fur seal populations, driven to virtual extinction in the 19th century, had recovered to a point where sustainable hunting could yield a good profit. Sustainability had never been the cornerstone of either the sealing or whaling industry. As it happened the fur seal population on the Kerguelens turned out to be unfindable if indeed it had recovered at all. The prospectus also considered, with little evidence but much optimism, that whale numbers would be comparable with South Georgia and the South Shetlands.

Granted in their agreement, also, was the right to maintain cattle herds and sheep flocks. The Kerguelens, fittingly also known as Desolation Land, would demand great resilience from both the livestock and their keepers. In fact, the hopes of exploiting agriculture didn't extend far beyond releasing 22 Icelandic sheep on Long island. The sheep, left to their own devices, survived, reproduced and grew too wild to catch. The experiment was not further developed. The leaseholders of the Kerguelens, the Bossière brothers attempted a more ambitious farming program. In mid-1913 1150 surviving sheep of the 1600 loaded at the Falkland Islands, were deposited at the bleak Port Couvreux with three hapless shepherds. A year later only 200 had survived.

This Storm, Bull and Co enterprise was very ambitious. It was far more than just sending a ship down south to slaughter elephant seals, the company were setting up a small, utterly remote and self-sufficient sub-Antarctic factory colony with two new whale catchers and an impressively large shore station.

The Company transport ship, *Jeanne D'Arc*, left Tønsberg on 25 August 1908, with upward of 100 crew and their prefabricated town, together with various livestock, prompting newspapers to describe it as the Noah's Ark Expedition.[14] In Durban, 23 African labourers were recruited. The colonists arrived at their bleak and desolate destination on 29 October 1908.

Once at the Kerguelens a suitable location for their settlement was chosen in Royal Sound on the Presqu'ile Jeanne d'Arc peninsula and an immediate start was made to the buildings. By early 1909 the flensing platform and the cookery buildings and 130-foot pier were completed. The guano factory followed in July while the manager had to wait over a year, until November 1909, for his residence.

Henrik Bull accompanied the expedition as far as Durban from there he sailed to Melbourne arriving in January 1909. He had just received word from the master of *Jeanne d'Arc*, Captain Ring, who had returned to Durban, advising that the expedition had successfully disembarked and unloaded the equipment. Henrik Bull, confident of the success of the endeavour, was likely seeking additional antipodean investors to help fill the company float that had not been fully subscribed.

In late February 1909 he was in Auckland, New Zealand spruiking the potential of whaling stations on the Auckland and Campbell Island groups. This had proved spectacularly unsuccessful when attempted by Charles Enderby, and the 1894 sojourn for whaling during Bull's Antarctic expedition had been equally disastrous. Henrik Bull, though, not unreasonably, saw developments in technology as being a catalyst to success. He referred to Captain Kristensen sighting upward of 50 whales in the vicinity of New Zealand's sub-Antarctic possessions. 'The *Antarctic* was not the ship to tackle these whales; an up-to-date whaling steamer would have secured the better part of the fifty.'[15]

He flagged his intention 'to offer the people in New Zealand who care to venture, the opportunity to take up about half the shares in the company'.[16] Probably fortunately for any New Zealanders swayed by this, the company to exploit whaling in sub-Antarctic New Zealand didn't go ahead.

The Kerguelen Islands operations commenced in 1909. In the first year the oil yield from both elephant seals and whales was promising. For the next few years sealing remained successful but whaling proved progressively disappointing. The location of the whaling station and the location of the whales often meant many hours of towing to the processing works. The manager recommended the purchase of a towing vessel, a suggestion taken up by the Company directors, incurring another substantial expense.

Each year, though, the whale catch diminished. To try and balance the books the company entered negotiations with a Glasgow consortium finally gaining a licence to conduct whaling in Walfish (now Walvis) Bay, a British enclave within German South-West Africa (now Namibia). The 1912 whaling at Kerguelen was dismal with only 4 whales captured. In April 1912 their whale catchers *Eclair* and *Etoile*, the towing vessel *Espoir*, transport *Jeanne d'Arc* and *Regent* (on charter) decamped with crew and supplies to the hopefully more fruitful whaling grounds off German South West Africa.

Unfortunately, they immediately encountered a series of problems. The station was only partially built, typhoid broke out, and some of the workers went on strike. Whaling finally got underway in August 1912 but the business was failing to show a profit and the directors decided to sell their transport *Jeanne d'Arc* and use *Espoir* in that additional role.

Meanwhile in Europe the gathering jealousies and rivalries between nations descended towards a war of unimaginable horror and devastation.

In late September 1914, on the African coast, the whaling crews found themselves fleeing from advancing German troops with the majority of the oil barrels remaining behind. This was the final straw for the company. Whaling and sealing ceased for the duration of the war and in 1920 the company didn't have the capital required to recommence. The business was sold to a South African company. Thus ended Henrik Bull's dreams of a whaling and sealing empire in the deep south. His son Ole, who had been so loyal and had followed his father's advice in the sealing and whaling business, pre-deceased his father, dying, aged 58, in 1928.[17]

Henrik Bull died on 1 June 1930 having outlived many of his contemporaries. The younger Borchgrevink only survived him by 4 years, while Kristensen died in 1911. None of the original members of the AEC in Melbourne survived him, and two of the most prominent members, Baron von Mueller and Crawford Pasco, died before Borchgrevink set out on the Southern Cross expedition for its first winter on the Antarctic mainland. The Norwegian press reported Bull's 80th birthday and published obituaries on his death. An article was even published to mark the centenary of his birth. A ship named *H.J. Bull* ventured to the Antarctic in 1935–36, surveying for whales much as Bull himself had done 40 years previously. On his 80th birthday, Bull received the Order of Merit from the Norwegian Geographical Society. A rocky outcrop in the Possession Islands and a nunatak off the east coast of the Antarctic Peninsula bear his name.

Chapter Eighteen

Legacy of the voyage

The Antarctic explorations by the major European nations at the beginning of the twentieth century swamped much of what came before, and both Bull and the AEC are rarely remembered today. They were, however, important in the exploration of the Antarctic. When little was happening in England, the AEC in Melbourne was lobbying the imperial government and the Australian colonial governments. The Committee were in discussion with a range of Dundee and Norwegian whaling companies, seeking and disseminating information on whaling in the Antarctic. They were also in contact with two of the biggest names in polar exploration, Fridtjof Nansen and Adolf Nordenskiöld. There was much positive correspondence with Erasmus Ommanney, and even Clements Markham found their work to be encouraging. The committee was able to convince the government of the colony of Victoria to have the Agent General in London act tirelessly on their behalf, and to lobby the other Australian colonial governments. The work was covered regularly in the Victorian press and also in the newspapers in the other Australian colonies and in England.

Finally, the AEC failed to achieve the goal of being a partner in an Antarctic expedition. As with much of history there are many 'what ifs', but despite hard work over many years, they were never able to convince the government of Victoria to commit reasonable funds to such an expedition. While there were significant private subscriptions, the most substantial from Sir Thomas Elder, who had offered £5,000, carried with it untenable conditions. In the end the AEC received vicarious reward from Bull's expedition, but even then, the Royal Societies had been unable to convince a local scientist to accompany the voyage and the ship *Antarctic* was not really suited to transporting additional people.

Had the Lords of Treasury accepted advice from the British Royal Societies and the Colonial Office rather than the Board of Trade, and contributed the paltry amount of £5,000, it would have surely ensured a commitment from the Australian colonies, and more certain and generous private contributions. With such funding a preliminary scientific / commercial expedition would have gone ahead, perhaps led by Allen Young. Similarly had the conditions required by Elder been more flexible then the proposed Nordenskiöld expedition, out of Melbourne with several Australian scientists, may have gone ahead.

Even the chance of being immortalised through Antarctic place names has been denied the Antarctic Exploration Committee. Kristensen named various points on his voyage for key members of the Committee. There was Baron von Mueller Cape and Potter Peninsula, in the Possession Islands, Kernot Peak and Griffiths Peak on Ross Island (probably Mt's Erebus and Terror), Pasco Island, (one of the Lyall islands). For Henrik Bull he named some rocks, a probably intentionally paltry recognition of the expedition manager. Bull's view was that 'as we followed another explorer's track and made no original discoveries of land, we abstained from any extensive naming of capes, islands etc. ...' Bull then suggests that Kristensen added all the names back in Melbourne 'thousands of miles from the infant to be christened' and felt those names 'have little right to appear on any chart'.[1] Most of them don't, although the name Bull Rocks survives. Kristensen's choice of names does illustrate the close association felt between the AEC and this expedition and the warm support and hospitality provided by the AEC.

Finally, the AEC ended with a whimper rather than a bang. One of its last acts was a donation of £250 in July 1899 to Scott's *Discovery* expedition.

Bull's expedition is now a footnote in the terrestrial exploration of the Antarctic. Even the disputed first step on the continent has been rendered of less relevance as evidence emerges concerning previous landings. At the time, however, it was considered very important and was the first confirmation of a landing on Antarctica. Kristensen, involved in disagreements with Bull during the voyage, and with Borchgrevink afterwards, also achieved more than he is generally credited. As Tonnesson and Johnsen noted:

> Public opinion merely noted that he had come back with his holds empty, without realising that he had carried out one of the major feats in the history of seamanship. Practically without hitch he had sailed a small vessel

of 226 gross tons across some of the world's most hostile seas, through pack ice and unfamiliar waters, without charts – he made them himself – and had opened the Antarctic continent for exploration.[2]

Even their ship *Antarctic* achieved pioneering feats in both north and south Polar Regions. Following Bull's expedition the ship ventured north transporting Dr A.G. Northorst's Swedish East Greenland Expedition in 1899. This expedition, as the name suggests, was investigating the barely known eastern coast of Greenland. The expedition mapped the area and did useful zoological, geological and botanic work. Part of their aim was to search for both Andrée and Sverdrup. As mentioned previously Swede Salomon Andrée and two companions set off on 11 July 1897 aiming, rather recklessly, to reach the North Pole by hot air balloon. Many expeditions of the time kept an eye out for them, but they were not seen alive again. Their remains were found on White Island in August 1930. Norwegian Otto Sverdrup was part of Nansen's 1888 expedition across Greenland. In 1893 he commanded *Fram* for Nansen's audacious attempt to float to the North Pole. After Nansen and Hjalmar Johnsen left the ship to attempt (unsuccessfully) to sled to the Pole, Sverdrup managed to break free after three years trapped in the ice and returned the ship and crew safely to Norway. From 1897 to 1902 Sverdrup commanded several expeditions mapping the area around Greenland. Despite various periods trapped in ice or overwintering on Ellesmere Island his expeditions were all successfully completed. Needless to say, Northorst's expedition didn't come upon either Andrée or Sverdrup, however they achieved their scientific aims.

Northorst sold *Antarctic* to G.C. Amdrup for the Danish East Greenland Expedition of 1900. This expedition included 5 naturalists and an artist. A group led by Amdrup landed at Cape Dalton where they set up a base and then explored the coast in an 18-foot boat. They sailed 800 kilometres to Tasiusak. There his party rendezvoused with *Antarctic*, returning to Copenhagen on 4 October 1900.

Antarctic was then purchased by Otto Nordenskiöld for his Swedish South Polar Expedition to the Weddell Sea and the Antarctic Peninsula. Unfortunately, she did not finally emerge from the Weddell Sea, having been crushed by ice in February 1903 when returning to collect the Swedish scientific party led by Otto Nordenskiöld.

Bull's hopes for Antarctic whaling were eventually realised, although not by him.

In the new century the Australian Antarctic Exploration Committee, Henrik Bull, and even Borchgrevink's first overwintering, were quickly overshadowed as the major European countries launched three simultaneous expeditions and the so called Heroic Age of Antarctic exploration began.

Largely forgotten, Henrik Bull and the Antarctic Exploration Committee are not major names in Antarctic history, but they are important and worthy of our attention.

Afterword

By the time Borchgrevink's expedition returned, the British were preoccupied with preparations for their National Antarctic Expedition. Clements Markham hadn't much liked Borchgrevink and was incensed that he had been able to arrange financial backing and raise an expedition in a few years, when Markham and his colleagues had been labouring unsuccessfully for decades.

The British National Antarctic Expedition left in 1901 as did two other national expeditions, the German South Polar Expedition and the Swedish South Polar Expedition. The British expedition was led by Robert Falcon Scott and included Ernest Shackleton. The expedition ship, *Discovery* was iced in and used as accommodation, a relief supply ship *Morning* was sent after the first year and then again in the second year accompanied by *Terra Nova*.

There were fears *Discovery* might have to be abandoned but in February 1904 the ship was able to break free of the ice. At the beginning of November 1902 Scott, Shackleton and Edward Wilson had made a first attempt on the South Pole and struggled towards 82° 17' before turning back.[1] The three men were in poor shape on their return with Shackleton suffering most and enduring the indignity of having to travel on a sledge at times. Worse was to follow when Scott sent him back to England on the relief ship *Morning* in early 1903 due to his ill health. This established a lasting enmity between these two contrasting personalities. The expedition had left England in August 1901 and finally returned in September 1904.

The German South Polar Expedition set sail from Kiel in August 1901. Their ship *Gauss* was caught fast in the ice pack in February 1902. Despite this, under the leadership of Erich von Drygalski, the expedition carried out an extensive scientific program and sent sledging teams across the frozen sea to explore the coast.

The Swedish expedition, under (Nils) Otto Nordenskiöld (Adolf's nephew), provided one of the most exciting stories of Antarctic exploration. The expedition, aboard Henrik Bull's old ship *Antarctic*, sailed to the Antarctic

Peninsula. The small scientific party (six men) landed at Snow Hill Island in February 1902. A prefabricated hut was erected, and the men settled to a year of exploration and observation. The ship returned to collect them the following summer but encountered impenetrable ice conditions. With the ship stuck fast and with no hope of reaching the scientists on Snow Hill Island, three of the crew cheerfully volunteered to cross the ice to advise the scientists. Relying on a speculative map drawn by James Ross 60 years previously, the three encountered open water and themselves were stranded without supplies or shelter. With great resourcefulness they built a rudimentary stone hut and killed enough penguins to provide food for the winter.

The ship *Antarctic* was crushed in the icepack and the crew (including the ship's cat), struggled across the ice to Paulet Island where they were able to construct a stone hut. One man died of a heart condition, but all other members of the three parties survived the winter. Miraculously they all met on the ice in November 1903 and were rescued by the Argentinian ship *Uruguay*.

These three expeditions heralded the commencement of the famous and much investigated Heroic era of Antarctic exploration when expeditions from many nations began terrestrial exploration of the continent. In 1902 the Scottish National Expedition, under William Speirs Bruce, set sail. Bruce had accompanied the Dundee whaling fleet to the Antarctic in 1892–93 and had been interested in joining Bull's expedition. His expedition wintered at the South Orkneys and explored mainland Antarctica due south of there. Bruce named it Coats Land after two of his financial backers.

Intrepid Frenchman Jean-Baptiste Charcot led an exploration of the west coast of the Antarctic Peninsula, sailing from France in August 1903. They wintered on Wandel Island (now officially Booth Island), finally leaving the Antarctic in February 1905. In 1908 Charcot led another expedition in a new purpose built ship *Pourquoi-Pas?* continuing his exploration of the western side of the Antarctic Peninsula. He finally returned to France in June 1910. He didn't go back to the Antarctic but he continued his love affair with the sea and with his ship. In September 1936 Charcot went down with his ship when *Pourquoi-Pas?* sank off Iceland.

In 1907 Shackleton was able to raise his own expedition and managed to get within 100 miles of the South Pole. On the journey he pioneered the

Beardmore Glacier route through the Antarctic mountains to the polar ice cap. His expedition included an ascent of Mount Erebus and a harsh trek to the South Magnetic Pole. Before the expedition Robert Scott rather unreasonably demanded that Shackleton not use Ross Island as a base. However, after exploring the Ross Sea coast Shackleton was unable to find a suitable alternative and erected his base on Ross Island. Scott's supporters judged this as poor form and it exacerbated the existing tension between the two men.

On turning back with the Pole within striking distance, Shackleton phlegmatically remarked later to his wife 'I thought you'd rather have a live donkey than a dead lion'.[2] This single quote perhaps sums up the difference between he and Scott. Scott's personality suggests he couldn't bear returning as a live donkey. Shackleton, a pragmatic optimist, didn't allow failures or setbacks to overwhelm him. He left them behind and always looked forward.

In 1909, Norwegian Roald Amundsen was an experienced explorer who had travelled in Greenland and, over 3 years (1903–1906), became the first to sail the Northwest Passage in his small boat *Gjoa*. During this voyage he observed and learned from the Inuit. He had been a mate aboard *Belgica* when the ship was trapped in the ice over the Antarctic winter in the 1897–1899 expedition. His intention in 1909 was to attempt the North Pole, but he was forestalled as first Frederick Cook, a *Belgica* shipmate of Amundsen, and then Robert Peary emerged from the Arctic claiming the North Pole. Cook's claim proved spurious, Peary's was accepted, although strong doubts have subsequently been raised regarding Peary's claim too. But with these two claims Amundsen immediately shifted his gaze south, only telling his men of his decision after they had set sail. At the time Robert Scott was about to commence his second major Antarctic expedition and was determined to conquer the Pole. Amundsen easily won the race, arriving at the South Pole on 14 December 1911.

Scott and four companions struggled to their goal, arriving on 17 January 1912 to the sight of the tent and flags the Norwegian's had left. On the desperate return journey firstly the strapping seaman Edgar 'Taffy' Evans died. Then Lawrence 'Titus' Oates, knowing he was weakening and slowing the party, famously walked from the tent into an Antarctic blizzard so as not to be a burden. Scott and his two greatest friends and confidantes, Henry 'Birdie' Bowers and Edward 'Bill' Wilson, struggled on. Weak from hunger and exhaustion and enduring brutal weather conditions, the three men died in their tent in late March 1912. In November 1912, a party sent out from their base on Ross Island, found their bodies and Scott's famous diary.

On 29 November 1910 a Japanese expedition, under Nobu (also expressed as Choku) Shirase, set sail from Tokyo aboard *Kainan Maru*. They docked at Wellington New Zealand on 7 February 1911 and continued south on 11 February. They reached the Ross Sea but just south of Coulman Island the ice proved impenetrable. The expedition wintered in Sydney. Professor Edgeworth David, noted geologist at Sydney University, who along with Mawson and Alistair McKay conquered the South Magnetic Pole on Shackleton's *Nimrod* expedition, provided generous support for the Japanese expedition. The expedition sailed south again in November 1911. This time they were able to push through the Ross Sea and make a landing on the ice barrier where they undertook a sledging journey 250 km inland. They arrived back in Japan in June 1912.

In 1911 Germany mounted a second Antarctic expedition under Wilhelm Filchner. The expedition was caught in ice, overwintering in the Weddell Sea.

In 1911 Douglas Mawson led the Australasian Antarctic Expedition, the main party was based in Adelie Land and a second party based in Queen Maud Land. Various parties set out on exploratory sled journeys. Mawson and two companions had been out for a month when Belgrave Ninnis, his dog team and a sled with most of their supplies, disappeared into a crevasse. Xavier Mertz died three weeks later. Mawson, with astonishing toughness and determination, struggled back to base on 8 February 1913, his relief ship having sailed away just hours earlier. Several of the expedition members had stayed behind in the hope their leader may have survived. The men spent another long winter at their base hut. Their ship *Aurora* returned in December 1913 to collect them. Mawson finally arrived back in Adelaide in February 1914.

Like many men, Ernest Shackleton could never shake the thrall of the Antarctic. With the Pole having been conquered he now set his sights on crossing the Antarctic from the Weddell Sea, through the Pole, to the Ross Sea. His crossing didn't ever commence, instead the expedition turned into one of the world's most famous survival stories. His ship *Endurance* was crushed in the Weddell Sea. The men camped on the ice until it broke up and then sailed in three whale boats to Elephant Island. Then in one of the whale boats Shackleton and five companions made an extraordinary open boat journey to South Georgia. Shackleton, ship's captain Worsley, and Antarctic veteran Tom Crean then crossed the precipitous South Georgia Mountains to the Norwegian whaling station at Stromness. Finally in late August 1916 Shackleton accompanied the Chilean tug *Yelcho* back to Elephant Island to rescue his men. All survived. Remarkably, in March 2022, the well-preserved wreck of *Endurance* was located.

On the other side of the Antarctic, Shackleton's Ross Sea party, despatched to lay store depots for his crossing, hadn't fared so well. Their ship *Aurora* had been carried away in a storm in May 1915, finally breaking free and reaching New Zealand in April 1916. The 10 men of the stores party, stranded on Ross Island, undertook brutal sledging journeys, assuming Shackleton's life depended on the store depots. Three men died. The remaining 7 were rescued in January 1917.

This is considered the end of the heroic era. Mawson, Shackleton, Scott and Amundsen were its' dominant figures and all four have fascinated historians and biographers. In 1979 Roland Huntford wrote a searing critique of Robert Scott, gleefully debunking the unrealistic mythologising that had taken place over the previous 7 decades. It was not Scott's fault, though, that others chose to posthumously idealise him. Certainly, a mature and realistic assessment of Scott's failures and strengths was overdue. Huntford's exhaustive book takes care of the failures, but beyond Scott's facility with the written word (and even the most hard-hearted Scott hater could fail to be moved by the final pages of his diary) Huntford finds few positives.

There is no doubt that Scott made errors, but decisions were perhaps harder out on the ice than the judgements of them in a comfortable northern European study nearly 70 years later. Huntford's book is detailed and stylish and was a boon for Antarctic publishing. His palpable dislike of Scott spawned a boom in publications defending and reassessing Scott.

Treatment of Shackleton, Amundsen and Mawson has been much gentler. In his writings on Amundsen and Shackleton, Huntford was much more inclined to mitigate their failures and laud their success. Shackleton was certainly an exceptional leader, particularly in a crisis, although it could be argued that the crises were partly of his own making. Amundsen was a superbly efficient and experienced explorer. Untroubled by a need to serve science his single-minded pursuit of the South Pole, at short notice, by an untried route, was a triumph. Lacking the charisma of Shackleton or the pessimism and burden of obligation that Scott felt so keenly, he is a more elusive, and perhaps less interesting personality. He died, as did Scott and Shackleton, exploring the icy extremes. In May 1926 he was aboard Umberto Nobile's airship *Norge*, when it floated over the North Pole. In 1928 Nobile returned in a new airship, *Italia*. This time it crashed. Amundsen accompanied one of the search aircraft. The plane disappeared.

The fourth of the big names, Mawson, an Australian, had, during Shackleton's *Nimrod* expedition (1907–09), been one of the group to make the first ascent of Mt Erebus and one the party of three to first get to the South Magnetic Pole. He was less interested in being the first to the South Pole though, and of the four, was the most genuinely committed to science. His great expedition 1911–14 explored the totally unknown area of Antarctica directly south of Australia. His story of survival, when one of his men and the sled with most of the equipment and supplies disappeared down a crevasse and his other companion later died, is one of the greatest survival stories. From 1929 to 1930 and also in 1931 he went south again, to consolidate Australia's claim to vast areas of the Antarctic. His major financial backer, Melbourne confectionary giant Mac Robertson was rewarded with a vast area of East Antarctic named for him. In fact notable features and vast areas of the Antarctic are named for financial backers of various heroic era expeditions.

In 1921 Shackleton went south one last time. In a valentine to the past he gathered many of his old shipmates and, with only vague aims, set sail for South Georgia. On 5 January 1922, while anchored off the Norwegian whaling station, Gryytviken, Shackleton died of heart failure on board his expedition ship *Quest*. He is buried on South Georgia.

By the late 1920s exploration had taken to the air with 1928 expeditions led by Australian adventurer Hubert Wilkins and American aviator Richard Byrd. American Lincoln Ellsworth embarked on aerial expeditions in the 1930s.

Perhaps the last expedition to link the heroic and modern eras was the 1934–37 British Graham Land Expedition led by South Australian John Rymill. The expedition ship was the beautiful schooner *Penola* often travelling under sail. The expedition also included dog teams, a biplane and a tractor. They definitively proved that Graham Land was a peninsula and also collected significant scientific data.

After the Second World War, Antarctic exploration and science became the preserve of national governments, and permanent national stations were established. The International Geophysical Year ran from 1 July 1957 to 31 December 1958 and focussed on the Antarctic where twelve nations established 50 research stations. The nations involved were those who had had significant involvement with Antarctic exploration in the 19th and early 20th centuries – Argentina, Australia, Belgium, Chile, France, Great Britain, Japan, New Zealand, Norway, South Africa, USA, USSR. Following this, in December 1959, the twelve nations signed the Antarctic Treaty, preserving the Antarctic as perhaps the only part of the world free of rampant exploitation and sabre rattling, where co-operative scientific programmes dominate the activity of participating nations.

In 1957 Vivian Fuchs led the Commonwealth Trans Antarctic Expedition, finally achieving Shackleton's dream of crossing the Antarctic from the Weddell Sea through the Pole to the Ross Sea. The journey took 99 days, the party reaching Ross Island on 2 March 1958. The Ross Sea stores party was led by Edmund Hilary who, after laying store depots, couldn't resist continuing to the South Pole, leading the first party to reach the Pole overland since Scott. The crossing was an enormous achievement, but with snow tractors, air support and communications, it lacked the romantic appeal of the Heroic Era.

The famous and much discussed expeditions of the Heroic Era can overshadow the contributions of the Antarctic Exploration Committee, Henrik Bull and Carsten Borchgrevink. Theirs, though, was an important and underestimated contribution, turning the gaze of large nations southward to Antarctica, after half a century of disinterest.

Notes

1. British and Russian circumnavigations

1. See Sankey, 1995, Knecht, 2008.
2. Cook, J, 1777, vol. 1, p. 2.
3. Ibid., p. 3.
4. Ibid., p. 35.
5. Cook /Beaglehole, 1961, p. 52.
6. Cook, 1777, vol. 1, pp. 248 & 250.
7. Cook, 1777, vol. 2, p. 237.
8. Ibid., vol. 2, p. 231.
9. Ibid., p. 289.
10. Variable English spellings of forename – Thaddeus, Fabian, Faddei (English publication of Bellingshausen's narrative and *Australian Dictionary of Biography* uses Faddei).
11. Dates altered to Gregorian calendar (G), 12 days ahead of Julian to avoid confusion with newspaper reports etc.
12. Bellingshausen, 1945, p. 14.
13. English spelling and attribution of ranks vary in different publications.
14. Ibid., p. 128 (note).
15. Arrival/ departure dates from *Sydney Gazette and New South Wales Advertiser*.
16. Charcot, Jean, 1911, p. 289.

2. Seals and discovery

1. Begg, 1979, p. 101.
2. Péron, 1971, p. 30.
3. Ibid., p. 31.
4. Ibid.
5. Ibid., p. 30.
6. Ibid., p. 33.
7. Reynolds, 1828, p. 193.
8. Hodgskin, 1820, p. 369.
9. Ibid.

10 Ibid., p. 373.
11 *Literary Gazette and Journal of Belles Lettres*, 24 November 1821, p. 746.
12 *Morning Chronicle*, 7 August 1820, p. 2.
13 Ibid.
14 Gould, R.T., 1941, p. 209.
15 Ibid., p. 224.
16 Christie, 1951, p. 90.
17 Stackpole, 1955, p. 51 (quote).
18 Christie, 1951, p. 93–4.
19 Stackpole, 1951, quoting Burdick p. 59.
20 Jones, A.G.E., 1975, p. 458.
21 Hobbs, 1939, pp. 44–5.
22 Rudmose-Brown, 1939, p. 173.
23 Gordon, 1988.
24 Harvey, unpublished letter 23 January 1832, A2588.

3. Enderby & Sons and the Third circumnavigation

1 Baker, 1967, p. 72.
2 Biscoe, 1833, p. 105.
3 Ibid., pp. 105–6.
4 Ibid., p. 106.
5 Cumpston, 1963, p. 175 [Cumpston notes that Biscoe's chronometers were inaccurate and 'that corrections of up to 2° of longitude ... eastwards should be made to all the positions in this area as recorded in Biscoe's Journal.'].
6 Ibid., p. 108.
7 Dalton, 1931, p. 385.
8 Biscoe, 1833, pp. 108–9.
9 Cumpston, 1963, p. 183.
10 Jones, 1971, p. 51 [quoted from Biscoe's journal].
11 Biscoe, 1833, p.109.
12 *Hobart Town Courier*, 14 May 1831, p. 2.
13 *Hobart Town Courier*, 17 Sept 1831, p. 2.
14 Biscoe, 1833, pp. 108–9.

15 Jones, 1971, p. 51.
16 Biscoe, 1833, p. 112.
17 Balleny, 1839, p. 517.
18 Jones, 1969, p.58.
19 *Sydney Gazette and New South Wales Advertiser*, 14 May 1839, p. 2.
20 Jones, A.G.E., 1964, p. 278.
21 Dumont d'Urville, 1987, p. 452.
22 Balleny, 1839, p. 520.
23 Ibid., p. 521.
24 Ibid., p. 526.
25 Ibid., p. 527.
26 Darwin, 1839, p. 529.
27 Darwin, 1860, p. 252 (note).
28 Mawson, 1932, pp. 117–8.
29 Balleny, 1839, p. 528.
30 Mill, 1905, p. 146.
31 *The Times*, 4 March 1845, p. 4.
32 Ibid., Oct 23, 1849, p. 5.
33 Enderby, 1849, p. 381.
34 McLaren, 1948, p. 71.
35 Melville, 1851, p. 493.

4. Three national expeditions

1 *Lancaster Gazette and General Advertiser*, 4 June 1831, p. 1.
2 Ibid.
3 Rosenman, Helen, ed., A biographical note on Dumont d'Urville from *Two Voyages to the South Seas* [Dumont d'Urville], 1987, p. xliii.
4 Dumont d'Urville, 1987, vol. 1 pp. 37–8.
5 Ibid., p. 272.
6 Ibid., vol. 2, pp. 318 & 319.
7 Ibid., p. 339.
8 Ibid., pp. 343–44.
9 Ibid., p. 476.

10 Wilkes, 1849, p. 344.

11 Dumont d'Urville, *Two Voyages to the South Seas*, 1987, vol. 2, p. 545.

12 Peck, 1909, p. 30.

13 Clark, 1873, p. 474.

14 *New York Times*, 12 May 1884, p. 2.

15 Ibid..

16 Reynolds, 1828, p. 193.

17 *Knickerbocker Magazine*, vol. 13 May 1839 pp. 377–92.

18 Reynolds, *c.*1838, pp. 3–4.

19 Pillsbury, 1910.

20 *Hobart Town Courier and Van Diemen's Land Gazette*, 21 February 1840, p. 2.

21 Wilkes, 1849, vol. 2, p. 296.

22 Ibid., p. 292.

23 *North American Review*, 1845, p. 70.

24 Ibid., p. 71–2.

25 Wilkes, 1849, vol. 2, p. 282.

26 Ross, 1847, vol. 1 pp. 278–9.

27 Ibid., p. 278.

28 Ibid., p. 280.

29 Ibid., p. 298.

30 Scott, 1905, vol. 2, p. 291.

31 Balch, 1906, p. 31.

32 Mawson, 1934, p. 80.

33 Ibid., p. 81.

34 Ibid., p. 113.

35 Lambert & Law (unpublished, Law papers) MS 9458, p. 8.

36 Mawer, 2006) (see discussion pp. 245–59).

37 *Sydney Herald*, 19 December 1840, p. 3.

38 Wilkes, 1849, vol. 3 pp. 273–4.

39 Ibid., pp. 285–6.

40 Stanton, 1975, p. 285.

41 Bertrand, 1971, p. 162.

42 *Spectator*, 28 June 1845, p. 613.

43 Philbrick, 2003, p. 421.

44 *North American Review*, 1845, p. 105.

45 Ibid., p. 106.

46 *Sydney Herald*, 19 December 1840, p. 3.

47 Stanton, 1975, p. 284 (quoted).

48 Bertrand, 1971) n. 39, p. 192.

49 Stanton, 1975, pp. 362–3.

50 Wilkes, Charles The Rebel Privateers [Letter] *New York Times*, 18 December 1863, p. 4.

51 BAAS, 1839) 8th Meeting held Newcastle August 1838, pp. xxi–xxii.

52 Ross, 1847, vol 1, p. xxii.

53 Ibid., p. 53.

54 Jones, 1972, pp. 201–4.

55 *Port Phillip Herald, 28* October 1845, p. 2.

56 Dickson 1850, p. 201.

5. Franklin, the Northwest Passage and the cooling of European interest in the icebound south

1 Barrow, 1846, p. 49.

2 Parl Pprs UK, 1875, p. 4.

3 *The Times*, 15 February 1849, p. 7.

4 Osborn, 1856, p. 300.

5 Parl Pprs, 1852, p. 3.

6 Ibid.

7 *North American Review*, 1857, pp. 99–100.

8 Osborn, 1856, p. 300.

9 Amundsen, 1908, pp. 105–6.

10 Rae, 1854, p. 246.

11 *The Times*, 23 October 1854, p. 7.

12 Ibid.

13 Dickens, 1854, p. 245.

14 *The Times* (Letters to the Editor E J H), 30 October 1854, p. 10.

15 Ibid. (Letters to the Editor Medicus), 1 November 1854, p. 9.
16 Ibid., 26 February 1857, p. 8.
17 Ibid., 15 April 1857, p. 6.
18 Ibid.
19 Ross, 2002, p. 66.
20 BAAS, 30th meeting June/July 1860, pp. 45–6.
21 BAAS, 31st meeting September 1861, p. 71.
22 Osborn, 1864–5, pp. 43–4\4.

6. HMS *Challenger*: An exploration beneath the waves
1 *The Times*, 5 Dec 1872, p. 3.

7. Britain revisits the Arctic
1 Markham, 1874, Introduction by Sherard Osborn, pp. xxiii–xxiv.
2 Loomis, 1972).
3 Markham, 1874, p. 210.
4 Parl Pprs UK, 1875, p. 17.
5 *BMJ*, 1877, p. 298.
6 *BMJ*, 1918, p. 606.
7 Markham, C., 1877, p. 551.
8 *Quarterly Review*, vol. 143, no. 285, 1877, p. 185.
9 Markham, C., 1877, p. 547.
10 Ibid., p. 547.

8. The Australian Antarctic Exploration Committee: The new champions of Antarctic exploration
1 BAAS, 30th meeting June/July 1860, p. 45.
2 BAAS, 31st meeting September 1861, p. 71.
3 *Argus*, 6 August 1857, p. 4.
4 *Argus*, 21 November 1857, p. 4.
5 *Hansard*, Victoria, 4 August 1857, p. 1033.
6 *Argus*, 20 August 1857, p. 5, 22 August 1857, p. 4.
7 *Hansard*, Victoria, 16 December 1857, p. 62.
8 Mill, 1902, p. 364.

9   *Argus*, 2 April 1868, p. 4.
10 Purnell, 1880, p. 423.
11 Ibid.
12 *Argus*, 8 August 1885, p. 5.
13 *Leader*, 10 January 1885, p. 16.
14 GSA. NSW & Vic 1883/4, p. 108.
15 Ibid., p. 112.
16 Mueller, 1998 (Letter dated 3 Nov. 1885 to John Buchanan), vol. 3, p. 419.
17 BAAS, 1887 (56th Meeting Sept. 1886), p. 278.
18 *Argus*, 28 January 1886, p. 6.
19 RGSA, Victoria, *Minutes*.
20 *Daily Telegraph* (Launceston), 17 December 1885, p. 3.
21 AEC, 1886.
22 Premier's Correspondence, Appendices 2, PROV.
23 *Observer*, 22 August 1886, p. 5.
24 *Argus*, 5 August 1886, p. 7.
25 *Argus*, 7 August 1886, p. 9.
26 Murray [1886] p. 527.

9. Northern whalemen and the London Agent General for Victoria

1   Premier's Correspondence, Appendices No. 9, PROV.
2   RSV, 1886, pp. 264–5.
3   Premier's Correspondence, Appendix No. 10, PROV.
4   Ibid., P87/765.
5   Ibid., P87/822.
6   RSV, Proceedings for 1886, pp. 280–2.
7   Premier's Correspondence, P87/765, PROV.
8   Ibid., P87/909.
9   Ibid., P87/1870.
10 Ibid., 1287/87.

10. Lords of the Imperial Treasury

1   *Argus*, 4 July 1887, p. 5.

2 Premier's Correspondence, letter 9 September 1887 (Agent General Berry), P87/3169, PROV.

3 Ibid., letter dated 17 September 1887, P87/4019.

4 *The Times*, 5 October 1887, p. 3.

5 Premier's Correspondence, letter dated 25 October 1887, PROV.

6 Ibid., Letter 16 November 1887, P88/677.

7 Ibid. (no visible file number).

8 *The Times*, 17 November 1887, p. 8.

9 RSV, AEC report, 25 November 1887, vol. 5 (2), pp. 44–5.

10 Premier's Correspondence, letter 30 November 1887, P88/677, PROV.

11 Ibid.

12 Premier's Correspondence, letter 2 December 1887, P88/656, PROV.

13 *Argus*, 2 March 1888, p. 5.

14 *The Times*, 15 October 1890, p. 3.

15 Premier's Correspondence, letter 22 February 1888, P88/588, PROV.

16 RGSA Vic, Report AEC, 31 July 1888, vol. VI, pt 2 1888, pp.14–15 Note the Geographical Society became 'Royal' at the beginning of 1887.

17 *Argus*, 3 November 1888, p. 7.

18 RGSA Vic, Report AEC, vol VII 1889, p. 47.

19 Ibid.

20 *Argus*, 21 September 1889, p. 10.

11. The Swedish Offer

1 *Argus*, 10 June 1890, p. 7.

2 RGSA Vic, vol. VII, pt 1, 1889, p. 32.

3 *Argus*, 19 July 1890, p. 4.

4 RGSA Vic, vol. VIII, pt 2, 1890, p. 79.

5 *Argus*, 26 July 1890, p. 13.

6 RGSA Vic, vol. XIII, part 1, 1890, p. 61.

7 Mueller, 1998, vol. 3, pp. 550–1, Gundersen to Baron von Mueller, 24 March 1890.

8 *Age*, 30 July 1890, p. 5.

9 RGSA Vic, vol. VIII, pt 2, 1890, p. 80.

10 RGSA Vic, vol. XIII, pt 2, 1890, p. 35.

11 *Science*, no. 7, 1890, pp. 252–8, and *Nature*, 16 October 1890, pp. 601–4, *The Times*, 11 October 1890, p. 4.

12 Potter, 1896, p. 144.

13 Ibid., p. 145.

14 *Age*, 1 Dec 1890, p. 6.

15 *Age*, 20 November 1890, p. 5. James Munro 1832–1908 only became Premier on 5 November 1890, he was one of many who was bankrupt during 1890s economic depression and his short period as premier ended on 16 February 1892, when he sailed to London to become Agent General, leaving behind massive debts. He returned at the end of 1892 to face his bankruptcy. His spectacular fall from grace and fortune was repeated across the colony indicating just how difficult it would be to raise Government or private funds for a high-minded scientific expedition to the Antarctic.

16 *Table Talk*, 26 December 1890, p. 11.

17 AAAS, vol. 3, 1891, p. 238.

18 Ibid., p. 250.

19 Ibid., p. 254.

20 *The Times*, 13 February 1891, p. 14.

21 Parkes (unpublished SL NSW), CYA925 CY, reel 77.

22 *Argus*, 28 May 1891, p. 5 .

23 Elder, 1893, pp. 159–60.

24 Mueller, 1998, vol. 3, pp. 606–7, Lindsay to Mueller, 27 April 1892.

25 RSV, vol. III, 1891 (meeting 13 November 1890), p. 150.

26 Potter, 1896, p. 147.

27 Ibid., pp. 147–8.

28 *Argus*, 4 July 1891, p. 12.

29 RSV, vol. IV NS, pt 2, 1892, pp. 205–6.

30 Mueller, 1998, vol. 3, p. 594, Mueller to Holtze.

31 Potter, 1896, p. 150.

32 *Argus*, 2 June 1892, p. 10.

33 *Argus*, 8 June 1892, p. 7.

34 *Argus*, 13 February 1892, p. 11.

35 *Argus*, 2 June 1892, p. 10.

12. The NSW government subsidy

1   AEC NSW minutes, 23 October 1891.
2   *Hansard*, NSW, 24 November 1891 pp. 2879.
3   *Hansard*, NSW, 24 February 1892, pp. 5629–30.
4   Mueller, 1998, vol. 3, pp. 630–1, Potter to Mueller 10 Dec 1892.
5   AEC NSW minutes, 13 December 1892, (unpublished) MLMSS 7540/1.
6   AAAS, vol. 5, 1894, p. 131.
7   Ibid., p. 132.

13. Henrik Johan Bull and an accidental triumph

1   Harboe-Ree_1995, p. 11.
2   Ibid.
3   Ibid.
4   *Evening Standard*, 9 June 1890, p. 7.
5   *Argus*, 28 November 1891, p. 11.
6   Ibid.
7   *Argus*, 1 December 1891, p. 10. *Terra Nova* was later used by Captain Scott in his final expedition, and certainly proved to be a durable vessel in hostile Antarctic conditions.
8   *Argus*, 1 December 1891, p. 10.
9   Bull, 1896, p. 5.
10 Ibid., p. 6.
11 RGSA Vic, meeting 9 August 1893, vol. 11, pp. 12–13.
12 RSV, vol. 6 NS, 1894, p. 212.
13 Bull, 1896, pp. 52–3.
14 Ibid., p. 80.
15 *Age*, 6 January 1894, p. 12 (3 quotes).
16 *Age*, 26 February 1894, p. 5.
17 *Argus*, 8 March 1894, p. 4.
18 *Premier's Correspondence* (PROV), 1894, P94/530.
19 *Age*, 26 February 1894, p. 5.
20 Bull, 1896, p. 82.
21 Ibid., p. 91.

22 Ibid., p. 92.
23 *Otago Witness*, 24 May 1894, p. 18.
24 *Otago Witness*, 2 August 1894, p. 17.
25 Bull, 1896, p. 102.
26 Ibid., p. 103.
27 RSV, 1893, vol. 6 NS p. 212.
28 Borchgrevink 1896, p. 433.
29 Bull, 1896, p. 228.
30 Ibid., p. 107.
31 *The Times*, 6 September 1895, p. 4.
32 Bull, 1896, p. 107.
33 Bull, 1896, p. 110.
34 *Mercury*, 4 October 1894, p. 2.
35 Kristensen, 1896, pp. 80–1.
36 Bull, 1896, p. 110.
37 Ibid., p. 124.
38 Bull and Kristensen differ on dates. Bull having the date they got into dock 27 November. *Otago Daily Times* 19 November 1894 confirms date of arrival at Port Chalmers as 18 November, Kristensen records 20 November as date they got to dry dock.
39 Kristensen 1896, p. 81.
40 Bull, 1896, p. 139.
41 Bull's dates vary slightly from Kristensen's, who seems more accurate in this regard.
42 Bull, 1896, p. 181.
43 Ibid., p. 185.
44 Kristensen 1896, p. 97.
45 Bull, 1896, p. 152.
46 Ibid., pp. 152–3.
47 Ibid., p. 153.
48 Ibid., p. 154.
49 Ibid., p. 209.
50 *Age* 13 March 1895, p. 6.

51 *Argus* 13 March 1895, p. 5.

52 Borchgrevink, C.E. (unpublished) 1895, p. 42.

53 Bull, H.J. (unpublished) 1895, p. 43.

54 Ibid., p. 45.

55 *The Times,* 25 December 1895, p. 10.

56 *Age,* 20 March 1895, p. 7.

57 Borchgrevink in the *Illustrated Australian News* ['A voyage in the Antarctic', 1 April 1895, pp. 22–23]; Bull in the *Australasian* 30 March 1895, pp. 601–2.

58 RGSA. Vic *Minutes.*

59 *Victorian Naturalist,* vol. X11, no. 1, April 1895, pp. 1–2.

60 Bull, 1896, p. 212.

14. Borchgrevink's ambition

1 Ibid., p. 213.

2 Mill, 1951, p. 142.

3 Borchgrevink, 1896a, p. 174.

4 Ibid., p. 175.

5 Greely, 1896, p. 431.

6 Ibid., pp. 431–2.

7 Quartermain, 1971, p. 9.

8 Borchgrevink, 1895, p. 41.

9 Bull, 1896, p. 180.

10 Kristensen 1896, p. 95.

11 *The Times,* 6 September 1895, p. 4.

12 Ibid., 7 September 1895, p. 7.

13 Ibid., 11 September 1895, p. 6.

14 Markham, 1895, p. 710.

15 *The Times,* 9 October 1895, p. 11.

16 Borchgrevink, 1896, p. 441.

17 *The Times,* 9 October 1895, p. 11.

18 Ibid., 6 January 1896, p. 14; 8 January 1896, p. 13.

19 Ibid., 11 January 1896, p. 13.

20 Bull, 1896, p. 212.

21 Speak, 2003, p. 37.

22 *The Times*, 24 Dec. 1895, p. 13.

23 *The Times*, 9 Jan. 1896, p. 6.

24 *New York Times*, 3 Feb. 1896, p. 2.

25 *Evening Star* (Washington), 4 April 1896, p. 23; and published in various newspapers.

26 *Pacific Commercial Advertiser* (Honolulu), 15 May 1896, p. 3.

27 *Los Angeles Herald*, 15 February 1896, p. 1.

28 Huntford, 2001, p. 463.

29 *South Australian Register*, 15 January 1897, p. 7; *Australasian*, 3 July 1897, p. 39.

15. A minor journey

1 *Table Talk*, 24 May 1895, pp. 3–4.

2 *Argus*, 14 March 1898, p. 6.

3 Evans, 1973, p. 791.

16. The First Overwintering

1 Roald Amundsen led the first party to reach the South Pole, famously beating Englishman Robert Falcon Scott's ill-fated party. Amundsen also was the first man to sail the Northwest Passage, over a three year period (1903–1906) in the small boat *Gjoa*, learning much from the Inuit on the journey. In 1928 Amundsen disappeared over the Arctic as a passenger in a search airplane, trying to find the survivors of the crashed airship *Italia*. Frederick Cook, who so distinguished himself on the *Belgica* expedition was later disgraced, firstly with a fraudulent claim at having conquered Mt McKinlay and then emerging from the Arctic claiming to have reached the North Pole in 1908. His claim was quickly contested as being false. Later he served jailtime in the US for fraud.

2 Harrowfield, 1991, p. 179.

3 Bernacchi, 1998, p. 101.

4 Ibid.

5 Patterson et al, 2020, p. 13.

6 Bernacchi, 1998, pp. 101, 149, 127.

7 Ibid., p. 127.

8 Ibid., p. 147.

9 Evans, 1974, p. 25.

10 Bernacchi, 1998, p. 128.

11 Bernacchi, 1901, p. 185.
12 *Mercury,* 19 April 1900, p. 3.
13 *The Times,* 26 June 1900, p. 7.
14 Hovey, 1902, pp. 471–2.
15 Evans, 1974, p. 27.
16 BM, 1902, p. 79.
17 *The Times,* 8 July 1902, p. 4.
18 Ibid., 17 July 1902, p. 6 .
19 Ibid.
20 Ibid., 19 July 1902, p. 6.
21 Ibid., 26 July 1902, p. 10.
22 Close, 1930, p. 181.

17. Henrik Johan Bull's later life

1 Bull, 1907, (unpublished) RHSV MS 000142.
2 Bull, 1901, (unpublished) SPRI MS101/27/3.
3 Bull, 1907, (unpublished) RHSV MS 000142.
4 Bull, 1907a, p. 691.
5 Harboe-Ree, 1995, p 3.
6 Ibid., p. 10.
7 Ibid., p. 12.
8 Ibid., p. 13.
9 Ibid., p. 7.
10 Bull, 1907a, p. 708.
11 Bull, 1907, (unpublished) RHSV MS 000142, p. 14.
12 Ibid., p. 12.
13 Marsh 1948 (Chapter 5).
14 *Cheltenham Chronicle,* 5 Sept 1908, p. 5.
15 *Star,* 25 February 1909, p. 4.
16 Ibid.
17 The figures of yields and information on the operations of A/S Kerguelen comes, with permission, from Odd Galteland's publication.

18. Legacy of the voyage

1   Bull, 1896, pp. 231–2.

2   Tonnessen, 1982, p. 155.

Afterword

1   Scott, 1904, vol. 2, p. 59 ('Observations give it as between 82.16 S. and 82.17 S')

2   Riffenburgh. p. 233.

Bibliography

Unpublished

Borchgrevink, C.E. 1895. *Address given at a meeting of the Australian Antarctic Committee in Melbourne, 19 March 1895.* [Rough Proof] (Prepared for Royal Geographical Society of Australasia (Victoria) but not published. (University of Melbourne)

Bull, H.J. (1907). Notes on the Crozet Islands – expedition to the islands in the schooner Catherine; read at the meeting of the Royal Geographical Society of Australasia (Victoria) 19 March 1907. Melbourne: Royal Historical Society of Victoria [RHSV] MS 000142

Bull, H.J. *Address given at a meeting of the Australian Antarctic Committee in Melbourne, 19 March 1895.* [Rough Proof] (Prepared for Royal Geographical Society of Australasia (Victoria) but not published (University of Melbourne)

Bull, H.J. 1896b. Letter to William Speirs Bruce, 10 February 1896. Cambridge: Scott Polar Research Institute (SPRI) MS101/27/1

Bull, H.J. 1901. Letter to William Speirs Bruce, 24 December 1901. Cambridge: Scott Polar Research Institute (SPRI) MS101/27/3

Harvey, Samuel. Letter dated 23 January 1832 in *James Kelly correspondence, legal documents*, etc., 1821–1851 State Library NSW A2588

Lambert, B.P. and P.G. Law. A new map of the coastline of Oates Land and Eastern King George V Land (copy of report with annotations) *Papers of Phillip Law* 16/006 Box # 63 Series 16 p 8 MS 9458 National Library of Australia

Law, Phillip. *Papers of Phillip Law* 16/006 Box # 63 Series 16 p.8 MS 9458 National Library of Australia

Parkes, Sir Henry. *Papers* State Library NSW CYA925 CY reel 77

Premier's correspondence. Public Records Office Victoria (PROV) VPRS 1163/P Unit 245

Royal Geographical Society of Australasia (Victoria)). [RGSA. Vic] 1883–1913. *Minutes*. Melbourne: Royal Historical Society of Victoria MS 000142 (1883–1886) MS 000688 (1886–1913)

Royal Geographical Society of Australasia. New South Wales Branch – Further records, 1883–192- ,[AEC NSW] *Antarctic exploration committee minutes* MLMSS 7540/1, State Library NSW

Articles

Amdrup, G.C. (1900). *The Danish East Greenland Expedition in 1900 The Geographical Journal*, 16 (6), 662–6

Baker, P.E. (1967). Historical and geological notes on Bouvetøya *British Antarctic Survey Bulletin*, (13), 71–84

Balch, Edwin Swift. (1906). Wilkes Land *Bulletin of the American Geographical Society*, 38(1), 30–2

Balleny, John communicated by Charles Enderby Esq. (1839). Discoveries in the Antarctic Ocean, in February 1839 Extracted from the journal of the schooner Eliza Scott...*Journal of the Royal Geographical Society of London* 9, 517–28

Barr, William. (1983). Geographical aspects of the first international polar year 1882–1883 *Annals of the Association of American Geographers*, 73(4), 463–84

Biscoe, John and Messrs. Enderby. (1833). Recent Discoveries in the Antarctic Ocean *Journal of the Royal Geographical Society of London* 3, 105–12

Borchgrevink, C.E. (1896). The first landing on the Antarctic continent. *Century Illustrated Monthly Magazine,* 51(3), 432–48

Borchgrevink, C.E. (1896a). The voyage of the Antarctic to Victoria Land. *Report of the Sixth International Geographical Congress: held in London, 1895,* 169–76

Borchgrevink, C.E. (1897). Antarctic exploration. *Strand Magazine,* 3(75), 344–52

[BMJ] (1877). *British Medical Journal* 1(845), 298

[BMJ] (1918). The cause and prevention of scurvy. *British Medical Journal,* 2(3022), 606

Bull, H.J. (1907a) Christmas House: the adventures of a shipwrecked crew. *Pall Mall Magazine,* 40, 689–709

Caswell, John Edwards. (1977). The RGS and the British Arctic Expedition. *The Geographical Journal,* 143(2), 200–10

Cawood, John. (1979) The magnetic crusade: science and politics in early Victorian Britain. *Isis,* 70(4), 492–518

Charcot, Jean. (1905). The French Antarctic Expedition. *The Geographical Journal,* 26(5), 497–516

Clark, P. (1873). The Symmes Theory of the Earth. *Atlantic Monthly,* 31(186), 471–480

Close, C. Meetings: Session 1929–1930. (1930). *The Geographical Journal,* 76(2), 180–92

Cumpston, J. (1963). The Antarctic Landfalls of John Biscoe, 1831. *The Geographical Journal,* 129(2), 175–84

Dalton, E.W. (1931). The First Sighting of the Antarctic Continent: A Critical Analysis of Biscoe's Discovery of Enderby Land. *Isis,* 16(2), 379–92

Darwin, C. (1839). Note on a Rock Seen on an Iceberg in 61° South Latitude. *Journal of the Royal Geographical Society of London*, 9, 528–29

Dickens, Charles (1854) The lost Arctic voyages. *Houshold Words*, (245) 361–65, (246), 385–92

Dickson, Walter. (1850) The Antarctic voyage of Her Majesty's hired barque, Pagoda. *Colburns United Service Magazine*, 2, 201–8, 402–8

Durey, Michael. (2008) Exploration at the edge. *The Great Circle*, 30(2), 3–40

Enderby, Charles (1849) Revival of the Southern Whale Fishery – The Auckland Islands. *The Colonial magazine and East India Review*, 16, 378–81

Evans, Hugh. (1973). A voyage to Kerguelen in the sealer Edward in 1897–1898. *Polar Record*, 16 (105), 789–91

Evans, Hugh. (1974). The Southern Cross expedition 1898–1900: a personal account. *Polar Record*, 17(106), 23–30

Evans, Hugh & A.G.E. Jones. (1975). A forgotten explorer Carsten Egeborg Borchgrevink. *Polar Record*, 17 (108), 221–35

Fogg, G.E. (2000). The Royal Society and the Antarctic. *Notes and Records of the Royal Society of London*, 54(1), 85–98

Gordon, Arnold L and Josefino C Comiso. (1988). Polynas in the Southern Ocean. *Scientific American*, 258(6). 70–7

Gould, R.T. (1941). The Charting of the South Shetlands, 1819–1828. *Mariner's Mirror*, 27(3) 206-242

Greely, A.W. (1895/6) Borchgrevink and Antarctic exploration *Century Illustrated Monthly Magazine* 51(NS 29) 431–2

Hall, R. (1900). Field notes on the Birds of Kerguelen Island. *Ibis*, 42(1), 3–34

Hamre, Ivar. (1933) The Japanese South Polar Expedition of 1911–1912. *Geographical Journal*, 82(5), 411–23

[Hansard. NSW] Parliamentary debates. Parliament Legislative Assembly New South Wales

[Hansard. Vic.] Parliamentary debates. Legislative Council and Legislative Assembly. Victoria

Harboe-Ree, Anders. (1995). The diary of Anders Harboe-Ree extracts translated and edited by Eva and Cathrine Harboe-Ree (includes letter from Henrik Bull). *Republica*, 2, 1–14

Harrowfield, D.L. (1991). Archaeology of Borchgrevink's stores hut, Cape Adare Antarctica. *New Zealand Journal of Archaeology*, 13, 177–97

Headland, R.K. [1996] An early Antarctic landing, Captain Copper's Log of the Levant, 1853. *American Neptune* 56(4). 371–81

Hedgpeth, Joel W. (1946). The voyage of Challenger *Scientific Monthly*, 63(3), 194–202

Hobbs, William H. (1932). Wilkes Land rediscovered. *Geographical Review*, 22(4), 632–55

Hobbs, William H. (1939). The discoveries of Antarctica within the American Sector as revealed by Maps and Documents. *Transactions of the American Philosophical Society*, NS 31(1), 1–71

Hobbs, William H. (1939a). The Pack-Ice of the Weddell Sea. *Annals of the Association of American Geographers*, 29(2), 159–70

Hobbs, William H. (1940). The discovery of Wilkes Land Antarctica. *Proceedings of the American Philosophical Society*, 82(5), 561–82

Hodgskin, Mr (1820) Account of the Discovery of New South Shetland. *Edinburgh Philosophical Journal*, 3, 367–80

Home, R.W. & Kretzer, H.J. (1991) The Flagstaff Observatory, Melbourne: new documents relating to its foundation. *Historical Records of Australian Science*, 8(4), 213–43

Hovey, Edmund Otis. (1902). Mr Borchgrevink and the Eruption of Mt Pelée. *Science*, 16(403), 471–72

Jones, A.G.E. (1964). John Biscoe (1794–1843). *Mariners Mirror*, 50(4), 271–81

Jones, A.G.E. (1968). Captain Peter Kemp and Kemp Land. *Mariner's Mirror*, 54(3), 233–44

Jones, A.G.E. (1969). New Light on John Balleny. *Geographical Journal* 135(1), 55–61

Jones, A.G.E. (1971). John Biscoe's Voyage Round the World, 1830–1833. *Mariner's Mirror*, 57(1), 41–62

Jones, A.G.E. (1972). First into the Ross Sea. *Antarctic*, 6(6), 201–4

Jones, A.G.E. (1975). William Smith and the discovery of the New South Shetland. *Geographical Journal*, 141(3) 445–61

Jones, A.G.E. (1985). British Sealing on New South Shetland 1819–1826: Part I, *The Great Circle* 7(1), 9– 22

Jones, A.G.E. (1985a). British Sealing on New South Shetland 1819–1826: Part I1, *The Great Circle* 7(2), 74–87

Kristensen, Leonard. (1896). Journal of the Right – Whaling Cruise of the steamship 'Antarctic' in the South Polar Seas under the command of Captain Leonard Kristensen during the years 1894–1895 *Royal Geographical Society of Australasia, Victorian Branch [RGSA. Vic] Proceedings* 12/13, 73–99

Knecht, Robert. (2008). France's Fiasco in Brazil *History Today*, 58(12), 34–9

Markham, C.R. (1877). The Arctic Expedition of 1875–1876. *Proceedings of the Royal Geographical Society of London*, 21(6), 536–55

Markham, C.R. (1895). The need for an Antarctic expedition. *The Nineteenth Century*. 38(10), 706–712

Mawson, Douglas (1914). Australasian Antarctic Expedition 1911–1914

Geographical Journal, 44(3), 257–84

Mawson, Douglas. (1932). The B.A.N.Z. Antarctic Research Expedition, 1929–1931. *Geographical Journal*, 80(2), 101–26

Mawson, Douglas (1934). Wilkes Antarctic landfalls. *Proceedings of the Royal Geographical Society of Australasia, South Australian Branch* Vol.34, 70–113

Mill, Hugh (HRM). (1902) Dr Von Neumayer and Antarctic Research. *Geographical Journal*, 19(3), 362–4

Murray, John (1886). The exploration of the Antarctic regions. *Scottish Geographical Magazine* 2(9), 527–48

Nathorst, A.G. (1899). The Swedish Arctic Expedition of 1898. *The Geographical Journal*, 14(1), 51–76

North American Review. (1845). [Review]. 61(128), 54–107

North American Review. (1857). [Untitled Article] 84(174), 95–122

Osborn, S., Wells, R., & Petermann, A. (1867). On the Exploration of the North Polar Region. *Proceedings of the Royal Geographical Society of London*, 12(2), 92–113

Parliamentary Papers (United Kingdom) [Parl Pprs UK] (1875). *Arctic expedition: papers and correspondence relating to the equipment and fitting out of the Arctic expedition of 1875 including report of the Admiralty Arctic Committee, presented to both houses of parliament by command of Her Majesty.* HMSO, Command Paper 1153

Parliamentary Papers (United Kingdom) [Parl Pprs UK] (1852) *Arctic Expedition. A Return of the Sailing Orders given to Edward Belcher relating to the Arctic Expedition Admiralty 6 May 1852 presented to House of Commons from order of 4 May 1852* House of Commons Sessional Papers. Vol 50, Paper 317

Patterson, D., Simmonds, J.G., & Snell, T.L. (2020). 'Savage beasts', 'great companions': the first dogs to winter on the Antarctic continent. *Society and Animals*, 28(5–6), 651–69

Peck, John Weld. (1909). Symmes Theory. *Ohio archaeological and historical publications*, 18, 29–42

Philbrick, Nathaniel. (2004). Young Ambition Charles Wilkes' Antarctic Adventure. *The Quarterly Journal of Military History*, 17(1), 84–93

Pillsbury, John Elliott. (1910). Wilkes and Dumont d'Urville's discoveries in Wilkes Land. *National Geographic Magazine*, 21 (2), 171–3

Potter, Rev. W. (1896) Brief survey of Antarctic exploration *Transactions* RGSA (Vic) 14, 117–58

Purnell, C.W. (1880). The Antarctic Regions, *Melbourne Review*, 5, 418–31

[*Quarterly Review* Unamed author]. (1877) Geographical results of the Arctic Expedition, *Quarterly Review*, 143(285), 146–86

Rae, John (1854). The lost Arctic voyages. *Household Words*, 10(246), 433–7

Ray, Dorothy Jean (1975). Early maritime trade with the Eskimo of Bering Strait and the introduction of firearms Arctic. *Anthropology*, 12(1), 1–9

Reynolds, J.N. (Jeremiah N.). (25 March 1828). On the expediency of fitting out vessels of the Navy for an Exploration of the Pacific Ocean and South Seas, *American State Papers Naval Affairs*, 3(363), 189–97

Ross, W. Gillies. (2002). The type and number of expeditions in the Franklin search 1847–1859. *Arctic*, 55(1), 57–69

Rudmose Brown, R.N. (1939). Antarctic history: a reply to Professor W.H. Hobbs *Scottish Geographical Magazine*, 55(3), 170–3

Sankey, Margaret (1995). Where was Goneville Land. *Parergon*, 12(2), 115–26

Schokalsky, J de (1907). A short Account of the Russian Hydrographical Survey *Geographical Journal* 29(6), 626–49

Stone, Ian (1994). Joseph Wiggins. *Arctic*, 47(4), 405–10

Victorian Naturalist (1895). 12(1), 1–2

Thomson, Robert (2001). First Ascent of Mt Lindesay – 'A climbing whodunit. *Queensland Review*, 8 (1), 1–20

United States of America. *Senate Journal*, 7 March 1822, 170–1

Newspapers

Age (Melbourne)
Argus (Melbourne)
Australasian
Hobart Town Courier
Hobart Town courier and Van Diemen's Land Gazette
Illustrated Australian News
Leader (Melbourne)
Morning Chronicle (England)
New York Times
Otago Witness (New Zealand)
Star (Christchurch)
Sydney Gazette and New South Wales Advertiser
The Times (London)
Table Talk (Melbourne)

Books & transactions

Amundsen, Roald. (1908). *The Northwest Passage Vol 2*. Dutton & Co: New York

Antarctic Exploration Committee [AEC]. (1886). *A memorandum of the objects to be served by Antarctic research*. Melbourne: The Committee

Arnaud, Patrick and Beurois, Jean. (1996) *The shipowners of the dream: the Bossiére leases and the exploitations of the French Companies in the Southern Indian Ocean (1893–1939)*. Marseilles: Mme. F. Jambois

Australian Dictionary of Biography. (1966–2012). Melbourne: Melbourne University Press

Australasian Association of the Advancement of Science [AAAS] *Report of meeting*...Sydney: AAAS

Barrow, John. (1846). *Voyages of discovery and research within the Arctic regions, from the year 1818 to the present time*. London: J. Murray

Begg, A. Charles and Neil C. Begg. (1979). *The world of John Boultbee: including an account of sealing in Australia and New Zealand*. Christchurch: Whitcoulls

Bellingshausen, Faddei Faddeevich. (1945). *The voyage of Captain Bellingshausen to the Antarctic seas 1819–1821* translated from the Russian; edited by Frank Debenham. London: Hakluyt Society

Bernacchi, L.C., and J. Crawford. (1998). *That first Antarctic winter: the story of the 'Southern Cross' expedition of 1898–1900 as told in the diaries of Louis Charles Bernacchi*. Christchurch: South Latitude Research in association with Peter J. Skellerup

Bernacchi, Louis. (1901). *To the South Polar regions*. London: Hurst and Blackett

Bertrand, Kenneth J. (1971) *Americans in Antarctica, 1775–1948*. New York: American Geographical Society

Borchgrevink, C.E. (1901). *First on the Antarctic continent: being an account of the British Antarctic expedition, 1898–1900*. London: G. Newnes, Ltd.

British Association for the Advancement of Science [BAAS] London

British Museum [BM]. (1902). *Report on the collections of natural history made in the Antarctic regions during the voyage of the Southern Cross*. London: British Museum

Bulkeley, Rip. (2014). *Bellingshausen and the Russian Antarctic Expedition, 1819–21* New York: Palgrave Macmillan

Bull, Henrik Johan. (1896). *The Cruise of the 'Antarctic' to the South Polar regions* London: Edward Arnold

Bull, Henrik Johan. (1892). *Svend Foyn Forebrag af H.J. Bull; Melbourne 22 April 1892*. Christiania: Truft I Centralteriet

Campbell, R.J.(editor) and C.W. Poynter. (2000). *The Discovery of the South Shetland Islands: The Voyages of the Brig Williams 1819–1820 as Recorded in Contemporary Documents and the Journal of Midshipman C.W. Poynter*. London: Hakluyt Society

Charcot, Jean. (1911) *The voyage of the 'Why Not?' in the Antarctic: the journal of the Second French South Polar Expedition, 1908–1910* English version by Philip Walsh. London: Hodder and Stoughton

Christensen, Lars. (1935). *Such is the Antarctic* translated by E.M.G. Jayne. London: Hodder and Straughton

Christie, E.W. Hunter. (1951). *The Antarctic problem: an historical and political study.* London: Allen & Unwin

Cook, J., Furneaux, T., Hodges, W., & Pringle, J. (1777). *A voyage towards the South Pole, and round the world: Performed in His Majesty's ships the Resolution and Adventure, in the years 1772, 1773, 1774, and 1775.* London: W. Strahan and T. Cadell

Cook, James (1961). *The Journals of Captain James Cook on his voyages of discovery. Vol 2 The voyage of the Resolution and Adventure 1772–1775* Edited by J.C. Beaglehole. Cambridge: Hakluyt Society

Darwin, Charles (1860). *Journal of researches during the voyage of H.M.S. Beagle.* London: Collins

Deacon, Margaret (1971). *Scientists and the sea.* London: Academic Press

Dumont d'Urville, Jules S-C. (1987). *An account in two volumes of two voyages to the South Seas Vol 1 Astrolabe and Zélée 1837–1840* Translated and edited by Helen Rosenman. Melbourne: University Press

Elder, T., *et al.* (1893). *Journal of the Elder Scientific Exploring Expedition, 1891–2 under command of D. Lindsay.* Adelaide: C.E. Bristow

Fornasiero, F.J., Lawton, L., West-Sooby, J., editors. (2016). *The art of science: Nicolas Baudin's voyagers 1800–1804.* Mile End, South Australia: Wakefield Press

Galteland, Odd. (2013). *A/S Kerguelen 1908–1921: the optimism, the dreams – and the dull working day.* Vestfoldmuseene IKS, Sandefjord: Cdr Chrsitensens Whaling Museum

Geographical Society of Australasia, New South Wales and Victorian Branches [GSA.NSW/Vic]. *Proceedimgs*

Headland, Robert Keith (2009). *A chronology of Antarctic exploration.* London: Quaritch

Hunt, Susan, *et al.* (2002). *Lure of the southern seas: the voyages of Dumont d'Urville 1826–1840* Sydney: Historic Houses Trust of NSW

Huntford, Roland (2001). *Nansen.* London: Abacus

Jones A.G.E. (1982). *Antarctica Observed.* Yorkshire: Caedmon of Whitby

Jones, A.G.E. (1992). *Polar Portraits.* Yorkshire: Caedmon of Whitby

Kish, George (1973). *North-east passage: Adolf Erik Nordenskiöld, his life and times.* Amsterdam: Nico Israel

Loomis, Chauncey (1972). *Weird and tragic shores: the story of Charles Francis Hall, explorer.* London: Macmillan

McLaren, Fergus B. (1948). *The Auckland Islands: Their Eventful History.* Wellington: A.H. Reed

Markham, Albert Hastings. (1874). *Whaling Cruise to Baffin Bay and the Gulf of Boothia and an account of the rescue of the crew of the Polaris.* London: S. Low, Marston, Low and Searle

Marsh, J.H. (1948). *No pathway here.* Cape Town: Howard B. Timmins for Hoddder and Stoughton (Online version unnumbered, retrieved 22 February 2021 http://rapidttp.co.za/pathway/)

Mawer, Granville Allen. (2006). *South by Northwest.* Wakefield Press

Mill, H.R. (1951). *An autobiography.* London: Longmans, Green

Mill, H.R. (1905). *The siege of the South Pole: the story of Antarctic exploration.* London: A. Rivers

Mitterling, Philip. (1959). *America in the Antarctic to 1840.* Urbana, Illinois: University of Illinois Press

Mueller, Baron Ferdinand von. (1998). *Regardfully yours: selected correspondence of Ferdinand von Mueller (3 volumes)* edited by R.W. Home. New York: Peter Lang

Neatby, Leslie H. (1970). *Search for Franklin* New York: Walker & Co.

Osborn, Sherard editor. (1856). *The discovery of the Northwest Passage.* London: Longman

Oxford Dictionary of National Biography. (2004). Oxford: University Press

Péron, François. (1971). *King Island and the sealing trade 1802* translated by Helen Mary Micro. Canberra: Roebuck Society

Philbrick, N. (2003). *Sea of glory: America's voyage of discovery: the U.S. Exploring Expedition, 1838–1842.* New York: Viking Penguin

Quartermain, L.B. (1971). *New Zealand and the Antarctic.* Wellington: Government Printer

Report of the Sixth International Geographical Congress: held in London, 1895. (1896). Edited by the secretaries. London: John Murray

Reynolds, J.N. (Jeremiah N.) and Dickerson, Mahlon (ca.1838) *Exploring expedition. Correspondence between J.N. Reynolds and the Hon. Mahlon Dickerson, under the respective signatures of 'Citizen' and 'Friend to the navy', touching the South Sea surveying and exploring expedition.* New York

Riffenburgh, Beau. (2004). *Nimrod.* London: Bloomsbury

Ross, James Clark. (1847). *A voyage of discovery and research in the Southern and Antarctic regions during the years 1839–1843.* London: John Murray

Ross, M.J. (1982). *Ross in the Antarctic: the voyages of James Clark Ross in Her Majesty's ships Erebus & Terror, 1839–1843.* Yorkshire: Caedmon of Whitby

Royal Geographical Society (with the Institute of British Geographers) [RGS] *Proceedings ... and Monthly Record of Geography*

Royal Geographical Society of Australasia, South Australian Branch [RGSA.SA] *Proceedings*

Royal Geographical Society of Australasia, Victorian Branch [RGSA. Vic] *Proceedings/Transactions*

Royal Society of Tasmania [RCT]. *Papers and Proceedings*

Royal Society Victoria [RSV]. *Proceedings*

Rudmose Brown, R.N. (1923). *A naturalist at the poles.* London: Seeley, Service & Co.

Sandler, M.W. (2008). *Resolute: the epic search for the Northwest Passage and John Franklin, and the discovery of the queen's ghost ship.* New York: Sterling

Scott, R.F. (1905). *The voyage of the 'Discovery'.* London: Macmillan

Speak, P. (2003). *William Speirs Bruce: polar explorer and Scottish nationalist.* Edinburgh: National Museums of Scotland

Stackpole, Edouard A. (1955). *The Voyage of the Huron and the Huntress: The American sealers and the discovery of the continent of Antarctica.* Mystic, Connecticut.: Marine Historical Association

Stanton, William. (1975). *The great United States Exploring Expedition of 1838–1842.* California: Berkeley University of California Press

Thomson, C Wyville. (1873). *The depths of the sea.* London: Macmillan

Tonnessen, J.N. and Johnsen, A.O. (1982). *The history of modern whaling.* Canberra: ANU Press

Wilkes, Charles. (1845). *Narrative of the United States Exploring Expedition.* Philadelphia: Lea & Blanchard

Acknowledgements

Thanks very much to Dominique for all your love, encouragement and support and also to my late parents, Joan and Dempsey for all that you have given me.

Much of the research that forms the basis of this book was gathered during a 3-month staff fellowship awarded by State Library Victoria. Many of the resources used for research were sourced from the collections of the Library and I am very appreciative to the Library.

Thanks very much to Nick and Anna and all at Australian Scholarly Publishing.

Index

Admiralty 3–4, 15, 18, 25, 59, 64, 66–78, 80, 83–4, 90, 102, 107, 112, 114
Agent General (London) 102, 107–08, 111, 116, 185
Amundsen, Roald 61, 74, 90, 166, 169, 191, 193–4
Antarctic
  first sighting 7, 13, 15, 52
  first landings 7, 16–17, 152–3, 155–6, 159–61, 168, 174–5, 186
Antarctic Exploration Committee (Victoria)
  conversazione 144
  formation of 97, 99
  fund raising 101, 104–05, 107, 111–13, 116–23, 126, 128–33, 141, 145, 185–6
  members 100, 116, 125, 126, 148, 184
Antarctic Exploration Committee (NSW)
  relationship with Victoria 133
Astrup, Eivind 149, 177
Auckland Islands *see* Enderby, Charles
Austin, Horatio 33, 77, 80, 90
Australasian Antarctic Expedition (1911–1914) 51
Australasian Association for the Advancement of Science 125, 135

Back River *see* Great Fish River
Balleny, John 26–9, 32–3, 49, 61
Barrow, John 66–9, 78
Baudin, Nicolas 11, 34–5
Baxter, William 108–09
Bellingshausen, Faddei 7–9, 15, 79, 167
Bernacchi, Louis 166–71, 174

Berry, Graham 102, 104, 106, 111–13, 116–17
Board of Trade (London) 112, 114–15, 186
Borchgrevink, Carsten Egeberg
  in Australia 150
  dispute with British Museum 173
  claims of first landing 152, 155, 159, 161
  at International Geographical Congress 158–60
  dispute with Kristensen 150, 152, 159–61, 174, 186
  later life 175–6
  member of *Antarctic* expedition 150, 152, 155, 175
  Mt Pelee 173
  Southern Cross expedition (British Antarctic Expedition) 163–4, 166–72, 175, 189
Bossières brothers 181–2
Boultbee, John 10
Bouvet de Lozier, Jean Baptiste 2, 4, 6, 34, 53, 63, 79
Bouvet Island 2–6, 22, 53, 63, 95
Bransfield, Edward 13–16
Bride, Thomas 97, 100
British Antarctic Committee 98, 101
British Antarctic Expedition 163, 166, 169
British National Antarctic Expedition 172, 189
British Natural History Museum 173
British, Australian and New Zealand Antarctic Research Expedition (1929–1931) 51
Bruce, David 104

Bruce, William Speirs 132, 135, 149, 161, 177–8, 190
Buddington, James 73
Bull, Henrik Johan
   AEC 140, 142, 144–5
   Antarctic expedition 144, 146–8, 150–5, 160, 178, 185, 189–90
   book 161, 177
   and Borchgrevink 150, 152, 155–8, 161, 177, 195
   early life 137
   and Kristensen 140, 144, 146, 148, 150–2, 156, 159, 161, 177–8, 186
Bull, Ole Olsen 180, 184
Burn Murdoch, William Gordon 141

Cape Adare 19, 152, 155, 159–60, 162, 167, 170–2, 174–6
Cape Ann 23–4
Cape Circumcision *see* Bouvet Island
Carpenter, Dr William 83, 85, 88
Carpenter, William Lant 83
Challenger Expedition 80, 82, 84–5, 100, 126, 148, 165
Charcot, Jean-Baptiste 8, 190
Christensen, Christen 104–05, 138
Christensen, Lars 6, 8, 51
Close, Colonel Sir Charles 176
Colbeck, William 166, 169–70
Collinson, Richard 71, 73–5
Colonial Office 112, 114–15, 186
Cook, Frederick 166, 191
Cook, James 1, 3–8, 12, 22, 46, 53, 63, 80
Crozet Islands 60, 142, 178–80
Crozier, Francis 59
Crummer, William 134
da Cuhna, Tristan 142

Davis, John 14, 16–18, 53
d'Entrecasteaux, Bruni 34
Dessen, H. F. 108–09
Dibbs, George 133–4

Dickens, Charles 75–6
Dickerson, Mahlon 44–5, 55
Dickson, Baron Oscar 120, 122, 125–6, 128–9, 135
Duffy, John Gavan 98, 100
Dumont d'Urville, Jules Sébastian César
   Adelie Land 34, 39, 47
   early life 34–5
   encounter with Wilkes expedition 34, 39–40, 45–7
   expeditions 18, 34, 36–40, 45–7
   and La Perouse 36–7
   later life 40, 79
   Weddell Sea 38

Elder, Thomas 127–30, 185–6
Ellery, Robert L. J. 99, 125, 129
Enderby, Charles
   Auckland Islands 30–1, 147
   expeditions 22, 25–6, 29–31, 183
Enderby Land 23, 33, 60, 147
Essomeric 1
Evans, Hugh 164–6, 169–71, 173

Faeroe Islands 83, 85, 106
Fairweather, James 104, 107
Fanning, Edmund 14, 43
Du Faur, Frederick Eccleston 134–5
Forbes, Edward 82
Foster, Henry 33
Foster, Michael 113
Fougner, Anton 167–8, 170–1
Foyn, Svend 117–18, 120, 140–1, 143, 146, 148–9, 152, 154–5, 161
Franklin, John 60, 64–6, 68–70, 73–8, 80–1, 84, 87, 89–90, 97–8, 102, 106, 158
   Franklin expedition 33, 64–5, 68–70, 73–8, 81
Franklin, Lady Jane 69–71, 75, 77, 106, 159
Freeman, Thomas 26, 28
French Company of the East Indies 2

Fréycinet, Louis 34–6

de Gerlache, Adrian 166
German South West Africa 183
Gillies, Premier Duncan 101–02, 111, 116
de Gonneville, Binot Paulmeyer Buschet 1–2, 34
Gonneville Land 2–3
Graham Land 33, 60, 194–5
Grand White Character and Plain Dress Ball 124
Great Fish River 75–7
Griffiths, George 98–9, 101, 105, 121–2, 125, 130, 132, 141–2, 144, 148–9, 156
Gubin (blacksmith) 9
Gundersen, Hans 117–18, 120–2, 128, 130, 144–5, 164, 166

Hagan, Andrew 142
Hanson, Nicolai 166–7, 170–1, 173–5
Harboe-Ree, Anders 178–81
Harvey, Samuel 19, 61
Heroic Age/Era 188, 190, 195
Hudson Bay Company 69

Imperial Treasury 109, 111, 115
International Geographical Congress 94, 126, 158–9, 172, 175
Inuit/'Esquimaux' 9, 60, 74–8, 87–8, 90, 124, 191

Jeffreys, Gwyn 83, 88
Jensen, Captain Bernhard 166, 171

Kerguelen Islands 12, 19, 60, 79, 84, 142–3, 148, 151–2, 164–5, 181–3
Kerguelen Whaling Company 181
Kernot, Professor William C. 99, 129, 156
King and Kangaroo Island emus 35
King William Island 74, 77–8, 81

Klövstad, Herlof 167
Kristensen, Leonard
    Antarctic expedition 140, 144, 146–53, 156–7, 160–1, 174, 177–8, 183, 186
    dispute with Borchgrevink 150, 152, 157, 160–1, 174
    later life 184

La Pérouse, Jean-François de Galaup 34, 36–7, 40
Lankester, Ray 173–4
Law, Phillip 52–3
Lazaref, Mikhail 7
Lindhagen, Georg (Daniel) 120, 123, 130
Lindsay, David 127
Love, Ernest F.J. 149
Lysle, William 26, 29

Macdonald, Alexander 97, 100, 144
Malolo Island 54
Marion Island 142, 181
Markham, Clements
    Arctic proposals 70, 82–4, 86, 89–90
    view of *Antarctic* expedition 160
    view of Borchgrevink 189
Maury, Matthew Fontaine 79–80, 91–2, 95
Mawson, Douglas
    expeditions 23, 29, 51, 135, 192, 194
    Sabrina Coast 29
    Wilkes Land 51–2
McClure, Robert 71–5
McFarlane, Andrew 14, 17
McLintock, Leopold 77, 109
Morgan, E. Delmar 126
Mt Pelée 173
von Mueller, Ferdinand 96–7, 99–100, 120–1, 124–30, 134, 138, 140, 144, 156, 184
Murray, John 84–5, 97, 103, 107, 109
Must, Ole 167, 170

Nansen, Fridtjof 119–21, 150, 162–3, 185, 187
Newnes, George 163, 166, 170, 172
Nordenskiöld, Adolf
and AEC 119–20, 122, 129, 164
expedition proposal 119–23, 125–6, 128–32, 135, 164
Northeast Passage 119
Nordenskiöld, Otto 187, 189
Northwest Passage 36, 59, 64, 66–7, 69–70, 73–5, 78, 83, 106, 191

Ommanney, Erasmus 70, 97–8, 107, 112, 123, 158, 166, 172, 185
Osborn, Sherard 70, 72, 80–3, 86, 88
Ouligback, William 75

Parkes, Premier Henry 126, 133–4
Parry, William Edward 42, 59, 64, 67–9, 88
Pasco, Crawford 99, 109, 116, 121–3, 126, 132, 145, 184
Patterson, Premier James 144–5
Paulmier, Abbe Jean 1
Peron, Francois 11–12
Peter 1 Oy 8, 95, 167
Port Jackson 8–9, 34, 36
Possession Island 61, 142, 152, 171–2, 179–80, 184, 186
Potter, William 126, 134–5, 145, 161
Prince Edward Island 12, 142

Rae, John 69–70, 74–7
Reid, Robert 130, 133–4
Reynolds, Jeremiah 12, 41, 43–4, 55
Richardson, Dr John 68–70
Romcke, Otto 139–40
Ross, Dr Andrew 134
Ross, James Clark 19, 28, 33, 38–9, 49–50, 53, 58–64, 66–7, 69–70, 95, 97, 127, 138–9, 154–6, 171, 190
Ross, John 59, 64, 66–8, 70, 90
Ross Sea 19, 50, 61, 63, 109, 154, 171, 191–3, 195
Rothschild, Lionel 164–5
Rowland, Charles 164
Royal Colonial Institute 112
Royal Geographical Society of Australasia 51, 99–100, 112–13, 127, 134
Royal Society, London 22, 64, 80, 83, 88–90, 113–15, 154, 175, 185
Rusden, Henry Keylock 101, 116, 129–30

Sabine, Edward 64
Sabrina Coast, Darwin 28, 33
Samuel Enderby & Sons 22
Sars, Michael 82
Savio, Persen 167–8
Scott, Robert 50, 61, 90, 169, 176, 186, 189, 191–5
Scottish National Antarctic Expedition (1902–1904) 149, 177, 190
sealing 10–11, 14–18, 20, 22, 25–7, 29–30, 43–4, 79, 109, 117–18, 138–40, 145, 147, 151–2, 161, 164, 166, 177, 180–1, 183–4
Selby, George W. 101
Shackleton, Ernest 61, 169, 189–95
Sharpe, Richard Bowdler 173–4
Shetland Islands 17, 53, 83
South Shetlands 9, 11, 14, 16–18, 25, 33, 43, 182
Shirreff, Captain 13
Shishmarev, Gleb 7, 9
Smith, William 12, 13–17, 23, 53
Storm, Bull and Co 180–2
Strachey, Richard 112–14
Symmes, John Cleves 40–3

Thomas Johannes Heftye and Sons 141
Tönsberg 108
Trapp, Blair and Co. 138
Tring Museum 164–5

Valparaiso 12–14, 46

Vasilev, Mikhail 7, 9

whaling 10, 21–2, 29, 51, 61, 70, 87, 95, 101–09, 117–18, 120, 122, 129, 132, 135, 137–40, 142, 144–5, 148, 151, 154, 156, 161–2, 180–1, 183–5, 188, 190, 193–4
Wiggins, Joseph 131
Wild, John James 85, 100, 126, 144, 148
Wilkes, Charles
   book 48–9
   conflict with crew 46, 50, 53, 55, 56–7
   court martials 48, 54–5, 57–8
   criticism of 48, 53, 55, 57–8
   later life 58
   Malolo Island massacre 54
Wilkes Land 50–1, 58
von Willemos-Suhm, Rudolf 84
Woods, Charles 77
Wyville Thomson, Charles 82

Young Island 28, 152, 154
Young, Allen 77, 106, 109, 113, 186

Ships

Adventure 3, 5
Agnes G. Donohue 181
Annawan 43
Antarctic 136, 140–5, 147–8, 150, 154–5, 158–9, 166, 172, 174–5, 177–8, 183, 185, 187, 189–90
Assistance 70, 72, 97
Astrolabe 36–7, 39
Beatrice L. Corcom 181
Belgica 166–7, 191
Blagonamyerenni 7–8
Breadalbane 71–2
Cap Nor 140
Cathrine 178, 180
Cecilia 14, 17–18
Chanticleer 33
Diligence 71
Dragon 14, 17
Eclair 183
Eclipse 105
Edward 164, 166
Eliza Scott 26, 28
Enterprise 69–71, 73–4
Erebus 28, 39, 59–60, 62, 64, 69, 78
Erik 105
Espoir 1, 183
Esquimaux 104
Etoile 183
Flying Fish 45–6, 54–5
Fortuna 104
Géographe 34–5
Hekla 177

Herald 70
Hersilia 14
Hertha Elida 104
Hope 105–06
Hopefull 26
Huntress 14, 16–18
Huron 14, 16–17
Intrepid 72
Investigator 70–4, 78
Jason 104
Jeanne D'Arc 182–3
La Boussole 36
Lady Emma 27
Lightning 83–5
Mirnyi 7–9
Naturaliste 34–5
North Star 71–2
Norvegia 6, 8, 23
Orestes 131
Otkryitie 7–8
Pagoda 64
Peacock 45–8, 54–5
Phoenix 71–2
Pioneer 70, 72, 80
Plover 65, 70
Polynia 104
Porcupine 83–4
Porpoise 39–40, 45–8, 52, 54
Pourquoi Pas? 8, 190
Prince of Wales 69
Regent 183
Relief 45–6, 55
Resolute 71–4, 78

Resolution 3–6
Rose 26, 71
Sabrina 26, 28–9
Scotia 177
Sea Gull 45–6, 54–5
Seraph 43
Shearwater 83–4
Solglimt 180–1
Southern Cross 166, 168, 171–3, 175–6
Terror 28, 39, 59–60, 62, 64, 69, 78
Venus 19, 61
Vincennes 45–8, 54
Vostok 7–9
Westye Egeberg 108
Williams 12
Zélée 37–8

227

www.ingramcontent.com/pod-product-compliance
Lightning Source LLC
Chambersburg PA
CBHW032126160426
43197CB00008B/535